Legalines®

Editorial Advisors:
Gloria A. Aluise
Attorney at Law
Jonathan Neville
Attorney at Law
Robert A. Wyler
Attorney at Law

Authors:
Gloria A. Aluise
Attorney at Law
Daniel O. Bernstine
Attorney at Law
Roy L. Brooks
Professor of Law
Scott M. Burbank
C.P.A.
Charles N. Carnes
Professor of Law
Paul S. Dempsey
Professor of Law
Jerome A. Hoffman
Professor of Law
Mark R. Lee
Professor of Law
Jonathan Neville
Attorney at Law
Laurence C. Nolan
Professor of Law
Arpiar Saunders
Attorney at Law
Robert A. Wyler
Attorney at Law

TORTS

Adaptable to Ninth Edition* of Epstein Casebook

By Gloria A. Aluise
Attorney at Law

*If your casebook is a newer edition, go to www.gilbertlaw.com to see if a supplement is available for this title.

THOMSON
WEST

EDITORIAL OFFICE: 1 N. Dearborn Street, Suite 650, Chicago, IL 60602
REGIONAL OFFICES: Chicago, Dallas, Los Angeles, New York, Washington, D.C.

SERIES EDITOR
Linda C. Schneider, J.D.
Attorney at Law

PRODUCTION MANAGER
Elizabeth G. Duke

FIRST PRINTING—2009

Legalines®

Features Detailed Briefs of Every Major Case,
Plus Summaries of the Black Letter Law

Titles Available

Administrative Law .... Keyed to Breyer
Administrative Law .... Keyed to Schwartz
Administrative Law .... Keyed to Strauss
Antitrust .... Keyed to Areeda
Antitrust .... Keyed to Pitofsky
Business Associations .... Keyed to Klein
Civil Procedure .... Keyed to Friedenthal
Civil Procedure .... Keyed to Hazard
Civil Procedure .... Keyed to Yeazell
Conflict of Laws .... Keyed to Currie
Constitutional Law .... Keyed to Brest
Constitutional Law .... Keyed to Choper
Constitutional Law .... Keyed to Cohen
Constitutional Law .... Keyed to Rotunda
Constitutional Law .... Keyed to Stone
Constitutional Law .... Keyed to Sullivan
Contracts .... Keyed to Calamari
Contracts .... Keyed to Dawson
Contracts .... Keyed to Farnsworth
Contracts .... Keyed to Fuller
Contracts .... Keyed to Kessler
Contracts .... Keyed to Knapp
Contracts .... Keyed to Murphy
Corporations .... Keyed to Choper
Corporations .... Keyed to Eisenberg
Corporations .... Keyed to Hamilton

Criminal Law .... Keyed to Dressler
Criminal Law .... Keyed to Johnson
Criminal Law .... Keyed to Kadish
Criminal Law .... Keyed to Kaplan
Criminal Law .... Keyed to LaFave
Criminal Procedure .... Keyed to Kamisar
Domestic Relations .... Keyed to Wadlington
Estates and Trusts .... Keyed to Dobris
Evidence .... Keyed to Mueller
Evidence .... Keyed to Waltz
Family Law .... Keyed to Areen
Income Tax .... Keyed to Freeland
Income Tax .... Keyed to Klein
Labor Law .... Keyed to Cox
Property .... Keyed to Cribbet
Property .... Keyed to Dukeminier
Property .... Keyed to Nelson
Property .... Keyed to Rabin
Remedies .... Keyed to Rendelman
Securities Regulation .... Keyed to Coffee
Torts .... Keyed to Dobbs
Torts .... Keyed to Epstein
Torts .... Keyed to Franklin
Torts .... Keyed to Henderson
Torts .... Keyed to Prosser
Wills, Trusts & Estates .... Keyed to Dukeminier

All Titles Available at Your Law School Bookstore

THOMSON

WEST

SHORT SUMMARY OF CONTENTS

TABLE OF CONTENTS AND SHORT REVIEW OUTLINE

I. INTENTIONALLY INFLICTED HARM: THE PRIMA FACIE CASE AND DEFENSES

A. INTRODUCTION

The body of law known as Torts is concerned with the allocation of losses resulting from the activities of people; it is an attempt to balance the utility of a particular type of conduct against the harm that it may cause, judged by the prevailing social and economic attitudes of the time. In a broad sense, a tort is a wrong, and a tortious act or omission is a wrongful act or omission. While no one definition satisfactorily defines, describes, or delimits "torts" generally, a tort usually arises through conduct, in the form of an act or omission, affecting a legally protected interest in person or property (or both), done with a certain state of mind (*e.g.*, intention, reckless disregard of the consequences, carelessness, etc.—although state of mind may be immaterial, as in strict liability cases), which causes damage.

1. **Prima Facie Case.** In order to recover in tort, the plaintiff must establish the essential elements of the tort. If the plaintiff's complaint sufficiently alleges these elements, he has stated a prima facie case, which means that if the allegations are all true, they are sufficient to allow recovery unless contradicted and overcome by other evidence. The tort is "defined" by the prima facie case.

2. **Tort vs. Crime.** A tort is distinguished from a crime in that the latter is a social harm defined and made punishable by the state. While the same act or omission may result in both a crime and a tort, a tort is a wrong to the individual while a crime is a wrong against the public at large, for which the state seeks redress. Torts may be committed by individuals, corporations, associations, and other entities. The party who commits a tort is commonly referred to as the tortfeasor.

3. **Damages.** If the elements of a tort are established by the plaintiff and if the defendant fails to raise an adequate defense, a court will award nominal damages if no injury has in fact been sustained, or damages in such amount as it deems reasonable to compensate the plaintiff for the loss suffered. No other or special damages (*i.e.*, damages not generally resulting from the tort but suffered by the plaintiff because of his particular circumstances, condition, etc.) need be shown for tort liability to attach to the defendant. However, if liability does attach to the defendant, any special damages caused to the plaintiff as a result of the defendant's act or omission may also be recovered. Further, if it appears that the act or omission of the defendant that forms the

basis of the liability was either motivated by an intention to injure or harm the plaintiff or constituted a willful and wanton disregard of the consequences, the court may, in addition, award punitive ("exemplary") damages against the defendant. (*See* discussion under Damages, *infra.*)

4. **The Policies of Tort Liability.** Judicial opinions resolve controversies between two parties. Thus, the premises underlying tort law are seldom discussed in depth. There are several, sometimes conflicting, values involved:

    (i)   Compensating individuals who have been injured;

    (ii) Preserving individual choice; and

    (iii) Determining the social cost-benefit of a given policy.

    For example, should the legal system force all persons to be vaccinated for polio? Even if there is some chance that a few will die from the vaccination? Should individual choice be allowed if the benefit to society is greater than the cost of loss of some individuals?

5. **Objectives of the Tort System.** There are many possible compensation systems: negligence; negligence plus liability insurance; strict liability; strict liability plus insurance; etc. Whatever system is employed, it should fulfill the following objectives:

    (i)   Be equitable (between those who receive benefits and those who bear the burden; among beneficiaries; among the cost bearers).

    (ii)   Contribute to the wise allocation of human and economic resources.

    (iii) Compensate promptly.

    (iv)   Be reliable.

    (v)   Distribute losses rather than leave them on single individuals.

    (vi)   Be efficient.

    (vii) Deter risky conduct.

    (viii) Minimize fraud.

    Each compensation system meets these objectives to some extent. For example, negligence law is founded on the notion of compensation-based fault. But fault is objective. Thus, the moral basis of liability is eroded. Objectification may be defended in that it reduces cost and error in administering the system. Also, fault is supported by commonly shared values of people. Possibly the system deters risky conduct.

6. **Intentional Interference with Person and Property.** One of the major classifications of tort liability is liability based on the intent of the defendant. However, intent means not only the desire to bring about the physical results, but also the knowledge or belief that certain results are substantially certain to follow from the defendant's conduct. The intent forming the basis of tort liability need not be immoral, malicious, or hostile; instead, it need only be an intent to affect a legally protected interest in a way that will not be permitted by law. The subjective knowledge or belief on the part of the defendant that certain results are substantially certain to follow from his conduct is determined on an objective rather than a subjective basis. That is, actual knowledge or belief, or lack thereof, on the part of the defendant is immaterial if a reasonable person in the position of the defendant would have believed that certain results were substantially certain to follow from the conduct of the defendant. Of course, the external, objective standard must have certain subjective inputs based upon the position of the defendant (*i.e.*, age, physical abilities, special skills, etc.), and it is on the basis of the theoretical reasonable person who possesses these same characteristics of the defendant that knowledge or belief for purposes of tort liability is determined.

B. PHYSICAL HARMS

1. **Battery.** In order for there to be a battery there must be intent, an act by the defendant, and a rude or offensive touching of the plaintiff.

   a. **Intent--**

Vosburg v. Putney, 50 N.W. 403 (Wis. 1891).

Facts. While sitting in a schoolroom, Putney (D) lightly kicked Vosburg (P) in the shin, unintentionally aggravating a previous injury. As a direct result of the kick, P permanently lost the use of his leg. P sued D alleging assault and battery and was awarded $2,800. On appeal, the verdict was set aside and the case was remanded for retrial. In the subsequent case, a judgment for $2,500 was granted. D appeals.

Issue. In an action for battery, must the plaintiff prove that the defendant intended to cause the harm that resulted?

Held. No. Judgment reversed and case remanded for new trial.

♦   In an action for assault and battery, the plaintiff need only show that the defendant either committed an unlawful act or that the defendant had an unlawful intention to commit the harm produced.

♦   Since the kick did not occur in the normal course of play on the school ground, the defendant does not have access to the implied license of the playground, which will excuse all injuries that are the result of boyish play.

♦ Because the kick took place during regular school hours in the schoolroom, the defendant's actions were unlawful and the court will infer an unlawful intent.

♦ As such, the defendant committed an assault and battery, and is therefore liable for all damages that result from his unlawful conduct.

Comment. Intentional conduct is an act that a reasonable person in D's position would know is substantially certain to lead to the damage of another's legally protected interests. This case also states the well-settled proposition that the tortfeasor must take his victim as he finds him; that is, the mere fact that the plaintiff is more susceptible to injury does not mitigate the tortfeasor's liability.

---

2. **Intentional Acts by Children.** Children are charged with what is expected of them, considering age, experience, intelligence, etc. They are liable only for what they are capable of, considering the foregoing factors. If they are capable of knowledge of the consequences of an act, they may be liable for those consequences. [*See* Garratt v. Dailey, 279 P.2d 1091 (Wash. 1955)]

3. **Transferred Intent.** The old common law form of action called "trespass" gave rise to five modern actions: battery, assault, false imprisonment, trespass to land, and trespass to chattels. Under the doctrine of transferred intent, if the defendant acts intending to cause one of these harms to X, the defendant will be liable on an intentional tort theory if *any* of the harms occurs to X, or even if they occur to another person entirely (*i.e.*, the plaintiff). This is true even though the plaintiff is unexpected and the harm is unexpected.

4. **Trespass to Real Property.** Every unauthorized entry of a person or thing on the land in the possession of another is a trespass. If the defendant intends to be on the plaintiff's land, whether the defendant's presence is based on mistake, ignorance as to the ownership, boundary of the land, claim of right, or some other matter, he is liable for trespass. To recover, the plaintiff need prove neither damages nor actual harm to the land.

   a. **Early case--**

Dougherty v. Stepp, 18 N.C. 371 (1835).

Facts. Plaintiff's (P's) offer of proof to establish an act of trespass was that the defendant (D) had entered on P's unenclosed land with a surveyor and chain carriers and surveyed a part of the land, claiming it as his own; D did not mark trees or cut bushes. Following the judge's instruction that there was no trespass, the jury found for D; P appeals.

Issue. Was the judge's instruction in error?

Held. Yes. Judgment reversed.

♦ Every unauthorized entry onto the land of another is trespass. For every unlawful entry the law infers damage, even if it is only the treading down of the grass.

---

b. Electronic communications excepted--

Intel Corp. v. Hamidi, 71 P.3d 296 (Cal. 2003).

Facts. Hamidi (D) used Intel's (P's) internal e-mail system, which was connected to the Internet, to send e-mails, criticizing P's employment practices, to between 8,000 and 35,000 employees on six specific occasions. D refused to stop when P requested that he do so. P brought an action against D seeking an injunction to prevent D from sending further e-mails to P's employees. The trial court granted summary judgment for P and issued a permanent injunction on a theory of trespass to chattels. The appeal court affirmed. We granted D's petition for review.

Issues.

(i) Does the tort of trespass to chattels encompass D's electronic communications, which neither damaged nor impaired the functioning of P's computer?

(ii) Should the tort be extended to encompass D's electronic communications?

Held. (i) No. (ii) No. Judgment reversed.

♦ To support a claim of trespass to chattels, there must be an interference that proximately causes some injury to the chattel or the plaintiff's rights to it. Only the actual damages suffered as a result of the impairment of the property or the loss of its use may be recovered. There must have been some actual injury in order for a trespass to chattels to be actionable. A harmless use or touching of personal property may be a technical trespass, but an interference, not amounting to dispossession, is not actionable without a showing of harm.

♦ In order to obtain injunctive relief, a plaintiff must show that the defendant's wrongful acts threaten to cause irreparable injuries that cannot be adequately compensated in damages.

◆ The tort of trespass to chattels does not encompass, and should not be extended to encompass, D's electronic communications, which neither damaged nor impaired the functioning of plaintiff's computer system. Without any actual damage, a cause of action for trespass to chattels will not lie; a mere momentary or theoretical deprivation of use is not sufficient unless there is a dispossession. Any request from an employee to be removed from D's mailing list was honored. Therefore, P's complaint was about the content of D's messages rather than the functioning of the company's e-mail system. P's claim regarding the loss of productivity caused by employees reading and reacting to the messages, and P's efforts to block the messages do not constitute an actionable trespass to P's personal property.

Concurrence. Using another's equipment, such as a mobile phone, to communicate with an authorized user of the equipment who does not object to the communication is trespass to chattels only if the communications damage the equipment or in some significant way impair its usefulness or availability.

Dissent. D sent as many as 200,000 e-mail messages to P's employees. Perusing and deleting these messages diverted workers from productive tasks and undermined the utility of the computer system. "There may . . . be situations in which the value to the owner of a particular type of chattel may be impaired by dealing with it in a manner that does not affect its physical condition." [Restatement (Second) of Torts §218] This is such a case.

5. **Conversion.**

   a. **Introduction.** Conversion is the intentional, wrongful acquiring, altering, damaging, transferring, using, or withholding of the personal property of another. The interest protected is that of possession, control, or right to control of a chattel. There must be more than a mere intermeddling for a conversion to lie.

   b. **Good faith and mistake.** Generally, neither good faith nor mistake will constitute a defense to conversion.

      1) **An absolute duty breached--**

Poggi v. Scott, 139 P. 815 (Cal. 1914).

Facts. Poggi (P) stored about 210 barrels of wine and some empty barrels in a locked room in the cellar of a building he rented. The empty barrels were near the door. Later, the owner's agent rented the whole building to the Sanitary Laundry Company ("Company") and P paid rent for the use of the cellar to the Company. P was a stockholder in the Company, and the Company deducted P's rent from the dividends due him upon his stock. P visited his wine about twice a month and racked it off once a year. The building was sold and the new owner was informed about both tenants. P was not told about the sale. When the Company vacated the premises, P's wine remained in the cellar, and P understood that he was liable for his rent to the owner's agent. A friend phoned P in November 1909, to tell him his wine was being carted away from the building. P came the next day, found the wine had been taken away, and went to the owner's agent to inquire. It was then he learned of the sale of the building to Scott (D). P sought out D, who informed P he knew nothing about the wine, but that he had sold some old barrels. D said he had been contacted by two Italians who wanted to buy the empty barrels in the cellar of his building. D had not known about the barrels and had visited the building with the Italians the next day. There had been no lock on the door and a number of barrels had been laying about, broken. There had been other whole barrels back further; D had tapped them and had thought they were empty. D had agreed to sell the barrels for $15 if the Italians would clean the whole cellar out. D had said if anything was discovered in the barrels, the price would be different, and the Italians had agreed. The Italians had carted off the wine and shipped it away. They were arrested for the theft of the wine. P sued to recover from D $2,000 damages suffered by him by reason of the unlawful conversion of some 200 barrels of wine. A nonsuit was granted on the ground that P had failed to prove a sufficient case for the jury. P appeals.

Issue. Is the grantee of a building who innocently sells property of a tenant of his grantor that was stored in the building liable for conversion?

Held. Yes. Judgment reversed.

♦ The basis of an action of conversion is neither in the knowledge nor the intent of the defendant. It is the unwarranted interference by the defendant with the dominion over the property of the plaintiff from which injury to the latter results. Good or bad faith, care or negligence, knowledge or ignorance are not the basis of the action. P need not show a wrongful motive or intent on the part of D, nor is negligence an issue.

♦ The tort consists of the breach of an absolute duty; the act itself (in some cases it must have caused damage) is unlawful and redressible as a tort.

♦ Here, there is no question of D's responsibility. D exercised an unjustifiable and unwarranted dominion and control over the property of another and loss resulted from his acts.

---

c. **What may be converted.** At common law, only property that could be lost could be the subject of an action for trover. This limited the action to *tangible* personal property. However, because of the need to protect intangible rights evidenced by commercial paper, the action for conversion was extended so that intangible rights merged with an instrument; *e.g.*, checks, notes, bonds, stock certificates, etc., were considered converted when the instrument evidencing such rights was converted. Today, some jurisdictions permit recovery for conversion of an intangible right (if it is of the type considered merged with an instrument) even though the instrument itself has not been converted (*e.g.*, refusal to transfer stock by a corporation). Under the general rule, intangible rights not considered merged with an instrument are not recognized as capable of being converted (*e.g.*, ideas, goodwill, etc.).

1) Body cells--

Moore v. Regents of the University of California, 793 P.2d 479 (Cal. 1990).

Facts. Moore (P), shortly after being diagnosed with hairy-cell leukemia, was treated by Dr. Golde, a physician at UCLA Medical Center, which was operated by The Regents of the University of California (Ds). P was told that his condition was life-threatening and that his spleen should be removed, but he was not told that his cells were unique and had scientific and commercial value. After P's splenectomy, Ds retained P's spleen for research purposes, and during seven years of follow-up tests, samples of P's blood, tissue, and other fluids were taken and used for research without his consent. Ds established a cell line from P's cells, obtained a patent for it, and entered into commercial agreements that earned Ds hundreds of thousands of dollars. P sued Ds for using his cells without disclosing their economic interests and without P's informed consent. The trial court sustained Ds' demurrers for the claim, but the court of appeals reversed. The Supreme Court of California granted review.

Issue. Does an individual own property rights in his own cells, such that use of the cells for medical research without his permission would constitute conversion?

Held. No. Judgment reversed in part.

♦   A conversion arises when the plaintiff establishes an actual interference with his ownership or right of possession. In this case, P certainly did not expect to retain possession of his cells after their removal, so he had no ownership interest on which to base a conversion claim.

♦   A balancing of policy considerations counsels against extending the tort of conversion to allow P to claim a property right to his biological materials. Problems in this area are better suited to legislative resolution.

♦   While the threat of conversion liability might help enforce patients' rights, the fiduciary-duty and informed-consent theories protect the patient directly, without impairing socially beneficial research.

♦ To satisfy his fiduciary duty and to obtain the patient's informed consent, a physician who is seeking a patient's consent for a medical procedure must disclose personal interests unrelated to the patient's health that may affect his medical judgment. Thus, in this case, P has stated a cause of action for breach of fiduciary duty or lack of informed consent but not for conversion.

Concurrence and dissent. P's complaint states a cause of action under traditional, common law conversion principles.

Dissent. The nondisclosure cause of action gives the patient the right to refuse consent but not the right to grant consent to commercialization on the condition that he share in the profits. A patient has a right to participate in such benefits. The nondisclosure cause of action is inadequate to reach a major class of the defendants, those outside the strict physician-patient relationship, *e.g.*, a researcher or a corporation participating in the commercial exploitation.

---

6. **Defenses to Intentional Torts.**

   a. **Consent.** Consent of the plaintiff or the existence of a privilege in the defendant will exonerate the defendant from liability for an act which, on its face, would otherwise give rise to tort liability. Of course, the burden is on the defendant to plead and prove the existence of a privilege or consent. Under the general rule, consent by the plaintiff to an act that would otherwise give rise to tort liability will act as a bar to an action based on the act. However, the consent must be effective to act as a bar. Problems often arise as to whether the plaintiff has in fact given, or has the capacity to give, consent.

      1) **Surgical operations and emergencies.** While a doctor is generally subject to the same rules with respect to invasion of another's rights, the law has developed certain exceptions. If, during an operation, a doctor discovers a condition in the plaintiff that requires immediate attention or that would require another operation to remedy, consent to the additional surgical procedure is deemed implied in law, unless the patient specifically limited the authority of the doctor prior to the operation. With respect to emergencies, the victim is assumed to consent to acts by a doctor consistent with what a reasonable person would desire under the same circumstances.

         a) **Action for assault and battery--**

Mohr v. Williams, 104 N.W. 12 (Minn. 1905).

Facts. P went to D, an ear specialist, to have an operation on her right ear. While P was under anesthesia, D found a more serious condition in P's left ear, ultimately dangerous, but not immediately critical, and operated on it instead of the right ear. P sued D for assault and battery. A verdict of $14,322.50 for P was held excessive by the trial court and a new trial was ordered.

Issue. Did D's conduct amount to an assault and battery?

Held. Yes. The new trial order is affirmed.

♦ The fact that D acted without wrongful intent and was not guilty of negligence does not relieve D from the charge of assault and battery. He wrongfully, and hence unlawfully, operated on P.

♦ The amount of damages depends on D's wrongful intent, etc.

Comment. P ultimately recovered nominal damages for the assault and battery. Generally, consent of a parent is necessary to operate on a minor, except in an emergency. (Query: How extreme an emergency is necessary?) Some cases have permitted minors to consent to operations minor in scope. In personal injury cases, when a person is unable to give consent and no one with authority to consent is available, sound professional judgment can be exercised.

---

b) **Informed consent.** It is generally held that consent must be informed and that mistake in the facts will vitiate apparent consent. Modern courts treat absence of informed consent as grounds for a negligence action rather than a battery action.

2) **Manifestation of intent.** Consent may be express or implied. When the plaintiff, by words or conduct, intentionally indicates that he is willing to permit an invasion of his rights by the defendant, there is express consent. Implied consent, on the other hand, may be either implied in fact, as where the plaintiff acts in such a way as would be understood by a reasonable person to be consent to invasion of his rights by the defendant, or implied in law, as where circumstances are such as to create the privilege in the defendant to invade the plaintiff's rights without liability (*e.g.*, doctor rendering emergency medical care to unconscious person).

3) **Mistake of fact.** The plaintiff's mistake as to the nature of the defendant's conduct will vitiate the plaintiff's apparent consent. For example, where the plaintiff submits to a body massage under the mistaken belief that the defendant is treating an illness and that the massage is a necessary part of the treatment, the plaintiff will

not be deemed to have consented to the defendant's offered indecent familiarities. Similarly, a person who accepts and eats candy poisoned by the defendant, without knowledge of the poison, does not consent to be poisoned by the defendant.

4) **Mistake of law.** Consent is ineffective if given under a mistake of law; *e.g.*, submitting to arrest under belief that an arrest warrant is valid, when in fact it is not.

5) **Fraud.** Consent procured by fraud is ineffective, *e.g.*, the body massage example above. However, fraud as to a collateral matter does not vitiate consent; *e.g.*, where the plaintiff consents to sexual intercourse with the defendant in return for a $10 bill, which is counterfeit, the fact that the plaintiff did not know the bill was counterfeit will not negate the consent if it is otherwise effective.

6) **Nondisclosure of material fact negating consent.** In cases of sexual transmission of disease, courts have generally refused to impose liability when a cheating husband has passed on a sexually communicable disease to his wife, as long as the husband did not know or have reason to know that he had the disease. In contrast, in a 1998 Maine case, the court found the defendant's conduct actionable where a husband of 31 years intentionally misrepresented or failed to affirmatively disclose his medical condition to his wife. [*See* McPherson v. McPherson, 712 A.2d 1043 (Me. 1998)]

7) **Duress.** Consent given in response to physical force or threats thereof against the plaintiff or a member of the plaintiff's family will be ineffective.

8) **Unlawful acts.** There is a split of authority concerning whether a voluntary participant to an unlawful act can be deemed to have "consented" thereto for the purpose of barring a subsequent action against a fellow participant for damages.

   a) **Serious injury—majority rule--**

Hudson v. Craft, 204 P.2d 1 (Cal. 1949).

Facts. Hudson (P), an 18-year-old boy, sued Craft (D), the promoter of an illegal carnival boxing concession, for the assault and battery P suffered when he was induced to engage in a boxing match and was injured. The trial court dismissed the complaint, holding that P had consented to the match and thus to the risk of injury. P appeals.

Issue. May a member of a class of persons protected under the law consent to an act contrary to the intent of the law?

Held. No. Judgment reversed.

♦ The law was intended to protect participants in boxing contests from serious injury and P was a member of the class afforded this protection. The promoter is liable as a principal in the assault and battery charge rather than as an aider and abettor.

Comment. A strong public policy to prevent a breach of the peace and protect the 18-year-old plaintiff from promoters was important to the decision of the case.

---

       b) **Minority view.** A party participating in an illegal act may not gain a right of action by such participation.

    9) **Athletic injuries.** Consent to participation in violent sports such as football is not a consent to all acts and injuries. Acts completely beyond the purpose of the sport are held to be done without consent.

  b. **Insanity--**

McGuire v. Almy, 8 N.E.2d 760 (Mass. 1937).

Facts. An insane person (D) was wrecking her room and threatened to kill anyone coming into the room. D's nurse (P) entered the room and tried to take a table leg away from D. P failed and was struck over the head with the leg. P brought a personal injury suit for her injuries. The jury returned a verdict for P. D appeals.

Issue. Can an insane person have the requisite intent for assault and battery?

Held. Yes. Judgment affirmed.

♦ Where an insane person, by her action, does intentional damage to another's person or property, the insane person is liable to the same degree that a sane person would be. Here, D is not morally to blame, but is legally at fault.

Comment. A truly insane person cannot act, since an act is an external manifestation of an inward will—a volitional movement. However, such persons are held liable for their actions as a matter of public policy. Why?

    (i) People legally charged with the care of incompetents will be more aware and watchful.

    (ii) An innocent victim should not have to bear the damages caused by an insane person when the insane person is able to make restitution.

capture chattels if he is entitled to immediate possession, return has been demanded and refused, he is in "fresh pursuit" (*i.e.*, he has been reasonably diligent in discovering his loss and in attempting to recover the chattel), the person from whom the recapture is effected is the wrongdoer or is not a bona fide purchaser from the wrongdoer, and the force used is reasonable under the circumstances.

a)   Property held under claim of right--

Kirby v. Foster, 22 A. 1111 (R.I. 1891).

Facts. Kirby (P) was a bookkeeper for Foster (D). Some money was missing and D deducted it from P's salary. P got control of some of D's money when P was assigned to pay some of the workers. Upon advice of his counsel, P retained the amount that had been deducted from his salary, returned the rest to D, and quit instead of paying the amount to the workers as instructed. D then struggled physically with P to retake the amount retained and P was injured. P prevailed in an assault and battery action. D petitioned for a new trial.

Issue. Was D justified in using force to regain the money from P?

Held. No. Judgment affirmed.

♦   D's purported right to retake by force will be a defense to assault and battery where D is entitled to possession and the taking or conversion was wrongful (without a claim of right).

♦   However, conflicting claims of right (as in the situation here) should be settled by legal process, not physical force.

---

b)   Conditional sales. There is no right to use force to recapture a chattel if the chattel was obtained in a legal manner in the first instance. If a contract contains a clause allowing the seller to repossess from the buyer for failure of payment, the seller can attempt repossession. But since there was no force or fraud on the part of the buyer (possession was given to the buyer peacefully and voluntarily), the seller has no right to use any force in recapture of the chattel.

(1)   Force defined. Force is any intrusion into the premises of the plaintiff or use of force against the chattel or force against the possessor. Breaking into a car, garage, home, etc., using a skeleton key or master key, hot wiring, intruding, or using any force against the chattel or the person is tortious. Watch for trespass to chattels or trespass to land, or false imprisonment or battery to the person, in recovery cases.

(2) **No right to self-help.** While the repossessor has a legal right, he must use the courts to enforce that right and has no right to take the law upon himself.

(3) **Contract clause.** A contract with a clause permitting use of force in repossession is void as contrary to public policy.

(4) **Damages.** Note that a repossessor may even be liable for conversion in some cases and may be subject to punitive damages.

c) **Damages by reason of the invasion of another's land to reclaim chattels.** If the defendant damages the plaintiff's land in recapturing his chattels, and the plaintiff had wrongfully obtained the defendant's chattels, the defendant will not be liable for the damage, provided the entry and force used to recapture the chattels was reasonable. On the other hand, if the plaintiff was not a wrongdoer and the chattel is on the plaintiff's land through an act of God or an act of a third party, the defendant will be liable for any damage done in reclaiming the chattel, although he is not liable for damage caused by the chattel being deposited on the plaintiff's land. If the defendant's chattel is on the plaintiff's land through the fault of the defendant, the defendant has no privilege of any kind to enter the plaintiff's land and reclaim it.

2) **Reentry upon real property.** The statute of Richard II made it a criminal offense for one entitled to possession of land to reenter by force. Today, there is a split of authority as to the requirement of pursuing a civil action.

a) **Majority view.** Under the majority view there is no privilege to use force in reentry, and the legal owner must rely on legal processes to regain possession. Why?

(1) There is a summary method to gain reentry.

(2) In a modern society, citizens should rely on the state to enforce their rights, not self-help.

        b)   **Minority view.** The minority view is that there is a privilege to use reasonable force in reentry, but (in the majority of these jurisdictions) the actor (i) may be subject to criminal prosecution if he harms the possessor, (ii) must protect the property of the possessor for a reasonable time, and (iii) cannot eject the possessor of land into a dangerous position.

      3)   **Removing trespassing chattels.** The person in possession of land or chattels is privileged to use reasonable force to remove chattels belonging to another in order to protect his interest in his own land or chattels. The "reasonableness" of the force applied to the trespassing chattels is in part determined by the relative value of the actor's property as opposed to the value of the trespassing chattels (*i.e.*, the actor is not privileged to totally destroy a valuable trespassing chattel in order to effect immediate removal when the damage caused to his property by a more time-consuming but orderly removal would be nominal).

  g.   **Necessity.**

      1)   **Public necessity.** One is privileged to enter land or interfere with chattels of another if it is reasonably necessary or if it reasonably appears necessary to avert a public disaster. To invoke the privilege, the following are required: (i) an immediate and imperative necessity and not just one that is expedient or utilitarian; and (ii) an act that is in good faith and for the public good. The privilege is conditional and it disappears when the act becomes unreasonable under the existing circumstances. The rationale behind this privilege is that when peril threatens the whole community, or so many people that there is public interest involved, one has a complete defense or privilege to act to protect the public interest. The defendant is not liable for any damage or destruction to the land or chattels involved, as long as this was done in the proper exercise of the privilege.

      2)   **Private necessity.** If there is no public interest involved and the defendant acts to protect his own interest, he is not liable for the technical tort and the landowner has no privilege to expel him.

        a)   **Scope of privilege--**

Ploof v. Putnam, 71 A. 188 (Vt. 1908).

Facts. P was sailing on Lake Champlain when a tremendous storm came up. P came upon D's island and tied his boat to D's dock to protect his boat and his family. D had his agent untie the boat and set it adrift in the storm. P's boat was destroyed, and his wife and children were injured.

Issue. Does the privilege to invade another's land and chattels by reason of private necessity supersede the privilege of the possessor of the land and chattels to use reasonable force to prevent the invasion?

Held. Yes. Judgment affirmed.

♦ There is a privilege to enter land and use chattels of another if there is a private emergency.

♦ Here, P's choice appeared to be to invade D's land and use his chattels or face the prospect of losing his own and his family's lives.

♦ The preservation of life is more important than a property right.

Comment. The private necessity privilege is narrower than the public one (*i.e.*, it must appear that the emergency is great and the interests being risked must be greater than those violated).

---

b) Liability for damage--

Vincent v. Lake Erie Transportation Co., 124 N.W. 221 (Minn. 1910).

Facts. Lake Erie Transportation Co. (D), following Vincent's (P's) instruction, moored its boat to P's wharf so that P's cargo could be unloaded. During unloading, a violent storm arose that prevented the boat from leaving the wharf. Thereafter, the storm threw the boat against the wharf and damaged the wharf. P sued to recover for damages. D appeals an order denying the motion for judgment notwithstanding the verdict.

Issue. May one who is forced by necessity to use the property of another do so without liability for injury to the property caused by his use?

Held. No. Judgment affirmed.

♦ The ship's master exercised ordinary prudence and care in keeping the ship moored to the wharf during the storm.

♦ In so doing, he deliberately protected the ship at the expense of the wharf.

♦ The damage to the wharf did not result from an act of God or unavoidable accident, but rather from circumstances within D's control.

♦ Having deliberately availed himself of P's property, as the storm gave D the right to do, D was liable for injury inflicted by his actions.

Dissent. Judgment for P should be reversed.

- ♦ The master exercised due care.

- ♦ The injury to the dock was an inevitable accident.

- ♦ The owner of the dock, who had entered into contractual relations with the owner of the ship, should bear the loss.

Comment. The invasion of the other person's property out of private necessity must protect an interest greater than the interest invaded. If this is the case, the party whose interests are invaded will be liable if he tries to expel the invading party.

C. EMOTIONAL AND DIGNITARY HARMS

1. **Assault.** An assault is an act, other than a mere speaking of words, that directly places the plaintiff in fear or apprehension of immediate harmful or offensive contact without consent or privilege. The elements of assault that make up the plaintiff's prima facie case are: (i) an act by the defendant; (ii) intent of the defendant; (iii) fear or apprehension of the plaintiff; and (iv) causal relationship. For liability to attach, there must be an absence of consent by the plaintiff and privilege of the defendant (discussed *infra*).

    a. **Act by the defendant.** This element of the tort is satisfied by some volitional, external movement of the defendant. This would preclude an unconscious act or a movement made by a person under the influence of drugs. This requirement also eliminates any pure reflex action by the defendant.

       1) **Words alone usually insufficient.** Words alone are usually not sufficient to create an assault. There must be an apprehension of immediate offensive touching by the plaintiff before there can be an assault. Words alone usually will not be sufficient to create the apprehension of the imminent touching; *i.e.*, unless there is some act or action that indicates the present ability and intention to do personal violence, there is no assault.

       2) **Absence of physical harm--**

I. de S. and Wife v. W. de S., 1348 [or 1349] Year Book, Liber Assisarum, folio 99, placitum 60.

Facts. W. (D) was beating with a hatchet on the door of I.'s tavern, which was closed.

I.'s wife (P) stuck her head out the window and ordered D to stop, whereupon D swung at her with the hatchet. There was no contact. P, however, sued for trespass.

Issue. Where a plaintiff is caused to fear for her safety (but not actually physically harmed) by an act of a defendant, is there a cause of action?

Held. Yes.

♦ There is a recovery for an assault, which is making another fearful of a harmful touching. The assault occurred when D struck at P with the hatchet.

Comment. Here, the court compensated P not for a physical injury, but for mental suffering, intentionally inflicted. Actual touching of the plaintiff was not necessary to recover for assault.

———————

b. **Intent.** The defendant must have intended to inflict a harm on the plaintiff or put him in fear of an immediate harmful or offensive touching. This can be shown even under "transferred" intent.

1) **Declaration of no assault--**

Tuberville v. Savage, 86 Eng. Rep. 684 (1669).

Facts. P put his hand on his sword, saying, "If it were not assize-time, I would not take such language from you," whereupon he was struck and injured by D. D claimed self-defense, alleging that P's acts were an assault.

Issue. If an aggressor's words negate a present intent to harm the other person, is that person justified in using force to defend himself?

Held. No.

♦ D's apprehension was not reasonable because P's words negated an intent to inflict injury. Here, the words explained away the action and so did not constitute an assault. Similarly, the words, "If you were not an old man, I would hit you," do not constitute an assault.

———————

c. **Apprehension.** The actions of the the defendant must actually put the plaintiff in apprehension of an imminent harmful or offensive touching. The standard laid down for this test is not subjective (was the plaintiff apprehensive?) but is based on what a reasonable person in the plaintiff's shoes might have thought (*i.e.*, would a reasonable person have been apprehensive?).

d.   **Causation.** The plaintiff's apprehension must have been caused by the actions of the the defendant.

e.   **Damages.** The damages recoverable are the same as for battery.

2.   **Offensive Battery.** The elements necessary to establish the tort of battery are as follows:

a.   **Act by the defendant.** Like an action for assault, there must be a volitional act by the defendant that causes the plaintiff's injury.

b.   **Intent.** The act done by the defendant must have been done with the requisite intent to commit the harmful or offensive touching.

1)   The general test used to determine intent is whether the defendant acted with the desire to cause, or substantially knew that his actions would cause, the touching that occurred. The defendant may be liable even if he does not believe that the touching will be harmful or offensive; an objective standard is applied to that element.

c.   **Harmful or offensive touching.** The action of the defendant must result in the infliction of a harmful or offensive touching to the plaintiff or to something that is so closely associated with the plaintiff as to be tantamount to a touching of the plaintiff. A harmful touching is one that inflicts any pain or injury, while an offensive touching is one that offends a reasonable person's sense of personal dignity (*i.e.*, is not expressly or impliedly consented to).

1)   **Offensive touching--**

Alcorn v. Mitchell, 63 Ill. 553 (1872).

Facts. At the close of a trial, in the presence of many people, D spat in P's face. P sued D for battery. The court assessed punitive damages of $1,000 against D. D appeals on the grounds that the award was excessive.

Issue. Can punitive damages be awarded for intentional torts?

Held. Yes. Judgment affirmed.

♦   Spitting in someone's face is a great affront.

♦   The law should protect against such affronts in the courtroom by awarding punitive damages.

♦ If there were no punitive damages in cases such as this, the only alternative form of retribution would be personal violence.

Comment. The defendant's contact with the plaintiff need not cause actual physical harm (*i.e.*, pain, injury, disfigurement, etc., to the person). It is sufficient that the contact be offensive or insulting. The legally protected interest is the plaintiff's right to be free from being touched without consent. The plaintiff need not know of the offensive touching at the time of contact. For example, if the plaintiff is kissed by the defendant while she sleeps, and would otherwise have been offended by such an act if she had been awake, there is a battery.

---

        d.   **Causation.** The action of the defendant must be the legal cause of or put in motion the force that results in the plaintiff's injury.

        e.   **Damages.** An award of damages is based on the commission of a harmful or offensive touching. The plaintiff can receive compensatory damages for all damages directly caused by the touching as well as for all consequential damages. Punitive damages are also recoverable when it appears that the defendant was motivated to intentionally harm the plaintiff. The plaintiff may recover nominal damages if no actual damages are proven.

        f.   **Relation to assault.** A battery usually consists of an assault and actual contact. However, there can be a battery (for purposes of tort liability) without an assault. Compare with criminal liability, where assault is generally viewed as a lesser included offense in a battery.

3.   **False Imprisonment.** False imprisonment is the total obstruction and detention of the plaintiff, of which he is aware, within boundaries for any length of time, with intent by the defendant to obstruct or detain the plaintiff or another, and without privilege or consent. The plaintiff's prima facie case includes the following elements:

(i)   Act by the defendant;

(ii)   Obstruction or detention of the plaintiff;

(iii) Intent; and

(iv) Causal relationship.

For liability to attach, there must be an absence of consent and privilege.

        a.   **No escape.** It is not necessary that the plaintiff be totally imprisoned to support an action for false imprisonment. False imprisonment will arise if there is no "reasonable avenue of exit" available to the plaintiff. An exit is not "reasonable" if it is:

1)   Unknown to the plaintiff; or

2)   Requires the plaintiff to take risks to escape, is dangerous, or is discomforting.

    b.   **Restriction insufficient.** Generally, it is not sufficient that a plaintiff is not allowed to go where he wishes if he can go somewhere else. Under certain circumstances, an exclusion (as from one's home) may be sufficient. Further, it is sufficient for a finding of false imprisonment that the plaintiff, allowed to move freely about several rooms in a house, is restrained from leaving the house, without consent or privilege.

    1)   **Partial obstruction--**

Bird v. Jones, 115 Eng. Rep. 688 (K.B. 1845).

Facts. Part of a public highway was enclosed for a sporting event. P was prevented from going over an enclosure by police who worked for D. However, while P was stopped from going where he wanted to go, he could have remained where he was, or could have taken leave in another direction. P brought an action for false imprisonment and, after a verdict for P, D sought a new trial.

Issue. Is total obstruction and detention necessary to constitute false imprisonment?

Held. Yes. New trial granted.

♦   Total obstruction and detention, not partial, is required to give rise to an action for false imprisonment. Imprisonment requires more than loss of total freedom to go wherever one pleases (as with a partial restraint). It must be a restraint of the plaintiff within defined boundaries by a will or power contrary to that of the plaintiff.

Dissent. If I am prevented from doing what I want to do, the fact that I am permitted to do something else is of no importance. Any restraint of the person by force, I understand to be imprisonment.

    c.   **Knowledge of the obstruction or detention.**

    1)   **Submission of will.** Obstruction or detention for purposes of false imprisonment must be against the will of the one restrained. Therefore, the majority holds that if there is no knowledge on the part of the plaintiff at the time of his detention, there can be no submission of his will and hence no false imprisonment. The fact that the plaintiff makes no resistance does not necessarily negate the element of submission against his will.

2) Restatement approach. The Restatement (Second) of Torts, section 42, allows recovery for false imprisonment where there is (i) knowledge of imprisonment, or (ii) damages resulting from the imprisonment, even though there is no knowledge.

d. Means of obstruction or detention. The means of obstructing or detaining the plaintiff may be by conduct, words, force, threats, or refusal to permit egress.

1) Apparent physical barriers. Locking a plaintiff in a room where there is another concealed and unlocked door will still constitute confinement of the plaintiff. As indicated above, the plaintiff must know of the available exit.

2) Submission where the plaintiff has the power to break confinement. If the plaintiff, who is bigger and stronger than the defendant and has the power to break the physical force or restraint placed upon him by the defendant, instead physically submits to the unlawful detention, the defendant nonetheless is chargeable with false imprisonment.

3) Duress. False imprisonment will also arise from duress of person or property, but threats of duress in the future are not sufficient. Self-imposed moral pressure only to clear one's self, or threats to have the plaintiff arrested if he leaves, are not sufficient for false imprisonment.

e. Words as a restraint. Words can restrain a person if he fears disregarding them, even if there is no physical restraint.

f. Escape. It is generally held that false imprisonment invites escape and that the plaintiff may recover for any injuries sustained in an escape attempt.

g. Intent. Intent of the defendant to obstruct or detain the plaintiff or another is a required element of false imprisonment. However, as noted, omission to carry out one's duty, thereby causing confinement, will give rise to false imprisonment. Hostile or malicious intent is not required.

1) Transferred intent. The doctrine of transferred intent applies to false imprisonment; *e.g.*, if the defendant intends to detain butcher

A in a frozen locker and, thinking A is inside, shuts the door on B, the defendant is subject to an action by B for false imprisonment.

h. **Causal relationship.** There must be a causal relationship between the act or omission of the defendant and the obstruction or detention of the plaintiff.

i. **Consent or privilege.** The defendant's act that was the legal cause of the false imprisonment of the plaintiff must have been without consent or privilege in order for liability to attach.

1) **Statutory privilege--**

Coblyn v. Kennedy's, Inc., 268 N.E.2d 860 (Mass. 1971).

Facts. Coblyn (P), 70 years old and five feet, four inches tall, went to the second floor of Kennedy's (D's) store to buy a sport coat. While having it fitted, he removed an ascot that he had worn and placed it in his pocket. After the fitting, P walked down to the first floor and to one of the store exits, where he paused to replace the ascot around his neck. As he did so, two of D's employees approached him and asked where he had obtained the scarf. One of them grabbed P by the arm and said that he had better see the manager. P complied. The sport coat salesperson confirmed that the scarf was P's, but P suffered a myocardial infarction. P sued for false imprisonment and was awarded $12,500 damages. D appeals, contending that there had been no imprisonment and that the detention was justified by a shoplifting statute that allows detentions of reasonable length where there are reasonable grounds to believe that larceny is being committed.

Issues.

(i) Does the demonstration of physical power which apparently can only be avoided by submission constitute imprisonment?

(ii) May a merchant detain a person without reasonable grounds for belief that the person had shoplifted?

Held. (i) Yes. (ii) No. Judgment affirmed.

♦ Any genuine restraint is sufficient to constitute an imprisonment. Here, the 70-year-old P could do nothing other than comply with the "request" of D's employees.

♦ The Massachusetts statute provides that a merchant may detain a person if there are reasonable grounds to believe the person has attempted to shoplift and if the detention is effected in a reasonable manner and for a reasonable time.

♦ "Reasonable grounds" is an objective standard and means the same as "probable cause."

♦ While D's employees may have had an honest suspicion, there was nothing in P's conduct to justify a reasonably prudent person in believing that P was a shoplifter.

---

j. Damages. When liability is established, the plaintiff may recover damages from the defendant even though no special damages (*i.e.*, injuries, loss of earnings, etc.) are proved. If special damages are proved, they are of course recoverable. Also, note that any injuries sustained in an escape attempt are recoverable.

4. Intentional Infliction of Emotional Distress. Emotional distress is characterized by physical injury or severe mental suffering by the plaintiff, resulting from emotional disturbance (without physical impact) caused by highly aggravated words or acts of the defendant done with intent to cause mental suffering or with knowledge or belief on the part of the defendant that such is substantially certain to result from such words or acts, and without consent or privilege.

a. Introduction. The words or acts must be severe, exceeding all socially acceptable standards, and must cause injury of a serious kind to the plaintiff. There is no longer a requirement that there must be some physical injury manifestations from the emotional disturbance caused by the defendant. On the other hand, the law recognizes that humans must occasionally "blow off steam," and ordinarily the defendants are not liable for mere insults that may cause emotional disturbance. One way that intentional infliction of emotional distress differs from negligent infliction of mental disturbance is that it is done with a more culpable state of mind.

b. Objections. Mental distress was recognized as an element of damages in early assault cases. However, it was not until relatively recent times (about the turn of the century) that the intentional infliction of mental distress, without any other accompanying tort (such as assault), gained recognition as a separate basis for finding tort liability. The relatively slow development of the law to recognize the plaintiff's peace of mind as a legally protected interest has been due to the following objections:

1) The character of the injury suffered in mental distress is difficult to determine; you cannot see mental anguish, whereas it is easy to see a broken arm, an unlawful restraint, etc.

2) The damages resulting from mental distress are of a subtle and speculative nature (peculiar, variable, hard to assess, etc.).

3) Mental distress lends itself to fictitious claims.

4) Recognition of the basis of liability will open up floods of litigation.

5) Permitting recovery for mental distress will encourage perjury, either through overstating the facts or fabrication.

c. **Modern trend.** Notwithstanding the objections cited above, the law seems to be moving toward an expansion of the circumstances under which liability for the infliction of mental distress will be found.

d. **Early evolution--**

Wilkinson v. Downton, [1897] 2 Q.B. 57.

Facts. Downton (D) as a practical joke told Wilkinson (P) that P's husband was injured with two broken legs. D said P's husband asked P to "fetch" him with two pillows. D's statements were false. P suffered weeks of severe emotional distress and physical illness precipitated by nervous shock. P had not been previously ill. P brought an action for personal injuries. The trial court found for P. D appeals.

Issue. Is extreme or outrageous conduct causing physical injuries actionable?

Held. Yes. Judgment affirmed.

♦ D's act was calculated to cause physical harm to P.

♦ An ordinary person of sound health and mind could have suffered as P did.

♦ The effect of D's acts was thus not too remote.

Comment. This case is the predecessor of the modern cause of action for the intentional infliction of emotional distress.

---

e. **Parasitic damages.** In *Bouillon v. Laclede Gaslight Co.,* 129 S.W. 401 (Mo. Ct. App. 1910), Bouillon (P) was ill and in danger of a miscarriage. An agent of Laclede Gaslight Co. (D) demanded entrance to P's home to read a meter. There was no meter in P's home, although there was one in her basement, which the meter reader normally reached through a rear entrance. A nurse refused to admit D's agent, at P's direction. The agent argued and demanded in an outrageous manner that he be admitted. Finally, he desisted. P miscarried, according to a doctor's testimony, as a direct result of D's agent's conduct. P's health was permanently impaired. The trial court directed a verdict for P. On appeal the judgment was affirmed. The court held that D did not commit an assault against P. However, the agent clearly trespassed onto P's property by putting his hand inside her apartment. Further, the court found a trespasser is liable for the natural, necessary, direct, and proximate damages of his wrong. Fright and mental distress may be such results of trespass. In this case, the defendant clearly committed a trespass. The case could be interpreted as merely allowing parasitic damages for the trespass that was committed.

f. **Outrageous conduct.** The Restatement (Second) of Torts defines this tort as one of outrageous conduct. The conduct must be extreme and the result of an intentional or reckless state of mind. The tort is applied in a variety of settings. In *State Rubbish Collectors Association v. Siliznoff*, 240 P.2d 282 (Cal. 1952), Siliznoff (D) was threatened with bodily harm if he did not pay the Rubbish Collectors Association (P) part of the proceeds of one of his accounts. D paid cash to one individual and gave P a series of notes. When P sued on the notes, D demanded the notes be cancelled due to duress and for lack of consideration, and cross-complained for general and exemplary damages because of assaults by P and its agents to compel D to join the association. P's argument that there was no assault because all threats related to actions that might happen in the future and there was no immediate harm failed; the appeals court noted a cause of action was established when, in the absence of privilege, it is shown that one intentionally subjects another to mental suffering connected to serious threats to his physical well-being, whether or not the threats are made under circumstances that constitute technical assault.

g. **Debt collection.** In *George v. Jordan Marsh Co.*, 268 N.E.2d 915 (Mass. 1971), George's (P's) complaint alleged that Jordan Marsh Co. (D) harassed her, mailed letters to her stating that her credit was revoked, and engaged in other "dunning tactics" in an effort to get P to pay her son's debt. P claimed she had never guaranteed her son's debt. P suffered two heart attacks and incurred medical expenses as a result of D's actions. The sufficiency of P's complaint was upheld. The court found on appeal that one who, without a privilege to do so, by extreme and outrageous conduct, intentionally causes severe emotional distress to another, with bodily harm resulting from such distress, is subject to liability for such emotional distress and bodily harm even though he has committed no heretofore recognized common law tort.

h. **Public figure.** *Hustler Magazine* (D) ran a parody about an interview with Jerry Falwell (P), in which he identified his "first time" as a drunken encounter with his mother in an outhouse. P sued D for defamation and intentional infliction of emotional distress. In *Hustler Magazine v.*

Falwell, 485 U.S. 46 (1988), the jury found that there was no defamation because the parody could not be understood as describing actual facts. The jury did find for P, however, on the emotional distress claim. The court of appeals affirmed, but the Supreme Court reversed, finding that P was a public figure and could not recover for emotional distress because of the same First Amendment concerns that arise in defamation. In the absence of establishing that a false statement of fact was made with "actual malice," *i.e.,* knowledge of falsity or reckless disregard as to truth or falsity, P had no basis for recovery.

II. STRICT LIABILITY AND NEGLIGENCE: HISTORIC AND ANALYTIC FOUNDATIONS

A. INTRODUCTION

Liability based on the negligence of the defendant is another of the major classifications of tort liability. The Restatement (Second) of Torts, section 282, defines negligence as "any conduct, except conduct recklessly disregardful of an interest of others, which falls below the standard established by law for the protection of others against unreasonable risk of harm." This section looks at the historical evolution of the law from strict liability to negligence.

B. THE FORMATIVE CASES

1. **Early English Law.** Early cases seem to suggest liability for all injuries without a requirement of any proof of fault.

    a. **Liability for direct injury--**

The Thorns Case, Y.B. Mich. 6 Ed. 4, f. 7, pl. 18 (1466).

Facts. D owned a hedge of thorns bordering P's property. D cut down the hedge and, against his will, some thorns fell on P's land. D went on P's land to remove the thorns as soon as he could. P sued for a continued trespass by the thorns and by D when he removed the thorns. P won. D appeals.

Issue. May a person be held liable for an act he might have avoided?

Held. Yes. Judgment affirmed.

♦   If a man does a lawful act and causes injury to someone else by that act, he will be held liable if he could have avoided the act.

♦   D could have avoided dropping thorns on P's property.

♦   He that is damaged ought to be recompensed.

Comment. The action of trespass provided relief for all direct injury to person or property. It covered intentional injuries (*i.e.*, intent to do the act) but did not require fault on the part of the defendant (*i.e.*, wrongful intent or negligence was not required). Only later was the concept of liability only for fault (negligence) recognized.

b. Intent or fault—possibly material--

Weaver v. Ward, 80 Eng. Rep. 284 (K.B. 1616).

Facts. Weaver (P) and Ward (D) were soldiers. In the course of a military exercise, D's musket accidentally and against his will discharged, wounding P. P brought an action in trespass for damages for the injury.

Issue. Must the plaintiff show intent or fault on the part of the defendant?

Held. No.

♦ The defendant is liable for direct injury unless it is utterly without his fault.

Comments.

♦ The court did state that "no man is excused from a trespass unless he is utterly without fault." Thus, the case indicates a shift in determination of liability through a recognition of the fact that a defendant might not be liable for an unavoidable accident occurring without his fault, notwithstanding that injury to the plaintiff was direct and forcible and otherwise would constitute a trespass.

♦ The court indicated a move toward looking at the defendant's intent or negligence instead of the artificial classification of the injury as direct or indirect. The shift was finally completed in the late 19th century, when it was recognized that no liability would lie for pure accident and that for a defendant to be held responsible for injury to the person, there must be fault on his part; *i.e.*, wrongful intent or negligence.

C. THE FORMS OF ACTION

1. **The Significance of the Forms of Action.** In the common law courts of the 13th century, only two writs were available for redressing torts. These were the writ of trespass and the writ of trespass on the case.

   a. **Trespass.** The writ of trespass provided relief for all direct and immediate forcible injuries to person or property. It covered unintentional as well as intentional injuries, required no proof of actual damages, and did not require fault on the part of the defendant (*i.e.*, wrongful intent or negligence was not required).

   b. **Trespass on the case.** The writ of trespass on the case provided relief for injuries that were intended but were either not forcible or not direct.

Usually the plaintiff was required to show actual damages and wrongful intent or negligence on the part of the defendant.

c. Liability for consequential damages--

Scott v. Shepherd, 96 Eng. Rep. 525 (K.B. 1773).

Facts. Shepherd (D) threw a lighted squib made of gunpowder into a crowded marketplace. The squib was thrown back and forth by several people, all of whom were attempting to prevent injury to themselves and their stalls. The squib finally was thrown to Scott (P). It blew up in his face, blinding him in one eye. P sued for trespass. D argued that he could not be liable for trespass because of the intervention of others, who were the actual cause of P's injuries. P argued that, once having set an instrument capable of causing injury in motion, D was liable for consequential injuries directly attributable to his acts. P received a verdict of £100.

Issue. Is a person liable for the consequential, but foreseeable, damages caused by his setting in motion a dangerous instrumentality?

Held. Yes. Judgment affirmed.

- The natural and probable consequence of D's action was injury to some person.

- D's act was one of general mischief, not being intended to injure any particular person, but to frighten all those in the area.

- D should know that anyone to whom the squib was thrown would throw it elsewhere to protect himself.

- Because both the final result (injury to some person) and the intervention of third parties were foreseeable, D is liable for the ultimate injury caused by his initial act.

Dissent (Blackstone, J.). If the action is to lie at all, it must lie as trespass on the case, not mere trespass. Trespass applies only to immediate damage, not consequential damages. Here, D's tort was completed when the squib initially came to rest. The intervention of other actors after that time vitiated D's liability.

Concurrence (De Grey, C.J.). The true question is whether the injury is the direct and immediate act of the defendant, and I am of the opinion that it is. Mischief was originally intended; whatever mischief follows, D is the author of it.

Comment. The courts finally had to confront the question of whether an action was to be brought in trespass or on the case when the injuries were the consequential results of a defendant's action. By the middle of the 19th century, the courts were allowing a plaintiff to bring an action on the case, whether the injury was the direct result or the consequential result of the defendant's acts. [*See* Williams v. Holland, 131 Eng. Rep. 848 (C.P. 1833)]

D. STRICT LIABILITY AND NEGLIGENCE IN THE LAST HALF OF THE NINETEENTH CENTURY

Strict liability is liability without fault. It is based on a policy of the law that the particular injured plaintiff must be given a right of recovery, notwithstanding that there is no fault in the conduct of the defendant. However, strict liability does not mean absolute liability. There still remain problems of causation, and there are some defenses.

1. American Evolution of Negligence--

Brown v. Kendall, 60 Mass. 292 (1850).

Facts. Brown's (P's) and Kendall's (D's) dogs were fighting. While attempting to separate the dogs, D struck P (who was standing behind him) in the eye with a stick. The trial court placed the burden on D to show that he exercised extraordinary care because he was not engaged in a necessary act. D's objection to this requirement was overruled, and judgment was rendered. D appeals.

Issue. Was the court correct in requiring D to show that he exercised extraordinary care?

Held. No. Judgment reversed.

♦ It was error to overrule D's objection. When a defendant is engaged in a lawful act and injures a plaintiff, the plaintiff may not recover damages if: (i) the plaintiff and the defendant exercise ordinary care, (ii) the plaintiff and the defendant fail to exercise ordinary care, or (iii) the plaintiff alone fails to exercise ordinary care.

Comments.

♦ The standard of care referred to by the court was not the subjective standard (*i.e.*, dependent upon the individuals involved) but an objective standard related to the degree of care prudent and cautious persons under similar circumstances would exercise. Further, the court pointed out that the plaintiff, and not the defendant, has the burden of proof (*i.e.*, the plaintiff has the burden of proving negligence, or fault, on the part of the defendant).

♦ The importance of this case is that it indicates the shift to finding liability on the part of a defendant only if he is legally at fault. The court stated that "if it appears that the defendant was doing a lawful act, and unintentionally hit and hurt the plaintiff, then unless it also appears to the satisfaction of the jury that the defendant is chargeable with some fault, negligence, carelessness, or want of prudence, the plaintiff fails to sustain the burden of proof, and is not entitled to recover."

---

2. **Abnormally Dangerous or Ultrahazardous Activities.** Certain activities are so dangerous that they involve serious risk of harm to others despite the use of utmost care to prevent harm. Strict liability is imposed upon those who engage in such activities. Ultrahazardous activities are those abnormal to the area, which necessarily involve a risk to persons, land, or chattels, and which cannot be eliminated by the use of utmost care. [Restatement (Second) of Torts, §520]

   a. **Construction of reservoir--**

Fletcher v. Rylands, 159 Eng. Rep. 737 (Ex. 1865).

Facts. Rylands (D) constructed a reservoir on his land which, when filled with water, burst, causing water to flow into coal mines on Fletcher's (P's) adjoining property. Unknown to D, there were old coal mine shafts under his property that were discovered by his employees during construction of the reservoir and that weakened the reservoir and permitted the flow of water to P's property. P sued for damages. D appeals a verdict for P.

Issue. Does a person who brings on his land something that will cause harm to another if it escapes have an absolute duty to prevent its escape?

Held. No. Judgment reversed.

♦ The damage here was not immediate; therefore, there was no trespass. Further, the reservoir was no nuisance in the ordinary meaning of the word. (The pond was not harmful to the senses.) Different legal liabilities arise from intentionally casting water on someone's land than from the ignorant escape of water from a reservoir.

Dissent (Bramwell, B.). P had the right for his mine to be free of water flowing onto it from D's reservoir. It makes no difference that the water flowed from D's land to P's land without D's knowledge.

---

b. On appeal to Exchequer Chamber--

Fletcher v. Rylands, L.R. 1 Ex. 265 (1866).

Facts. Same as the preceding case.

Issue. Same as the preceding case.

Held. Yes. Judgment of the trial court for P is affirmed.

- ◆ One who brings onto his land anything likely to do mischief if it escapes keeps it at his peril, and is prima facie answerable for all damage that is the natural consequence of its escape.

- ◆ He can only excuse himself by showing that the escape was the plaintiff's fault.

- ◆ But for D's act, no mischief could have accrued.

- ◆ This case is distinguishable from traffic and other cases that require proof of a defendant's negligence for recovery. They involve situations where people have subjected themselves to some inevitable risk. Here, there is no ground for saying that P took upon himself any risk arising from the use to which D chose to put his land.

c. On appeal to House of Lords--

Rylands v. Fletcher, L.R. 3 H.L. 330 (1868).

Facts. Same as preceding case. The Exchequer had reversed but the Exchequer Chamber had affirmed the trial court. D appeals.

Issue. Same as the preceding case.

Held. Yes. Judgment affirmed.

- ◆ An owner of land may use it for any purpose for which it might, in the ordinary course of enjoyment, be used. Thus, if the water had accumulated naturally and run off onto adjoining land, there could be no complaint.

- ◆ Nevertheless, a landowner who introduces onto the land that which in its natural condition was not upon it does so at the peril of absolute liability for consequences arising therefrom.

d. The *Rylands* Rule.

1) The rule of *Rylands* is that a landowner is liable to adjacent land-owners when he brings onto his land an unnatural, artificial device that causes something to escape from the land and harms another's land or chattels. After initial disfavor, the rule gradually became accepted by a majority of American courts. One court that did not was Texas, which in *Turner v. Big Lake Oil Co.,* 128 Tex. 155 (1936), rejected strict liability in favor of a negligence standard on facts similar to *Rylands.* Reservoirs of the type built were common in that part of Texas, according to the court.

2) The jurisdictions are split as to applying the doctrine to personal injury as well as to property damage.

3. Early Application in America--

Brown v. Collins, 53 N.H. 442 (1873).

Facts. Collins's (D's) horse became frightened, bolted out of D's control, ran onto Brown's (P's) land and destroyed a post. P sued for the damages caused by the escaped horse. P argued that D was strictly liable for the damage, or, in the alternative, under *Rylands v. Fletcher,* was liable for anything that escaped from D's land and caused injury to P.

Issue. Will New Hampshire adopt the doctrine of *Rylands v. Fletcher,* that a landowner is strictly liable for damages caused by something escaping from his land if the landowner is totally without fault and has not been negligent?

Held. No. Judgment for D.

♦ D was totally without negligence; his horse caused damage without D's will, intent, or desire.

♦ Everything a person brings onto his land is capable of causing some damage if it escapes. For example, a spark from a person's fireplace could escape and burn down the neighborhood. But no court in America would hold the owner of the fireplace liable in such circumstances.

♦ Adoption of a rule making a person liable for the natural consequences of the escape of things he brings onto his land would also have to apply to any action disturbing the order of nature that subsequently caused damage to another. But not all damage is actionable. To hold so would obstruct progress and improvement by discouraging persons from interfering with nature's own patterns, fearing, as they would, that consequential damages caused by their actions would impose liability on them. A certain amount of interference in our property rights is the price we pay for living in a society that strives for progress.

♦ If no negligence exists on which the consequential damage is based, no action will lie.

Comment. Naturally, if one intends to enter the land of another, unintentional damage caused thereby is actionable. Likewise, if some force is set in motion with the intention of invading A's property, but it in fact invades B's property and causes damage, liability exists. The court in *Brown* appears unwilling to adopt a test of strict liability for escaping substances, although it would be willing to impose liability if the property owner is negligent. In the fireplace example, liability might exist if the owner were somehow negligent in letting sparks escape from his chimney. As mentioned, the *Rylands* rule has recently found greater acceptance in American courts.

4. Statutes and Strict Liability--

Powell v. Fall, 5 Q.B. 597 (1880).

Facts. Fall (D) operated a steam engine along a highway in accordance with statutes. D's steam engine blew sparks on Powell's (P's) hay rick, causing it to be destroyed. P sued and recovered a judgment.

Issue. Does the existence of a statute protect D from a strict liability action?

Held. No. Judgment affirmed.

♦ There was no legislative intent to exempt D from liability.

♦ It is just and reasonable that when D uses a dangerous machine he should pay for the damage it causes.

♦ If use of the machine is profitable, D ought to pay compensation for the damage.

Comment. D had claimed that the legislature had authorized his business on the public roads. Because of this legislation, D claimed that he could only be sued for failure to use reasonable care. Some cases have indicated that the existence of a statute may have an impact on use of strict liability. Where the act itself is authorized by statute, some courts have required proof of fault for liability to attach.

5. **Strict Liability and Intentional Torts.**

    a. **Early cases.** Early decisions may have viewed trespass to land as a strict liability tort. Since landowners had a right to possession of the land, any invasion of that right was actionable.

    b. **Modern cases.** Recent decisions have removed trespass to land from the area of strict liability. In order to recover for trespass to land, some proof of intent or negligence may be necessary.

E. STRICT LIABILITY AND NEGLIGENCE IN MODERN TIMES

1. **The Cricket Case--**

Stone v. Bolton [1950] 1 K.B. 201 (C.A.).

Facts. Stone (P) was struck and injured by a cricket ball hit over a high fence. P sued Bolton and all home team members (Ds) both for public nuisance and common law negligence. Ds argued that in the past 30 years, only a dozen or so balls had been hit over the fence and P's injury was, therefore, not a reasonably foreseeable risk. The trial court found for Ds. P appeals to the intermediate appellate court.

Issue. Was P's injury a reasonably foreseeable risk such as to be actionable, even if the risk was extremely slight?

Held. Yes. Judgment reversed.

♦   The hitting of a cricket ball over the fence was known from practical experience to be an actual possibility.

♦   It is reasonable to expect that what has happened several times before would happen again; although it may not have been likely to happen often, it was certain to happen.

♦   Because Ds knew such an accident was foreseeable, they were under a duty to prevent injury, either by building a higher fence or by not playing on the field.

♦   The hitting of a cricket ball over the fence, causing P's injuries, was a breach of Ds' duty and therefore P has a cause of action against Ds.

2. **On Appeal--**

Bolton v. Stone, [1951] A.C. 850.

Facts. Same as in *Stone v. Bolton*, above. This is the appeal from the intermediate appellate court's holding.

Issue. Did the acts of Ds cause a substantial risk of harm to P?

Held. No. The court of appeals is reversed and the trial court is affirmed.

♦ The proper test to decide this case is not merely the foreseeability of the accident, but rather the substantiality of the risk imposed by Ds' acts.

♦ Although the court feels sorry for P, negligence is more concerned with culpability than with fairness.

♦ The court of appeals applied a standard of strict liability. That standard is applicable only when the risk is very substantial. Here, the risk is very small and, in addition, it is the type of risk that is a part of living in a social environment.

♦ Where the risks are, as here, only slight, and the use of property is reasonable, a property owner is not liable for injuries to passersby caused by the use of his land.

Comments.

♦ Under negligence theory, P should not recover since without foreseeability there can be no negligence. This is the position taken by this case. *Stone v. Bolton* points out the division courts feel between their duty to the law and their desire to compensate an innocent victim.

♦ In *Rinaldo v. McGovern*, 587 N.E.2d 264 (N.Y. 1991), P's windshield was struck and shattered by a golf ball driven by one of two golfers who intended to drive his ball straight down the fairway. There was no evidence of anything other than ineptness. P charged Ds with negligence and failure to warn. The trial court's dismissal was affirmed. The court reasoned that a warning would have been all but futile. It is unlikely P would have heard the warning, much less have had the opportunity to act upon it. The possibility that the warning would have been effective, the court stated, was too remote to justify submission of the case to a jury. The possibility that a golf ball will fly off in a direction not contemplated by the golfer is a risk inherent in the game. To provide an actionable theory of liability, a person injured by a mishit golf ball must affirmatively show that the golfer failed to exercise due care by adducing proof, for example, that the golfer "aimed so inaccurately as to unreasonably increase the risk of harm."

---

3.   **Traffic Accidents--**

Hammontree v. Jenner, 97 Cal. Rptr. 739 (Cal. Ct. App. 1971).

Facts. Jenner (D), an epileptic who had not had a seizure in 14 years and who was under medication and regular medical treatment, suffered a seizure while driving and caused injuries to Maxine Hammontree and her husband (Ps). Ps argued both negligence and strict liability to a jury, but elected to stand only on strict liability before the case went to the jury. The trial court judge refused to instruct the jury on strict liability and on his own motion instructed the jury on negligence. The jury found no negligence. Ps appeal.

Issue. Did the trial court wrongfully refuse Ps' strict liability instruction where such liability was premised on D's sudden illness resulting in Ps' injuries?

Held. No. Judgment affirmed.

♦　　Strict liability principles will not be imposed in automobile-related accidents such as this. Products liability cases are not apposite since their purpose is to place liability on manufacturers of defective goods. In addition, to impose strict liability would also require establishing a comprehensive plan detailing how the new rule should operate. Such a detailed plan could not be implemented judicially without a case-by-case construction, causing damage to injured persons because of the delay.

♦　　Negligence law has traditionally been applied in sudden illness cases involving automobile accidents. That law has generally not imposed liability on the driver who is suddenly stricken unconscious by an unexpected illness.

♦　　Here, D, after being without a seizure for 14 years, had no reason to expect, as long as he was under proper medical treatment, that he would ever suffer another seizure.

Comment. Of course, if the driver had had knowledge of the onset of an incapacitating illness, negligence could be found. Some courts do find strict liability for traffic accidents even though this court did not.

III. THE NEGLIGENCE ISSUE

A. INTRODUCTION

1. **Elements.** The elements of a plaintiff's prima facie case based on negligence of a defendant are the following:

    (i)   Act or omission of the defendant;

    (ii) Duty owed by the defendant to exercise due care;

    (iii) Breach of duty by the defendant;

    (iv) Causal relationship between the defendant's conduct and the harm to the plaintiff (both actual and proximate cause); and

    (v)   Damages.

    Each of the above elements must be alleged by the plaintiff, and the plaintiff has the burden of proving the allegations by a preponderance of the evidence. Each of these elements will be discussed in detail below.

2. **Act or Omission by Defendant.** As in intentional torts, the act of the defendant must be the external manifestation of her will (*i.e.*, volitional movement) in order to support a cause of action based on negligence. However, liability in negligence may also be based on the failure or omission of the defendant to act if she is under an affirmative duty to act.

B. THE REASONABLE PERSON

As noted previously, a defendant is bound only to use that care that is commensurate with the hazard involved.

1. **The Standard of Care.** In general, the standard of care that must be exercised is that conduct which the average reasonable person of ordinary prudence would follow under the same or similar circumstances. The standard of conduct is an external and objective one, and has nothing to do with individual subjective judgment, although higher duties may be imposed by specific statutory provisions or by reason of special knowledge or skill on the part of the actor. Since the standard is an external one, being a fool is no excuse; likewise, being an expert is no excuse if a reasonable person of ordinary prudence would do otherwise. The reasonable person standard takes no account of the personality of the particular person involved.

2. **The Reasonable Person.**

a. Best judgment immaterial--

Vaughan v. Menlove, 132 Eng. Rep. 490 (C.P. 1837).

Facts. D built a hay rick on his premises near the boundary adjacent to P's barn, stables, and cottages. D was repeatedly warned of the danger, but ignored the warnings. The hay rick eventually caught fire (through spontaneous combustion), and the fire spread to P's barn, stables, and then to P's cottages, destroying all of the structures. The court found for P.

Issue. Is there a cause of action for negligence if a person acts in conformity with his own best judgment, although his actions are less reasonable than those of a person of ordinary prudence?

Held. Yes. Judgment affirmed.

♦   The question of whether D acted honestly and bona fide to the best of his judgment is immaterial, as the rule by which D's conduct is measured requires in all cases a regard for caution such as a person of ordinary prudence would observe.

Comment. It would be very difficult administratively to determine in each case whether a defendant has acted according to his own best subjective judgment.

---

b. Physical infirmities--

Roberts v. Ring, 173 N.W. 437 (Minn. 1919).

Facts. Roberts's (P's) son, age seven, was struck while crossing a busy street by an automobile driven by Ring (D), age 77. Evidence at trial indicated that D was driving only four to five m.p.h., but that his sight and hearing were defective. In the charge to the jury, the trial judge stated that the age and infirmity of D should be taken into account in determining whether he was negligent. The judge also charged that, in considering whether P's son was contributorily negligent, the standard is the degree of care commonly exercised by the ordinary boy of his age and maturity. The jury found for D. P appeals.

Issue. Should the standard of care be lowered to take into account the defendant's physical infirmities?

Held. No. Judgment reversed.

♦ Although D may not have been driving at a negligent rate of speed, he may have been negligent in failing to keep a proper lookout or failing to stop promptly.

♦ The charge to the jury suggested that D's infirmities might tend to relieve him from the charge of negligence. On the contrary, they weighed against him. To the extent they were proper to be considered at all, they suggest that D should not have been driving. Having engaged in the act of driving, D's negligence is judged by the standard of a reasonable person, without consideration of D's infirmities.

---

c. **Aggravated negligence.**

1) **Degrees of care or negligence.** The care that the reasonable person must exercise will vary according to the risk involved; *e.g.*, more care must be used when handling explosives than when handling lumber; common carriers must exercise a "high degree of care" with regard to their passengers. Although some cases and authors have taken a different approach and emphasized the "degree of negligence" concept, the majority view is that there are no different "degrees of negligence," just circumstances requiring more or less care.

2) **Gross negligence.** Statutes speaking of gross negligence or recklessness are usually interpreted to mean something equivalent to conscious and deliberate disregard of a high degree of probability—a state of mind between negligence and intention. One author has likened the difference to that between those who are "negligent" and those who are "damned negligent."

d. **Children.** The usual objective standard of care has been somewhat modified in the case of children.

1) **Majority rule.** The majority view is that the standard is based on what may be expected of children of like age, intelligence, and experience.

2) **Common law.** At common law, a child under age seven was presumed to be incapable of negligence, between the ages of seven and 14 rebuttably presumed incapable, and over 14 presumed capable.

3) **Minority rule.** A minority of the jurisdictions still have arbitrary age limits.

4) **When driving a car.** Some jurisdictions still make the age, intelligence, and experience allowance when a child is driving a car or engaging in other "adult" activity, but the better-reasoned cases hold children to an adult standard in such situations. [*See* Restatement (Second) of Torts, §283A]

5) **Application of "adult activity" rule--**

Daniels v. Evans, 224 A.2d 63 (N.H. 1966).

Facts. The representative of the estate of Daniels (P) brought suit for the decedent's estate. The decedent was killed when the motorcycle he was riding collided with Evans's (D's) auto. The court held for P and D appeals the verdict, contending that the instruction by the trial court that the decedent, a minor, "is not held to the same degree of care as an adult" was improper because the decedent was engaged in an activity normally undertaken by adults—driving.

Issue. When a minor undertakes a potentially dangerous adult activity, like operating a motor vehicle, will he be held to an adult standard of care?

Held. Yes. Judgment reversed.

♦ Minors are entitled to be judged by standards commensurate with their age and experience when engaged in activities appropriate to their age and experience.

♦ While a person may observe a child at play and may anticipate childish conduct, a driver must be able to expect adult conduct from other drivers. He has no notice of the other driver's youth and even if he did, he could usually not protect himself from youthful imprudence.

♦ Statutes that require traffic law obedience make no exception for minors.

♦ Furthermore, the adult standard should be applied to minor motor vehicle operators whether they are charged with primary or contributory negligence.

Comment. This case states the well-accepted rule that where a minor participates in an activity that can result in grave danger and is usually performed by an adult (for example, in this case, the driving of a motor vehicle), the lower standard of care will not apply, but the minor will be held to the higher standard that is applied to the adult without allowing for his age. This opinion overruled the prior decision of *Charbonneau v. MacRury,* 153 A. 457 (N.H. 1931).

---

e. **Mental capacity.** A person with a mental incapacity is held to the same standard of care as a person of ordinary intelligence because of the difficulties that would occasion determining the degree of disability. Re-statement (Second) of Torts, section 283B, states that insane persons are held in all respects to the reasonable person standard of a sane person, the only exception being where malice or intent is necessary for the cause of action.

1) **Insanity--**

Breunig v. American Family Insurance Co., 173 N.W.2d 619 (Wis. 1970).

Facts. American's (D's) insured (Veith) suffered an insane delusion while driving. She saw Breunig's (P's) truck coming and, believing that God was operating her car, stepped on the gas to become airborne. Instead, she crashed into P's truck, injuring P. From a judgment for P, D appeals, arguing that there was no negligence by Veith because there was no evidence that she had known or had warning that she would experience the seizure. The court held for P.

Issue. Are some forms of insanity a defense to a negligence action?

Held. Yes. But judgment for P is affirmed here.

♦ Although there is no negligence where one is afflicted with a sudden unforeseeable delusion that blurs understanding (the delusion being similar to a heart attack, stroke, etc.), here, D's insured had a history of delusions. Therefore, the insanity defense does not apply.

Comment. Where D's insanity prevents P from understanding the danger and taking action, D will not be permitted to assert contributory negligence as a defense.

---

f. **Physical attributes.** The physical attributes of the reasonable person are deemed to be identical to those of the actor.

1) **Blindness--**

Fletcher v. City of Aberdeen, 338 P.2d 743 (Wash. 1959).

Facts. Fletcher (P), blind since youth, fell into an excavation ditch dug by the city (D). A barrier that would have given P notice of danger had been removed by a city worker, who negligently failed to replace it after finishing his work. P brought a negligence action against D. D argued that it met its duty of care by erecting the original barriers and that it did not owe a higher standard of care to P just because P was blind. A jury found for P.

Issue. Was it error for the court to fail to instruct that P's blindness did not impose any higher burden of care on the city?

Held. No. Judgment affirmed.

♦ The duty of maintaining sidewalks and adjacent parking strips is a continuous one. That duty was breached when the city worker failed to replace a barrier protecting pedestrians from the ditch.

♦ The city is charged with the knowledge that its streets and sidewalks will be used by the physically infirm as well as by the physically able.

♦ The physically disabled are obliged to use that same standard of care as would a reasonable person with the same disability; the city is obligated to provide protection for all persons of whom it has notice will use its facilities in a reasonable manner.

♦ Blind persons are entitled to use city streets and sidewalks just as those who are not blind; the city must provide adequate protection for the sightless just as it does for the sighted.

Comment. The court relies on an implicit finding that P was a reasonable person under these standards.

---

g. **Voluntary intoxication.** The courts will not make allowance for voluntary intoxication (alcohol, drugs, etc.) in determining the standard. However, the rule may differ if involuntary intoxication is involved. Note also that if P is voluntarily drunk, D may have the benefit of contributory negligence as a defense.

In *Robinson v. Pioche, Bayerque & Co.,* 5 Cal. 460 (1855), Robinson (P), while intoxicated, fell into a hole dug in the sidewalk in front of Pioche, Bayerque & Co.'s (D's) store. The hole was not covered or barricaded. P sued for negligence. The court held that a plaintiff's intoxication does not excuse gross negligence on the part of the defendant. An intoxicated person is as much entitled to a safe street as a sober one, and actually needs it much more. D's failure to either barricade or cover the hole in front of its store was gross negligence. P's intoxication does not vitiate the gross negligence of the defendant. *Note:* The court considered the purpose for which D was required to erect a barricade around the hole. Because that purpose was to protect pedestrians, D had a duty to protect all pedestrians.

h. **Wealth.** In *Denver & Rio Grande Railroad v. Peterson,* 69 P. 578 (Colo. 1902), the court held that wealth is not a consideration in defining the standard of due care to warehousemen. The care owed by a warehouseman is the same whether he is rich or poor. A contrary decision would completely destroy any duty owed by one who is extremely poor. *Note:* If wealth were a factor in determining the duty of care owed by another, a person injured by another's negligence would have to first determine the financial standing of the person causing his injury. This would be an unworkable standard.

C. CALCULUS OF RISK

A calculus of risk test balances the likelihood and severity of an injury against the burden of taking steps to prevent it.

1. **Standard of Care.** In general, the standard of care that must be exercised is that conduct that the average reasonable person of ordinary prudence would follow under the same or similar circumstances. The standard of conduct is an external and objective one, and has nothing to do with individual judgment, although higher duties may be imposed by specific statutory provisions or by reason of special knowledge or skill on the part of the actor. Ideally, the reasonable person standard would complement the calculus of risk test rather than deviate from it.

2. **Unusual Conditions--**

Blyth v. Birmingham Water Works, 156 Eng. Rep. 1047 (Ex. 1856).

Facts. Birmingham Water Works (D) was sued for negligence when a water hydrant that it installed 25 years earlier sprang a leak in an extraordinary frost, and water flooded Blyth's (P's) home, causing damage. In installing the water mains, D took precautions to make them safe against such frosts as experience indicated might occur. The jury found for P.

Issue. Did D take reasonable precautions so as not to be negligent?

Held. Yes. Verdict entered for D.

♦ D did all that a reasonable person under like circumstances would be expected to do. The result of the unusual conditions was an accident for which D cannot be held liable.

Comment. Negligence is an act or omission that falls below the care that a reasonable person would have shown under the same conditions. In *Blyth,* the conduct was not unreasonable in relation to the known foreseeable risks involved. A defendant can often rely on past history and experience as to what is foreseeable. Further, some risks are too small to demand that a reasonable person take precautions (*e.g.*, extraordinary weather conditions).

---

3.   **Emergency.** The reasonable person confronted with an emergency may act differently than she would if there were no emergency. This does not mean that there is a different standard applied; this only indicates that the emergency conditions are added to the circumstances that are taken into consideration in determining how a reasonable person would act when confronted with the situation.

a.   **Risks taken by rescuer--**

Eckert v. Long Island Railroad, 43 N.Y. 502 (1871).

Facts. Eckert's (P's) deceased attempted to rescue a small child from the path of a negligently operated train owned by Long Island Railroad (D). The child was thrown to safety but P's deceased died from injuries sustained in the rescue. A wrongful death action was brought. D argued that P's deceased's contributory negligence barred his recovery. The trial court jury found for P. D appeals.

Issue. In the absence of rash or reckless judgment, will an attempt to save another person from death or serious injury caused by another's negligence, which involves placing the rescuer in a position of possible death or serious injury, give rise to contributory negligence so as to bar the rescuer from recovery for damages caused by the original negligence?

Held. No. Judgment affirmed.

♦   The law places a very high value on human life and does not want to discourage acts to preserve life, even if those acts involve some danger to the rescuer.

♦   A person's acts in trying to save another will not be considered negligent (so as to cause contributory negligence) unless they are rash or reckless.

♦   Here, P's deceased did not have time to deliberate or weigh the risks. Evidence was presented from which the jury could properly conclude that P's deceased's acts were reasonable and that therefore his acts did not bar recovery for D's negligence.

Dissent. P's deceased voluntarily, and while in full control of his capacities, chose to assume the risk involved with this rescue. His voluntary assumption of that risk, under such circumstances, bars any recovery by his personal representative.

Comment. With the advent of comparative fault, most states have done away with the defense of assumption of risk, either by statute or by judicial decision. It is now simply part of the calculation of fault.

---

        b.   **Caveat.** The emergency doctrine is limited. It does not apply where D creates the emergency herself or where D should have anticipated it.

    4.   **Foreseeability.** Foreseeability of risk, harm, or injury is frequently a key element in the determination of the acts necessary to avoid liability for negligence. As stated earlier, the risk reasonably perceived defines the duty owed.

    5.   **Reasonableness of the Risk.** The reasonableness of the risk is usually determined by balancing certain factors. These factors include the magnitude of the risk, the value of objects placed at risk, the value of objects sought, and the necessity of obtaining the desired goals. [Terry, Negligence, 29 Harv. L. Rev. 40, 42-44 (1915)]

    6.   **"Ordinary Care" and the Jury--**

Osborne v. Montgomery, 234 N.W. 372 (Wis. 1931).

Facts. Osborne (P) was riding his bicycle when he struck Montgomery's (D's) opened automobile door. There were allegations that D was negligent and that P was contributorily negligent. An "ordinary care" instruction was given by the court. Although the court instructed the jury that it should determine the case based on the "ordinary care" that most persons would exercise in their dealings with other people, it failed to provide operative definitions of "ordinary care." The jury awarded P damages of $2,500. On appeal, the instruction was challenged as not providing sufficient guidance to the jury.

Issue. Was the trial court's failure to provide an operational definition of "ordinary care" reversible error?

Held. Yes. Judgment reversed and case remanded on the issue of damages.

♦   We are constantly doing things that, although they injure others, do not involve our negligence and do not result in liability.

♦   Such acts are not negligent because they conform to what the mass of mankind would do in similar circumstances.

♦ The fundamental premise of liability results from a balancing of societal interests against the risk created by particular conduct. If the societal interest outweighs the risks, the jury should be instructed that it must determine whether a
defendant's conduct conformed to what a person in similar circumstances would
do.

Comment. The court offers the illustration of a firetruck driver who drives at a high
speed on a crowded street. Society's interest in his driving under such conditions outweighs the risks of his speed. Thus, we do not consider his acts to be actionable negligence.

---

7. **Duty Owed to Two or More Classes--**

Cooley v. Public Service Co., 10 A.2d 673 (N.H. 1940).

Facts. Public Service Co. (D) maintained uninsulated power lines above and at right
angles to telephone lines operated by the defendant telephone company. During a severe storm, the power lines broke and fell onto the telephone lines. Cooley (P) was
talking on the phone at that instant and while so talking a very loud noise came through
the telephone, causing neurosis with fairly severe physical injuries. P brought an action for personal injuries. Evidence at trial indicated that either of two safety measures
the power company could have used to prevent P's injury would have increased the
risk that people on the ground below the wires would be electrocuted. A jury found for
P against the power company, but not against the telephone company.

Issue. Where the the defendant owed a duty of due care to two classes of people, did it
breach that duty when it protected only the class that was in the more serious danger?

Held. No. Judgment reversed.

♦ The risk of injury to that class of people walking near the power lines was
significantly greater than the risk to people listening on the telephone. In addition, the gravity of danger to the first class was significantly greater.

♦ By using the safety devices suggested by P, the risk and gravity of danger to
those on the street would be increased. The court will not sanction decreasing
emotional harm to one class at the risk of increasing physical harm to another
class.

♦ Where two classes of people cannot both be protected from injury, that class
most likely to suffer the greater harm should be protected, even at the expense
of some injury to the other class.

Comment. The court's analysis rests on an assumption that emotional harm, at least the type of harm suffered by this plaintiff, is somehow less significant than physical harm, or that the risk of such harm is less than the risk of physical harm. Although that assumption might be made, more evidence than was discussed by the court would be needed to support it.

---

8. **Reasonable Persons and the Recognition of Unacceptable Risk--**

United States v. Carroll Towing Co., 159 F.2d 169 (2d Cir. 1947).

Facts. On the afternoon of January 4, a barge of the United States (P) broke from its mooring and sank, allegedly because of Carroll Towing's (D's) negligence. P's employee in charge of the barge, the bargee, was not on the barge when it broke loose and had been ashore for 21 hours. The accident occurred in the full tide of war activity, when barges were constantly being towed in and out of the harbor. P sued for damages. D contended that P was also negligent in that its employee, the bargee, was not on the barge when it broke loose. P appeals the verdict for D.

Issues.

(i)   Was P's employee, the bargee, negligent in being ashore?

(ii)   If so, did that negligence contribute to the loss of the barge?

Held. (i) Yes. (ii) Yes. Judgment affirmed.

♦   The barge owner's liability depends upon whether his burden of adequate precautions (B) is less than the probability that the barge will break away (P) multiplied by the gravity of resulting injury if it does (L). If B < PL, the barge owner is negligent.

♦   The harbor was crowded; it was not beyond reasonable expectation that work might not be done carefully.

♦   Under such conditions, it is a fair requirement that the barge owner have a bargee aboard during working hours.

Comment. The main question in a negligence case is whether a reasonable person would have realized the risk involved in a course of action but still not have changed his conduct. If so, then no negligence can be inferred. Because of the balancing of specific factors in this case, discussion of the opinion has frequently centered on an ability to analyze the decision in terms of economics. The balancing of burdens against risks to be avoided translates easily into a cost-benefit analysis.

---

9. **Emergency Standard.** In an emergency, a person is expected to act as a reasonable person would under the emergency circumstances.

  a. **Sudden emergency doctrine discouraged--**

Lyons v. Midnight Sun Transportation Services, Inc., 928 P.2d 1202 (Alaska 1996).

Facts. Lyons (P) sued after his wife was killed by one of Midnight's (D's) drivers in an automobile accident. Both parties' experts offered conflicting testimony regarding the probable speed of D's vehicle and what would have been the safest course of action to follow in the circumstances surrounding the accident. The jury was given an instruction regarding the standard of care in an emergency: In a sudden and unexpected dangerous situation, not resulting from a person's own negligence, the person must act as a reasonable person would under the same conditions. The jury found that the driver had been negligent, but his negligence was not a legal cause of the accident. P appeals.

Issue. Did the court err in giving the jury the sudden emergency instruction?

Held. Yes. Judgment affirmed because error was harmless.

♦ The giving of the instruction was harmless error since the jury decided that D's negligence was not the legal cause of the injury.

♦ However, we disapprove of the instruction's further use. It adds nothing to the established law that the duty of care is what is reasonable under the circumstances. It arose as a means of mitigating the "all or nothing" rule of contributory negligence, which has since been replaced by a comparative fault system.

♦ The instruction should not be used unless a particular set of facts warrants more explanation of the standard of care than is required.

10. **Negligence and the common carrier--**

Andrews v. United Airlines, 24 F.3d 39 (9th Cir. 1994).

Facts. Andrews (P) was hit in the head and seriously injured by a briefcase that fell from the overhead luggage compartment in United Airlines's (D's) airplane as passengers were retrieving their luggage upon arrival at the gate. P does not claim airline staff was involved, nor does P know what caused the briefcase to fall. However, P claimed the injury was foreseeable and the airline did nothing to prevent it. In a diversity action, applying California law, the court dismissed upon summary judgment. We review de novo.

Issue. Is the hazard encountered by P serious enough to warrant more than a warning to use caution when opening overhead bins?

Held. Yes. Judgment reversed and case remanded.

♦   While D is a common carrier and owes the duty of utmost care and the vigilance of a very cautious person to its passengers, it is not an insurer. The degree of care it must exercise is that which can be reasonably exercised considering the character and mode of conveyance and the practical operation of its business.

♦   One of P's witnesses testified that as a result of 135 reports of items falling from overhead bins in 1987, D announces to its passengers upon arrival that items stored in overhead compartments might have shifted during flight, and passengers should use caution when unloading. However, another of P's witnesses, a safety and human factors expert, testified that the announcement is ineffective because passengers cannot see falling items until bins are opened, and that D could have outfitted the bins with netting.

♦   While it is a close question, we conclude that P has made a sufficient case to overcome summary judgment. D is aware of the hazard; the case turns on whether D has done all that human care, vigilance, and foresight reasonably can do under the circumstances. A jury might decide either way based on the record before the district court; therefore, summary judgment was not appropriate.

D.   CUSTOM

1.   **Introduction.** Custom in the community is admissible as evidence of the standard of care, but it is never conclusive. A custom may be found to be negligent.

a.   **Old view--**

Titus v. Bradford, B. & K. Railroad Co., 20 A. 517 (Pa. 1890).

Facts. Titus, a brakeman for Bradford, B. & K. Railroad Co. (D), was killed while switching a car from a broad gauge track to a narrow gauge track. Evidence showed that this was an industrywide practice, that decedent knew of the dangers involved, and that he willingly accepted those risks as part of his employment. In a personal injury action by Titus's representative (P), the trial court found for P. D appeals.

Issue. Was D negligent in using procedures adopted industrywide?

Held. No. Judgment reversed.

♦ The standard of negligence in this case is what the industry custom is; D is not obligated to a higher standard of care than is imposed by that custom. Evidence showed that it was an industrywide practice to switch back and forth from a broad gauge to a narrow gauge track.

♦ D is not required to use new or better equipment if that equipment was not part of the custom of the railroad industry.

♦ The decedent knew the dangers of such work and willingly accepted them as part of his employment.

Comment. Although this standard may still be used by a few courts today, the majority of courts impose a higher standard of care when the plaintiff knows of inherent dangers of an industrywide custom. To decide otherwise would allow an entire industry to keep its safety standards artificially low just by refusing to raise the industrywide standards.

---

b. **Modern view.**

1) **Custom not conclusive--**

Mayhew v. Sullivan Mining Co., 76 Me. 100 (1884).

Facts. Mayhew (P), an employee of Sullivan Mining Co. (D), fell through an unguarded and unlighted ladder hole cut in a platform inside a mine owned by D. D attempted to introduce evidence that unguarded ladder holes were an industrywide custom. The trial court refused to allow that evidence to be introduced. The lower court verdict was for P. D appeals.

Issue. Did the lower court err in refusing to allow evidence of an industrywide custom that would tend to show that D was only adhering to that custom in its allegedly negligent acts?

Held. No. Judgment affirmed.

♦ Negligence is negligence, regardless of how great a portion of an entire industry believes otherwise. Even if D had been able to prove that, from the beginning of time, it was the custom in this industry to cut such holes and leave them unprotected, that action would still be negligent.

♦ One does not exercise care by following industry custom if the industry custom is itself negligent.

Comment. The key here is probably that the accident was foreseeable and the condition could have been easily corrected. Although mining is hazardous, the mining company cannot impose greater risks than necessary. If a risk is avoidable, the company must make efforts to avoid it.

_____

2) Radios for navigation--

The T.J. Hooper, 53 F.2d 107 (S.D.N.Y. 1931).

Facts. D owned and operated two tugs, which were towing barges owned by P and carrying coal. The tugs, like others, were not equipped with a radio receiver and the tug master was unaware of reports of an impending storm. The storm sank the tugs and destroyed the barges and cargo. The cargo owners sued the barge owners (Ps) who, in turn, sued D for damages to the cargo and barges. There was evidence that the tug master, had he heard the weather report, would have turned back. The trial judge rendered the decision.

Issue. Was there a duty to supply radios for navigation?

Held. Yes. Judgment for Ps.

♦ There were no statutes governing this situation, but that is not conclusive on the issue. "Seaworthiness" is not dependent on statute.

♦ Radios were not new and untried; others were using them and were familiar with their importance.

♦ Although most owners did not supply radios, evidence showed that approximately 90% of the tugs operating used radios privately owned by members of the crew.

♦ The practice of using the radios had become almost universal, and the owners, therefore, had a duty to supply them.

_____

3) **On appeal--**

The T.J. Hooper, 60 F.2d 737 (2d Cir. 1932).

Facts. Same as above. The trial court found the tugs unseaworthy and D jointly liable with the barge owners to the cargo owners. D petitioned for exoneration from or limitation of liability.

Issue. Is adherence to a trade custom an absolute defense to negligence?

Held. No. Judgment affirmed.

♦   The fact that most tugs were not equipped with receivers is not the final answer. An industry may not set its own tests for reasonable prudence. The court must, in the end, say what is required.

♦   Tugs towing several barges cannot easily maneuver and are very vulnerable to bad weather.

♦   Although the whole industry has lagged in the installation of receivers, they are required by reasonable prudence to install them.

---

c. **Profession or trade.** A professional is held, at a minimum, to the standard of care customarily exercised by members of that profession or trade.

1) **"Same or similar."** Generally, the standard of members of a defendant's profession in the "same or similar" communities is applicable. Older cases limited the standard of care for physicians to that of other doctors in the same community. Most cases employ the "same or similar" standard.

2) **Medical care--**

Lama v. Borras, 16 F.3d 473 (1st Cir. 1994).

Facts. Lama (P) sought treatment for back pain from Dr. Borras and Asociacion Hospital del Maestro (Ds). The doctor scheduled P for surgery, but prior to surgery, the doctor neither prescribed nor enforced components of conservative treatment, such as bed rest. The doctor had P enter the hospital one week before surgery to clean out P's lungs because P was a heavy smoker. During the surgery, the doctor attempted to remove extruding material from P's disc, but P's symptoms returned several days after the operation. To remedy the "recurrence," the doctor operated again. He did not order pre- or post-operative antibiotics. Two days after the surgery, P's wound was bleeding, a symptom of infection. Three days after surgery, P experienced pain at the site of the wound, and the next day it bled again. The hospital instructed the nurses to make notes on P's chart only when important changes occurred and not record qualitative observations for each of the day's three shifts, so a more complete account of P's evolving condition is not available. Five days after surgery, P was screaming in pain. The next day, P's problem was diagnosed as an infection and antibiotics were prescribed. P was hospitalized for several months undergoing treatment. P moved to Florida and filed a diversity tort action in Puerto Rico alleging that the doctor was negligent in (i) failing to provide proper conservative medical treatment, (ii) premature and otherwise improper discharge after surgery, (iii) performance of surgery, and (iv) failing to properly manage the infection. P also alleged that the hospital was negligent in its failure to maintain proper medical records. The jury found for P and rejected Ds' motions for judgment as a matter of law and for a new trial. Ds appeal.

Issue. Did P introduce legally sufficient evidence to support each element of negligence?

Held. Yes. Judgment affirmed.

♦　　To establish a prima facie case of medical malpractice in Puerto Rico, P must show the basic norms of knowledge and medical care applicable to physicians, prove that medical personnel failed to follow these norms in treatment, and show a causal connection between the omission and the injury.

♦　　Regarding the doctor's failure to provide conservative treatment prior to the first operation, the doctor's expert agreed with P as to the standard of treatment, and although the doctor testified that he did give conservative treatment, there was sufficient evidence to the contrary. Evidence showed that the doctor admitted P only to have a week of smoke-free relaxation, not for absolute bed rest.

♦　　Regarding causation, the Puerto Rico Supreme Court has suggested that when a physician negligently exposes a patient to risk-prone surgery, the physician is liable for the harm associated with the foreseeable risk. It is undisputed that the type of infection P developed was foreseeable.

♦　　While both P's and Ds' experts agreed that conservative treatment would eliminate the need for surgery in the overwhelming number of cases, each party's expert differed regarding P's extruded disc. However, the jury was free to credit some witnesses more than others and could have reasonably found that the doctor's failure to administer conservative treatment was the "most probable cause" of the first surgery.

♦　　The hospital's system of note-taking could have delayed the diagnosis of P's excessive bleeding, which could have prevented the infection from becoming as serious as it did; the jury could properly find that system to be the proximate cause of the resulting harm to P.

Comment. The principles cited in *Lama* are applied in all common law jurisdictions. As acknowledged in *Kalsbeck v. Westview Clinic, P.A.*, 375 N.W.2d 861 (Minn. App. 1985), a "doctor must use that degree of skill and learning which is normally possessed and used by doctors in good standing in a similar practice in similar communities and under like circumstances."

---

d. Physician's duty to disclose risk--

Canterbury v. Spence, 464 F.2d 772 (D.C. Cir. 1972).

Facts. Canterbury (P), while a minor, submitted to a laminectomy (operation on the spinal cord) performed by Dr. Spence (D). Prior to the operation, D did not tell P of the seriousness of the operation; D did, however, tell P's mother that the operation was a serious one but "not any more serious than any other operation." During the course of the operation, D found P's spinal cord to be in very poor shape. D did what he could and left P to recuperate. A couple of days after the operation, and contrary to D's instructions, P was left to "void unattended." While trying to do so, P fell out of the bed and onto the floor. His spine was further injured and D performed emergency surgery. Despite extensive medical care, P had extensive back pain, hobbled on crutches, and was a victim of paralysis of the bowels and urinary incontinence. Four years after the operation (two years after attaining his majority), P brought this suit charging D with negligence in performing the laminectomy, failure to inform P of the risk, and charging the defendant-hospital with negligent postoperative care. P did not produce witnesses as to proper postoperative care and produced only D, as an adverse witness, as a witness to the operations and procedures. The trial court granted both the defendants' motions for summary judgment. P appeals.

Issue. Does a physician have the duty to disclose the risks involved with a proposed treatment?

Held. Yes. Judgment reversed and case remanded.

♦ The majority of states hold that, if it is the standard of care in the community, a physician has a duty to disclose.

♦ This view is unacceptable since it does not take into account the patient's right to self-determination. Prevailing medical practice should itself define the standard of care.

♦ Full disclosure of every risk of treatment, no matter how remote or small, is not required.

- ♦ A better standard is an objective one. "A risk is thus material when a reasonable person, in what the physician knows or should know to be in the patient's position, would be likely to attach significance to the risk or cluster of risks in deciding whether or not to forgo the proposed therapy."

- ♦ Dangers, such as infection, that are inherent in every operation need not be disclosed, nor do dangers that the patient has already discovered.

- ♦ There are two exceptions to the rule:

  - (i) If the patient is unconscious or otherwise incapable of consenting (a relative should be consulted if possible); and

  - (ii) If the risk disclosure poses such a threat of detriment to the patient as to make treatment infeasible. This is a carefully *limited* exception.

- ♦ Breach of the duty to disclose does not itself establish liability. There must be a causal connection between the breach and the patient's injury. Again, an objective standard is adopted. The standard is what a prudent person in the patient's position would have decided if suitably informed of all perils bearing significance. If the prudent person could reasonably be expected to decline the treatment if the risks were disclosed, then there is sufficient causation.

- ♦ Neither expert nor layperson testimony is necessary to competently establish a physician's failure to disclose.

- ♦ Here, the reasonableness of P's disclosure should have gone to the jury.

Comment. Many states now have statutes requiring and defining informed consent for medical procedures.

E. STATUTES AND REGULATIONS

1. **Introduction.** Statutes that affect a defendant's conduct may be either civil or criminal. If the plaintiff is provided a civil remedy under a statute, she will not have to be concerned with establishing negligence. When the defendant's conduct violates a criminal statute that does not provide a civil remedy, the plaintiff might still obtain a remedy through a negligence action. When a court adopts a standard of care embodied in a criminal statute, the rationale is that a reasonable person always obeys the criminal law. For the plaintiff to establish negligence under a criminal statute, she must show that she is among the class of persons protected by the criminal statute and that the statute was enacted to protect members of the class from the type of injury the plaintiff suffered. Thus, the statute must clearly define the conduct or duty required and the class or individuals to whom it applies.

2. **Ability to Right a Wrong.** Whenever a statutory enactment provides an advantage for a person, or gives a person a right, the person shall also have a remedy to regain the advantage given to him or to have satisfaction for the injury done him. [*Anon.*, 87 Eng. Rep. 791 (K.B. 1703)]

3. **Effect of Violation.** Depending upon the jurisdiction, violation of a statute can have several effects. The *majority view* finds violation of a statute to give rise to a conclusive presumption of negligence (*i.e.*, negligence per se). In California, violation is deemed to give rise to a rebuttable presumption of negligence. In still other jurisdictions, violation is deemed merely evidence of negligence. However, if the plaintiff's claim is based on violation of the statute as negligence, the defendant generally has available the defenses of contributory negligence and assumption of risk.

   a. **Statutory duties--**

Osborne v. McMasters, 41 N.W. 543 (Minn. 1889).

Facts. A drugstore clerk employed by D sold the decedent poison without a "poison label." The label was required by law. The decedent later took the poison and died. In P's negligence action, a verdict was returned against D. D appeals.

Issue. Does a statutory right of action exist?

Held. Yes. Judgment affirmed.

♦ The statute created a duty in D to use reasonable care to protect customers from taking the wrong drug. D failed to use reasonable care and is therefore chargeable with negligence on the theory of respondeat superior. There was no common law right of action; the statute created such a right. There was a breach of a statutory duty meant to protect this class of people from this type of injury. The injury was the proximate cause of death.

   b. **Negligence per se--**

Martin v. Herzog, 126 N.E. 814 (N.Y. 1920).

Facts. P's deceased was thrown from the wagon he drove and was killed when D failed to drive his car to the right of the center of the highway. The accident occurred at night. The wagon had no lights, a statutory violation. P sued D for damages resulting from his negligence. D was denied a jury instruction that the absence of a light on the wagon was prima facie evidence of contributory negligence. The trial court found for P; the appellate division reversed and ordered a new trial. P appeals the reversal.

Issue. Is the unexcused violation of a statute negligence in itself?

Held. Yes. Order of appellate division affirmed.

- ♦ Unexcused omission of the statutorily required lighting is negligence in itself.

- ♦ To omit safeguards prescribed by statute for the benefit of others is to fall short of the duty of diligence toward the rest of society.

- ♦ The trial court erred in giving the jury the power to relax the duty which P's intestate owed to other travelers.

Comment. Note that the majority rule that violation of a safety statute is per se negligence may have an exception—it may not be negligence where, under all the circumstances, actions that violate a statute are the most reasonable thing to do.

---

c. **Licensing statutes--**

Brown v. Shyne, 151 N.E. 197 (N.Y. 1926).

Facts. D was practicing without a license as a chiropractor in New York. In so doing he was guilty of a misdemeanor. P, after nine treatments from D, became paralyzed. P sued for damages resulting from D's negligent treatment. D appeals a jury verdict of $10,000, contending that it was improper to instruct the jury that they might infer negligence from the violation of the licensing statute.

Issue. May negligence be inferred from a chiropractor's violation of the statute requiring licensing of medical practitioners?

Held. No. Judgment reversed and new trial granted.

- ♦ The statute is intended to protect the public from unskilled practitioners.

- ♦ Nevertheless, the violation of the statute was not the proximate cause of P's injuries; it has no direct bearing on the injury.

- ♦ P must prove that D failed to exercise the care and skill that would have been exercised by a qualified practitioner. This may not be inferred from the fact that D was unlicensed.

Dissent. The judgment should be affirmed.

- ♦ The jury was properly charged and had ample evidence with which to connect P's injury with D's acts.

- In practicing medicine, D violated the law.

- The law did not recognize D as a physician; the court should not either.

- If his act was the direct and proximate cause of the injury, he is liable irrespective of negligence.

Comment. This case shows the effect of licensing statutes in the majority of courts.

---

d.   No private right of action--

Uhr v. East Greenbush Central School District, 720 N.E.2d 886 (N.Y. 1999).

Facts. Education Law section 905 requires school authorities in the state of New York to examine students between eight and 16 years of age for scoliosis at least once in each school year. The principal issue on this appeal is whether the statute authorizes a private right of action. During the 1992-1993 school year, Uhr was a seventh grade student at a middle school in the East Greenbush Central School District (D). In October 1992, Uhr was screened for scoliosis with negative results. She was not screened the following year. In 1995, Uhr was screened and the examination proved positive. By that time doctors concluded that her scoliosis had progressed to the point that surgery was required rather than just the braces that often can be used after an early diagnosis. Uhr underwent surgery in July 1995. Uhr's parents (Ps) filed an action, asserting that D violated the education law and was negligent for failing to examine Uhr during the 1993-1994 school year, thereby allowing her ailment to progress to her detriment. The trial court granted D's motion for summary judgment, holding that the education law does not create a private right of action, and that Ps had otherwise failed to state a claim for negligence. The appeal court affirmed. The Court of Appeals granted leave to appeal.

Issue. Does the education statute authorize a private right of action?

Held. No. Judgment affirmed.

- In determining whether a private right of action may be fairly implied where the statute is silent, as it is here, we ask (i) whether the plaintiff is one of the class for whose particular benefit the statute was enacted; (ii) whether recognition of a private right of action would promote the legislative purpose; and (iii) whether creation of such a right would be consistent with the legislative scheme.

- Uhr is a member of the class for whose benefit the statute was enacted.

- The legislature amended the statute to include scoliosis screening in addition to vision and hearing testing in order to promote early detection.

◆ We do not agree with Ps that a private right of action is consistent with the statute and necessary for its operation. There is a powerful official enforcement mechanism to ensure compliance with the statute and to indicate the legislature contemplated administrative enforcement of the statute. The Commissioner of Education has been charged with the duty to implement the statute and adopt rules and regulations for such purpose. In addition, the commissioner has power to withhold public funding from noncompliant school districts.

◆ An implied private right of action would not be consistent with this scheme. The statute immunizes D from any liability that might arise from the screening program. It provides that a school district "shall not suffer any liability to any person as a result of *making* such test or examination." In addition, in 1994, D amended the statute after a court ruling held that the statute did not impose liability for a school district's failure to notify parents of a child's positive results of the screening. That court further stated in dicta that the legislature intended to remove liability for both making the tests and failing to make the tests. The legislature responded by amending the statute to provide that parents be notified of positive test results within 90 days after the test. Because no other amendments were made, it is obvious the legislature agreed with the court's interpretation of the immunity provision.

◆ In instituting the program, the legislature also took cost into consideration. Orthopedists and other professionals volunteered their time and expertise to train existing school personnel on the relatively simple examination procedure. In predicting its cost, the legislature anticipated minimal financial impact on school districts. Permitting a private right of action against the government would have direct and obvious financial consequences to the public.

◆ In order to imply a private right of action, we must have clear evidence of the legislature's willingness to expose the governmental entity to liability that it might not otherwise incur. The case before us reveals no such legislative intent.

F. JUDGE AND JURY

1. **Introduction.** If an act was negligent as a matter of law (negligent per se), the judge will so instruct the jury. Thus, the "proper" standard of care is given the effect of law by the courts. If an act is not negligent per se, the judge will leave it to the jury to determine whether the act was negligent. This procedure has been adopted in order to prevent juries from being overly swayed by their emotions. The following cases highlight this distinction.

2. **Negligence Per Se--**

Baltimore & Ohio Railroad v. Goodman, 275 U.S. 66 (1927).

Facts. Goodman (decedent) drove his truck at 10 m.p.h. up to a blind railroad crossing that did not have signals or guard rails. By the time he saw the approaching train operated by the railroad (D), it was too late to stop. Goodman's heirs (Ps) sued in wrongful death. D argued that Goodman's own negligence caused his death. The trial court refused to direct a verdict in favor of D. A jury found for Ps. D appeals.

Issue. If the evidence shows that a plaintiff failed to take reasonable precautions for his own safety, does the trial court commit error in not directing a verdict for the defendant?

Held. Yes. Judgment reversed.

♦　　　A person approaching a railroad crossing knows the train cannot stop for him; he must stop for the train.

♦　　　If a driver cannot be sure of his safety, he has an obligation to get out of his vehicle and look both ways down the track.

♦　　　Goodman failed to take reasonable precautions for his own safety and was, therefore, negligent; his own negligence was the proximate cause of his death.

♦　　　If the decedent proximately causes his own injuries, the trial court should direct a verdict for D.

3.　　**Rule of Law--**

Pokora v. Wabash Railway, 292 U.S. 98 (1934).

Facts. Pokora (P) approached a railroad crossing in his truck. He stopped, looked, and listened as well as possible, but did not get out of his truck, which would have been necessary to see sufficiently both ways, as the view was partially blocked by parked boxcars. As P proceeded across the tracks, he was struck by Wabash's (D's) train coming from the direction where his view was partially impaired. The trial court directed a verdict for D. P appeals.

Issue. Was P negligent as a matter of law?

Held. No. Judgment reversed and case remanded.

♦　　　To get out of the vehicle and look down the tracks is likely to be futile and possibly even dangerous.

Comment. The case points out that there are no ironclad rules as to what is negligent conduct; the duty varies with the circumstances. It is usually negligence as a matter of law not to stop, look, and listen, but not always. The holding of this case is just the opposite of the last case. This holding is the better of the two. A plaintiff should be given the chance to let a jury decide the extent to which his negligence contributed to his woe.

---

4. **Federal Employers Liability Act ("FELA").** FELA subjects every railroad to liability in damages for an employee's injuries due to the railroad's negligence, or from any defect or deficiency due to negligence in any premises or equipment. "Assumption of risk" was eliminated as a defense to a FELA action. Further, FELA limits the extent that an employer can argue "contributory negligence" as a defense. Determining the employer's negligence, then, is the key to the employee's action. In *Wilkerson v. McCarthy*, 336 U.S. 53 (1949), Wilkerson (P), an employee of Denver & Rio Grande Western Railroad (D), slipped while walking across a narrow board over a pit in D's repair shop. The board had oil and grease on it. Access to the board was chained off to prevent its indiscriminate use as a shortcut. After P brought an action for damages under FELA, a state court directed a verdict for D because no evidence of D's negligence was presented. The Utah Supreme Court affirmed. The United States Supreme Court reversed. The Court found that there was evidence from which the jury could have found negligence on the part of D, and, therefore, the question should have gone to the jury.

G. PROOF OF NEGLIGENCE

1. **Introduction.** If people of reasonable intelligence may differ as to the conclusion to be drawn, the issue must be left to the jury; if not, the court will decide. Generally, the burden of proof (*i.e.*, the risk of non-persuasion) is on the plaintiff, and if the evidence she introduces is not greater or more persuasive than that of her adversary, she must lose. The burden of going forward with presenting proof, on the other hand, is established by presumptions, and the failure to rebut a presumption may result in a directed verdict.

   a. **Circumstantial evidence.** Circumstantial evidence is the proof of one fact, or group of facts, that gives rise to an inference by reasoning that another fact must be true.

   b. **Res ipsa loquitur ("RIL").** RIL, directly translated, means "the thing speaks for itself." In situations where (i) it is highly probable that the injury would not have occurred in the absence of someone's negligence, (ii) the indicated source of the negligence is within the scope of a duty owed by the the defendant to the plaintiff, and (iii) neither the plaintiff nor any third party appears to have contributed to the plaintiff's injuries, an inference is permitted that the defendant was negligent, without any direct proof, and the defendant then has the burden of going forward and introducing evidence to overthrow the inference. The courts recognize RIL because of the existence of a necessitous plaintiff and the defendant's better access to the evidence concerning the cause of the injury.

1) **Application.** Res ipsa loquitur is applicable if:

   (i) The accident is the kind that will not normally occur without someone's negligence;

   (ii) The cause of the harm was in the complete control of the defendant; and

   (iii) The plaintiff did not in any way voluntarily bring about the harm.

   If these three elements are proven, the plaintiff need prove nothing else to establish liability.

2) **Type of occurrence--**

Byrne v. Boadle, 159 Eng. Rep. 299 (Ex. 1863).

Facts. P was walking on the street when a barrel rolled out of D's window, striking and injuring P. There was no other evidence. P was nonsuited by the trial court.

Issue. Can P get the case to the jury by showing only that there was an accident and it was caused by the barrel?

Held. Yes. Verdict for P.

♦ All that is necessary is that reasonable persons would say that more likely than not there was negligence.

---

3) **Burden on defendant.** RIL puts the burden on the defendant to explain away the negligence. However, the doctrine does not apply if negligence of the defendant is no more likely than another explanation; *e.g.*, where an auto inexplicably runs off the road, but is subsequently found to have a flat tire.

   a) There must be some evidence of negligence, but control of the instrumentality by the defendant gives rise to an inference that it happened from lack of care if it would not ordinarily happen without a lack of care.

    b)   The doctrine does not apply unless reasonable persons could not disagree that 51% of the probabilities point to the defendant's liability.

    4)   **Explanation of all possibilities.** A plaintiff need not explain away all possibilities as long as she shows that such an accident ordinarily does not occur without negligence.

    5)   **Exclusive custody or control--**

Colmenares Vivas v. Sun Alliance Insurance Co., 807 F.2d 1102 (1st Cir. 1986).

Facts. Colmenares Vivas (P) arrived in the airport in Puerto Rico with his wife. While P and his wife were riding an escalator in the airport, the handrail stopped, but the foot platform continued moving. P was thrown down the steps. P sued the Puerto Rico Ports Authority (D) and the Ports Authority's insurance carrier, Sun Alliance Insurance. The insurance carrier sued Westinghouse as the company that had a contract with D to maintain the escalators. The trial court ruled that there was no evidence of negligence and issued a directed verdict for D. P appeals.

Issue. Did D have sufficient custody or control of the instrumentality of the injury in order to allow the action to go to the jury under the doctrine of res ipsa loquitur?

Held. Yes. Judgment reversed and case remanded for a new trial.

♦   The first element of RIL is that the injury must be one that ordinarily does not occur in the absence of negligence. Here, the handrail stopped and the steps kept moving. Clearly, it appears that someone was negligent in maintenance and repair of the escalator.

♦   The instrumentality of the injury must be in the exclusive custody or control of the defendant.

♦   D had control over the entire airport area.

♦   Although Westinghouse did maintenance on the escalators, D had a nondelegable duty over them. The escalators were in a public area and D had to maintain them in a safe condition.

♦   Since the elements of RIL were met, the case should have been submitted to the jury.

Dissent. The mere fact that an escalator malfunctions does not necessarily mean that there was negligence. This type of equipment is complex and may malfunction even in the absence of negligence.

---

6)   Departure from the rule of exclusive control--

Ybarra v. Spangard, 154 P.2d 687 (Cal. 1944).

Facts. Ybarra (P) consulted Dr. Tilley (D), who diagnosed appendicitis and arranged for an appendectomy, which was performed by Dr. Spangard (D) at a hospital owned by Dr. Swift (D). Prior to the operation, P was wheeled into the operating room by Gisler (D), a nurse, and his body was adjusted on the operating table by Dr. Reser (D), an anesthetist, who pulled P to the head of the operating table and laid him back against two hard objects at the top of his shoulders. P awoke the next morning attended by Thompson (D) and another nurse. P immediately felt sharp pain between his neck and right shoulder that spread to his lower right arm, although he had never suffered pain or injury there before. P's condition worsened (after his release from the hospital) to paralysis and atrophy. P sued to recover damages for personal injuries due to negligent malpractice. Dr. Reser and the nurses were employees of Dr. Swift; the other doctors were independent contractors. They contend that P must show by what instrumentality he was injured and which D controlled it. The lower court entered judgments of non-suit as to all Ds.

Issue. If a person is rendered unconscious in order to undergo surgical treatment and in the course of the treatment receives an unexplained injury to a part of his body not the subject of treatment, is it the burden of each of those who were charged with the patient's well-being to demonstrate that they exercised due care toward the patient?

Held. Yes. Judgment reversed.

♦   If a person is rendered unconscious to receive medical treatment and an un-treated part of his body is injured, those entrusted with his care have the burden of initial explanation.

♦   Every D in whose custody P was placed for any period had a duty of ordinary care to see that he was not unnecessarily injured.

♦   Any D who negligently injured P or neglected P so that he could be injured would be liable.

♦   An employer would be liable for the negligence of his employees; a doctor in charge of the operation would be liable for negligence of anyone who assisted in the operation.

♦   Each D had within his control one or more instrumentalities by which P might have been injured.

♦   It is unreasonable to insist that P, who had been rendered unconscious, identify the negligent D.

Comment. Because all of the defendants would be motivated to protect each other, the court departs from the normal res ipsa loquitur doctrine (that the plaintiff must show that the cause of the harm is under the exclusive control of the defendant) in order to smoke out the evidence. Under this court's theory, the hospital attendant who rolled P back to his hospital room after the operation could be sued.

———————

7) **Three views of the effect of RIL.**

   a) **Permissible inference.** Under the majority view, a permissible inference arises, the strength of which varies with the circumstances of the case. The jury may accept or reject the inference.

   b) **Presumption of negligence.** Under another view, a presumption of negligence is raised and, unless the defendant shows evidence to rebut, the court must find negligence as a matter of law.

   c) **Shifting of burden of proof.** Under a third view, the burden of proof shifts to the defendant, making the defendant introduce evidence to support his defense. If the defendant's evidence is sufficient to support a finding of fact in his favor, the burden of proof shifts back to the plaintiff, who then must prove the defendant's negligence.

8) **The Restatement.** The Third Restatement is strongly opposed to maintaining the exclusive control requirement. Citing it as a poor proxy for negligence, the Restatement gives the example of a vehicle whose brakes fail to operate one day after the vehicle is purchased. The driver has exclusive control, but there is ample justification for placing the blame on the manufacturer. [Restatement (Third) of Torts §15, comment b]

9) **Defense against RIL.** Inspection is not a defense to RIL. A defendant can defend against RIL by: (i) offering alternate explanations for the injury to the plaintiff other than the defendant's negligence, (ii) showing that such injuries happen frequently without the negligence of anyone, or (iii) showing that the defendant did not have control of the situation, or that another person had control.

IV. PLAINTIFF'S CONDUCT

A. CONTRIBUTORY NEGLIGENCE

1. **Basics of Doctrine.** Contributory negligence is conduct on the part of the plaintiff that contributes, as a legal cause, to the harm he has suffered, where that conduct falls below the standard to which he must conform. Contributory negligence is much like negligence itself—the criteria are the same—but it involves a person's duty to exercise reasonable care for his own safety rather than the safety of others. While the formula for determining negligence and contributory negligence is the same, the results are not necessarily the same. The same act may be negligent when done by the defendant yet not so when done by the plaintiff. The standard of care, as in negligence, is determined by what the reasonable person would have done under the same or similar circumstances.

2. **Effect of Contributory Negligence—Traditional Rule.** For those states still retaining contributory negligence, the prevailing rule is that the plaintiff's action for negligence is barred by his own negligent conduct if such conduct is a substantial factor in bringing about his injury. Thus, its effect is to give the defendant a complete defense—*i.e.*, no liability to the defendant.

3. **Burden of Proof.** The burden of pleading and proving contributory negligence is on the defendant.

4. **Avoidable Consequences Distinguished.** Contributory negligence should be distinguished from "avoidable consequences." If the plaintiff fails to act as a reasonable person in order to mitigate his damages, he will be barred from recovering for the damages that could have been avoided. Note that this doctrine is a rule as to damages and not as to liability.

5. **Limitations on Defendant's Use of Contributory Negligence as a Defense.** Although contributory negligence will normally act as a complete defense, there are several circumstances or situations in which the defendant will not be allowed to use it.

    a. **Limitation to the particular risk.** The defense of contributory negligence is not available to the defendant if the plaintiff's injury did not result from a hazard with respect to which the plaintiff failed to exercise reasonable care.

    b. **Injuries intentionally or recklessly caused.** Contributory negligence is not a defense to intentional torts, willful and wanton conduct, or reckless misconduct.

    c.   **Violation of statute.** Generally, contributory negligence is as much a defense to negligence resulting from violation of statute as any other type of negligence.

       1)   With certain types of statutes, however, contributory negligence is not allowed as a defense. The purpose of such statutes is to place the entire responsibility upon the defendant to protect a limited class of people (*e.g.*, child labor laws). If contributory negligence were recognized, such purposes would be defeated. These special statutes usually have three characteristics: (i) they are strict liability statutes, (ii) contributory negligence is not a defense, and (iii) assumption of risk is no defense.

       2)   On the other hand, if the legislative purpose behind the statute is to establish a standard of ordinary care toward the plaintiff, contributory negligence is a bar to recovery, for this would not subvert the statute's purpose.

6.   **Contributory Negligence Found--**

Butterfield v. Forrester, 103 Eng. Rep. 926 (K.B. 1809).

Facts. Butterfield (P) was injured when he failed to use ordinary care to guide his horse around an obstruction that Forrester (D) had negligently placed in the road. P's action for damages was dismissed, and P appeals.

Issue. Since P failed to use ordinary care in avoiding the accident, may he still recover damages from D?

Held. No. Judgment affirmed.

♦   Two things must occur to support this action: (i) an obstruction in the road by the fault of the defendant, and (ii) no want of ordinary care to avoid it on the part of the plaintiff. One person being at fault (here D) will not dispense with another's duty to use ordinary care.

---

7.   **Contributory Negligence Not Found--**

Beems v. Chicago, Rock Island & Peoria Railroad Co., 12 N.W. 222 (Iowa 1882).

Facts. Beems's (P's) deceased signaled for the Railroad's (D's) employees to slow the train while he uncoupled the cars. The train was not slowed and he was killed while trying to perform his job. In the action for negligence, D claimed P's deceased was contributorily negligent. After a judgment for P, D appeals.

Issue. Was P's deceased contributorily negligent as a matter of law?

Held. No. Judgment affirmed.

♦   The deceased's acts were not necessarily contributory negligence.

♦   Even though the deceased got his foot caught, unless he was contributorily negligent, D cannot escape liability for a negligent act.

---

8.   **Proof of Contributory Negligence--**

Gyerman v. United States Lines Co., 498 P.2d 1043 (Cal. 1972).

Facts. Gyerman (P), a longshoreman working in a warehouse owned by United States Lines (D), was injured when sacks of fishmeal fell on him. Before beginning this particular job, P notified D's supervisor that the sacks were improperly stacked and that, because of this improper stacking, his risk of injury was greatly enhanced. D's agent replied that nothing could be done to correct the problem. P was injured three days later. The trial court found that D was negligent in its failure to stack the sacks in a safe manner, but it also found that P was barred from recovery because of his contributory negligence in continuing to work in the face of obvious danger. P appeals.

Issue. Did D bear his burden of proving that P's alleged contributory negligence was the proximate cause of P's injuries?

Held. No. Judgment reversed.

♦   The record supported a finding that P failed to use ordinary care for his own protection.

♦   Regarding the causation question, the burden of proof in a civil action rests on each party as to each fact essential to his own claim or defense.

♦   The burden of proving all aspects of the affirmative defense of contributory negligence, including causation, rests on D, unless the elements of the defense may be inferred from P's evidence.

♦   The fundamental question, then, is whether P so caused the harm of which he is complaining that the law will view his conduct as the cause of the harm.

- That determination requires an examination of the facts in the record. According to the trial court's findings, P's sole negligence was in failing to report the safety violation to his union supervisor. In order to establish causation under those circumstances, the record would have to show that, had P reported the safety violation, the condition would have been changed.

- The record does not show that the safety violation would have been corrected; therefore, P does not appear to have been contributorily negligent.

- On remand, the trial will be limited to establishing whether, in fact, P was contributorily negligent, including the issue of whether that negligence was the cause of P's injuries.

Comment. Other cases involving worker safety violations have attempted to allow recovery to the plaintiff on various theories of violations of statutory duties to provide a safe place of work. Failure to report a safety violation does not usually bar a plaintiff's recovery.

---

9. No Duty to Protect Property from Negligence of Another--

LeRoy Fibre Co. v. Chicago, Milwaukee & St. Paul Railway, 232 U.S. 340 (1914).

Facts. Seven hundred tons of straw belonging to LeRoy Fibre Co. (P) was destroyed by fire caused by sparks from a train operated by the railroad (D). The jury found that D was negligent in operating a locomotive that emitted large quantities of sparks and live cinders. But, in accordance with its instructions, it found that P was contributorily negligent for stacking the straw within 100 feet of D's right-of-way. P appeals.

Issue. Is contributory negligence an appropriate defense where P's negligence is alleged to be the violation of a duty to use its property in such a manner that it cannot be injured by the wrongs of another?

Held. No. Judgment reversed.

- The rights of one person in the use of his property cannot be limited by the wrongs of another.

- Although property adjoining D's right-of-way is subject to some risks, it is not subject to risks created by the wrongful use of the railroad's property or its negligent operation of trains on the property.

- In order to find P contributorily negligent in this case, we would have to impose on it a duty to use its land in such a manner that it could not be harmed by the wrongs of another. We cannot properly do so.

Concurrence (Holmes, J.). The question of P's contributory negligence is one of fact. A jury could find that P did not act in a reasonable manner in placing its straw so close to D's right-of-way.

Comment. Holmes's concurrence, if applied, would result in further complication of negligence cases since the jury would have to decide what is a reasonable manner of protecting one's self from another's negligent acts.

---

10. Seat Belts--

Derheim v. N. Fiorito Co., 492 P.2d 1030 (Wash. 1972).

Facts. Derheim (P) was injured in a collision between his car and Fiorito's (D's) truck when the truck made an illegal left turn. In P's personal injury action, D attempted to raise the defense that P was contributorily negligent in failing to use available seat belts. The trial court refused to admit such evidence and entered judgment for P. After its decision, the case was immediately certified to the Washington Supreme Court.

Issue. May the defendant in an automobile accident case allege the contributory negligence of the plaintiff in failing to use seat belts?

Held. No. Judgment affirmed.

♦ The seat belt defense does not fit neatly into the defense of contributory negligence. Contributory negligence is normally considered to be that negligence on the part of the plaintiff that contributes with the negligence of the defendant to cause the plaintiff's injuries. The failure to buckle up is conduct arising before a defendant's negligence and does not, therefore, act in concert with a defendant's negligence to cause injury.

♦ Contributory negligence in Washington completely bars a plaintiff's recovery. In a situation where the plaintiff did not cause the accident, such a bar would be unjust.

♦ The seat belt defense also does not fit into the assumption of risk or the doctrine of avoidable consequences categories.

♦ In addition, the consequences of allowing evidence of a seat belt defense would burden the courts with additional expert witnesses and would require the analysis of the use of all safety devices equipped in the car.

♦ It would be extremely unfair to mitigate the damages of one who was completely without fault in an accident, especially where there is no statutory duty to wear seat belts. Also, because not all vehicles in the state must be equipped with seat belts, such a distinction would create a preferred class of those who chose not to install seat belts. Those people would not need to be concerned with contributory negligence while those whose vehicles were so equipped would face the possibility of no recovery even though an accident was not their fault.

Comments.

♦ The real reason the court seems to have reached this decision is because contributory negligence, no matter how slight, barred recovery in the state of Washington at that time. The court was not willing to impose such a burden on the innocent victim of an automobile accident.

♦ Not all cases follow the example above. Some may, for example, allow the evidence of no seat belt use to be used to mitigate damages.

B. LAST CLEAR CHANCE

1. **Introduction.** This doctrine was promulgated to ameliorate the harsh effects of contributory negligence as a complete defense. It applies where a defendant was negligent and the plaintiff, through his contributory negligence, placed himself in a position of either "helpless" or "inattentive" peril. If the defendant "had the last clear chance" to avoid the accident, the plaintiff can recover despite his contributory negligence.

    a. **Last clear chance of train engineer--**

Fuller v. Illinois Central Railroad, 56 So. 783 (Miss. 1911).

Facts. Fuller (P) was riding a wagon over a stretch of railroad track. P had his head down and did not observe Illinois Central Railroad's (D's) oncoming train. The train was late and traveling faster than usual. P was in plain view at approximately 660 feet from the crossing and D's engineer could have stopped the train within 200 feet. The track was straight; there were no obstructions. A whistle blast was given approximately 20 seconds before the train crashed into the wagon, killing P. At trial, judgment was given for D. P appeals.

Issue. Will the contributory negligence of an injured party defeat an action if it is shown that the defendant, by the exercise of reasonable care and prudence, might have avoided the consequence of the injured party's negligence?

Held. No. Judgment reversed and case remanded.

♦ The party who has a last clear opportunity of avoiding the accident, notwithstanding the negligence of his opponent, is considered solely responsible for it.

♦ Even if the engineer had not made an effort to check his train, but had contented himself with giving the alarm at the point when he did see, or could have seen P, by the exercise of reasonable care on his part, the catastrophe in all probability could have been avoided.

---

2. **Classification.** Last clear chance situations may be classified into four categories, in each of which both the plaintiff and the defendant are negligent.

    a. **Where the plaintiff is helpless.**

        1) If the defendant discovers the plaintiff and his peril and fails to use reasonable care to avoid injuring the plaintiff, the defendant is liable to the plaintiff.

        2) If the defendant fails to discover the plaintiff or his peril and is negligent in not doing so, the defendant is liable to the plaintiff.

    b. **Where the plaintiff is inattentive.** In "inattentive peril" cases, the plaintiff could have recognized the peril if he had been looking and could have protected himself.

        1) If the defendant discovers the plaintiff and his peril and the plaintiff's inattentiveness, yet fails to exercise reasonable care, the defendant is liable to the plaintiff.

        2) If the defendant does not discover the plaintiff or his peril or his inattentiveness, the defendant will not be liable under the prevailing view, even if he could have discovered the situation by conducting himself as a reasonable person under the circumstances.

3. **Antecedent Negligence.** The general rule is that where the defendant, because of his negligence at some time prior to his discovery of the helpless or inattentive plaintiff, is unable to exercise his "last clear chance," he will not be held liable. The defendant must be negligent in failing to exercise an actual last clear chance to avoid injury to the plaintiff for the doctrine to apply; *i.e.*, it is the defendant's negligence after he discovers, or in the exercise of reasonable care should have discovered, the plaintiff's danger that is critical.

C. IMPUTED CONTRIBUTORY NEGLIGENCE

1. **Introduction.** Under the theory of imputed negligence, if X is negligent and if there exists a special relationship between X and Y, the negligence of X may be "imputed" or charged to Y, even though Y has had nothing to do

with X's conduct and may even have tried to prevent it. (*See* discussion, *supra,* on vicarious liability and Restatement (Second) of Torts section 491, comments b and g.) The effect of "imputed negligence" may be either to make Y vicariously liable to Z (who has an action against X for negligence, which negligence may be imputed to Y—*e.g.*, in master-servant situation) or to bar recovery by Y against Z where X has been contributorily negligent and such contributory negligence is imputed to Y (*e.g.*, driver (X) and passenger (Y) vs. other driver (Z), where both drivers were negligent and Y seeks recovery from Z, who defends on the basis of imputed contributory negligence).

2. **Passenger vs. Driver, Spouse vs. Spouse, and Child vs. Parent—Imputed Contributory Negligence.**

    a. **Introduction.** At one time, contributory negligence was imputed to the plaintiff passengers, spouses, and children to bar recovery against a defendant. In general, this position has been reversed—totally in the case of children; almost totally in the case of spouses; and, in the case of passengers, to the extent that some special relationship must be shown before it will apply. Of course, any of these parties may be negligent on their own.

    b. **Evolution from the old rule--**

Mills v. Armstrong (The *Bernina*), 13 App. Cas. 1 (H.L.E. 1888).

Facts. The Mills's (Ps') decedents were on the ship, the S.S. *Bushire*, which collided with the S.S. *Bernina* due to the mutual negligence of those in charge of each ship. Ps brought a wrongful death action. The trial court imputed the contributory negligence of those in charge of each ship to the decedents (sailors who merely worked on the ships); Armstrong (D) relied on *Thorogood v. Bryan,* 137 Eng. Rep. 452 (1849), which held that a passenger in an omnibus is identified with the driver and, hence, cannot recover if injured by the driver's negligence. Thus, D argued that since Ps' decedents were like passengers (they did not navigate the ship), they could not recover. The court of appeals reversed the trial court and found for Ps. D appeals.

Issue. May a passenger recover if injured or killed due to a driver's (navigator's) negligence?

Held. Yes. Judgment affirmed.

♦   The doctrine of identification as stated in *Thorogood* is incomprehensible. While two people may be so bound together by a legal relation (*e.g.*, master-servant) that the acts of one are regarded at law as the acts of the other, certainly the driver-passenger relationship in a public vehicle is not such a relationship.

♦ While a passenger may select the conveyance, it is not reasonable to hold that the passenger cannot recover for the negligence of the driver in whom the passenger has put his trust.

♦ Just because the driver's employer cannot maintain an action if he were injured while in an omnibus operated by his driver (since theirs is a master-servant relationship), that does not mean that a passenger should not be able to do so. The passenger is not analogous to the master.

D. ASSUMPTION OF RISK

1. **Introduction.** The defense of assumption of risk arises when the plaintiff voluntarily encounters a known danger and by his conduct expressly or impliedly consents to take the risk of the danger. In such case, the defendant will be relieved of responsibility for his negligence.

2. **Need Not Be Negligence.** The plaintiff's voluntary assumption of risk need not be a negligent act on his part—*e.g.*, a spectator at a baseball game may be held to assume the risks of flying balls, but there is no negligence in going to a baseball game.

3. **Unreasonable Assumption.** On the other hand, the plaintiff's action may constitute contributory negligence where the plaintiff is unreasonable in assuming the risks of the defendant's conduct.

4. **Knowledge Required.** The plaintiff may be contributorily negligent for failing to discover danger that a reasonable person should be aware of. However, there can be no assumption of risk where the plaintiff had no knowledge or awareness of the particular danger involved.

5. **Must Be Voluntary.** The plaintiff's assumption of risk must be voluntary, and if the defendant's acts leave the plaintiff with no reasonable alternative to encountering the danger, then there is no assumption of risk.

6. **Rejection of Theory.** Writers have consistently attacked assumption of risk. Some courts have come out rejecting assumption of risk completely by stating that one must either find contributory negligence, or the plaintiff's consent to negligence, which simply means that the defendant owed him no duty. That is the approach that most courts adopting comparative negligence have followed.

7. **Assumption of Risk by Employee--**

Lamson v. American Axe & Tool Co., 58 N.E. 585 (Mass. 1900).

Facts. Lamson (P) painted hatchets for American (D). Upon installation of new racks, P complained that there was a danger that hatchets might fall. He was told by D to work with the new racks or quit. P continued to work and was injured when a hatchet fell. P sued for negligence and the trial court entered a directed verdict for D. P appeals.

Issue. Were P's acts assumption of risk?

Held. Yes. Judgment affirmed.

♦   P knew and understood the risk and voluntarily continued to work.

♦   The fear of losing his job was not sufficient to remove the voluntariness of the consent.

Comment. Assumption of risk, contributory negligence, and the fellow servant rule were three defenses that routinely barred recovery by an injured employee who sued his employer for negligence. The passage of Worker's Compensation statutes, however, provided recovery for injured employees without use of the negligence system, thereby avoiding those defenses.

----

8.   Assumption of Risk of Amusements--

Murphy v. Steeplechase Amusement Co., 166 N.E. 173 (N.Y. 1929).

Facts. Murphy (P) got on an amusement park ride known as the Flopper. The Flopper had a moving belt that made people fall. P fell and sued Steeplechase (D) for negligence. P obtained a verdict and D appeals.

Issue. Was P's decision to get on the Flopper assumption of risk?

Held. Yes. Judgment reversed.

♦   P clearly saw the dangers of the ride.

♦   No additional warnings were necessary since P could observe all risks.

♦   The ride was not so dangerous as to require that it be closed.

----

9.   Exculpatory Agreements--

Dalury v. S-K-I Ltd., 670 A.2d 795 (Vt. 1995).

Facts. Robert Dalury (P) was injured when he struck a metal pole that was part of a control maze for a ski lift line owned by S-K-I Ltd. and others (Ds). P had signed an exculpatory agreement releasing Ds from all liability for negligence, and P's signed photo identification card contained the same release terms. The trial court granted Ds' motion for summary judgment. P appeals.

Issue. Are exculpatory agreements that require skiers to release ski areas from all liability resulting from negligence void as contrary to public policy?

Held. Yes. Judgment reversed and case remanded.

- *Tunkl v. Regents of University of California*, 383 P.2d 441 (Cal. 1963), outlined the leading judicial formula for determining whether an exculpatory agreement violates public policy: (i) it concerns a business generally thought of as one appropriate for public regulation; (ii) the service performed by the party seeking exculpation is of great importance to the public, sometimes a matter of practical necessity; (iii) the service is available for any member of the public or for anyone falling within certain established standards; (iv) because of the nature of the service, in the economic setting of the transaction, the party seeking exculpation holds a decisive advantage in bargaining power against a member of the public seeking the service; (v) the provider of the service uses a standardized adhesion contract of exculpation with no alternative provisions; and (vi) as a result of the transaction, the person or property of the purchaser is under the seller's control, subject to the risk of the seller's or his agent's carelessness. However, no one formula can apply to every factual situation.

- We do not agree with Ds' characterization of their service as a purely private matter that implicates no public interest. Whether or not Ds provide an essential public service does not resolve the public policy question in the recreational sports context. Ds' facility is open to and advertised to skiers of all skill levels. Thousands of people buy lift tickets every day throughout the season and use lifts, ski trails, and other services. When a seller invites the public to use its services, a legitimate public interest arises.

- The basis of the public policy implications rests in the law of premises liability. A business owner has a duty of care to provide safe premises in suitable condition for its customers. A ski area owes its customers the same duty as any other business. Those who own or control the land have the responsibility for maintenance of the land.

- Ds have the expertise and opportunity to foresee and control hazards. Only Ds can inspect their premises, train their employees, and insure against risks. An important incentive for ski areas to manage risk would be removed if defendants were permitted to obtain broad waivers of their liability, and the public policy underlying business invitee law would be undermined.

- Vermont's "Acceptance of inherent risks" statute places responsibility for the inherent risks of a sport on the participant if the risks are obvious and necessary. But a ski area's own negligence is neither an inherent risk nor an obvious and necessary one. Thus, a skier's assumption of risks inherent in skiing does not affect a ski business's duty to warn skiers about risks or correct dangers that, in exercising reasonable prudence under the circumstances, could have been foreseen and rectified.

E. COMPARATIVE NEGLIGENCE

1. **Explanation of the Theory.** Comparative negligence is a civil law doctrine. In admiralty law, it is followed in all countries adopting the 1909 Brussels Agreement, but United States Admiralty Law did not adopt it until 1975. [*See* United States v. Reliable Transfer Co., 421 U.S. 397 (1975)] In the United States, comparative negligence is generally a creature of statute. Such statutes provide for apportionment of damages between negligent parties who injure one another in proportion to their fault (*e.g.*, $10,000 damages; P 30% at fault—P would be entitled to $7,000).

   a. Some form of comparative negligence has been adopted in over 40 jurisdictions.

   b. Such legislation is an attempt to provide a system where an act of contributory negligence would not be a bar to recovery.

   c. Courts are very reluctant to apportion damages between a negligent plaintiff and a negligent defendant in the absence of such a statute.

2. **Pure Comparative Negligence--**

Li v. Yellow Cab Co. of California, 532 P.2d 1226 (Cal. 1975).

Facts. Li (P) made a left turn across three lanes of oncoming traffic to enter a service station without waiting for a safe opening in the oncoming traffic. Yellow Cab's (D's) employee, who was driving in the oncoming traffic, sped through a yellow light and struck P's automobile crossing in front of him. P sued for personal injuries, alleging negligence. The court found P contributorily negligent and, therefore, barred P from recovery. P appeals.

Issue. Should contributory negligence, which precludes P from recovering for injury if he is the least bit negligent, be abolished and a pure comparative negligence standard be judicially adopted?

Held. Yes. Judgment reversed.

- ◆ "[L]iability for damage will be borne by those whose negligence caused it in direct proportion to their respective fault."

- ◆ Codification in 1872 of judicially created contributory negligence does not preclude courts from rejecting the doctrine.

- ◆ The doctrine of last clear chance is abolished.

- ◆ Assumption of risk is subsumed by pure comparative negligence.

- ◆ The new rule is applicable in the present case and any for which trial has not yet begun.

Comment. Pure comparative negligence means a plaintiff can collect from a defendant even if the plaintiff was more negligent than the defendant. Many state legislatures have adopted a 50% rule, whereby a plaintiff can collect under a comparative negligence method only if the plaintiff's negligence was less than that of the defendant.

---

3. **Strict Liability Statute.** In *Bohan v. Ritzo*, 679 A.2d 597 (N.H. 1996), Bohan was riding his bicycle past Ritzo's house when he saw a small dog about two feet away from the bicycle and coming toward him. Fearing the dog was coming to bite his right leg, Bohan stuck out his right leg to discourage the dog. At the same time, he looked to the right and down at the dog and removed his right hand from the handlebar. The bicycle's front tire jackknifed and Bohan lost his balance and fell. The dog did not bite or make contact with Bohan, but his injuries required two complex surgeries and he was out of work for seven and one-half months. Bohan sued under a statute imposing strict liability on dog owners for "damages occasioned by their dogs." The jury awarded Bohan $190,000. On appeal, the court found Bohan had alleged not merely the presence of the dog, but "specific mischievous actions" by the dog that were causally related to P's injuries. Furthermore, the court found that the statute did not require an actual bite or physical contact. If the legislature had intended strict liability to be limited to those occasions, the court noted that it could have so specified.

   The court also noted that the trial court was correct in refusing Ritzo's request for jury instructions and special verdict forms regarding comparative fault because Ritzo offered no evidence of conduct by Bohan that a jury could consider in diminishing Bohan's award of damages. The record did not show that Bohan put himself in a dangerous situation, or provoked the dog. Bohan had no time to think about any evasive action that might give rise to characterizing Bohan's response as "misconduct."

V. MULTIPLE DEFENDANTS: JOINT, SEVERAL, AND VICARIOUS LIABILITY

A. JOINT AND SEVERAL LIABILITY

1. **Joint Tortfeasors.** Joint tortfeasors are persons who either act in concert to cause injury to a plaintiff or act entirely independently but cause a single indivisible injury to the plaintiff. Joint tortfeasors are jointly and severally liable for the damage they cause.

    a. **No recovery allowed--**

Union Stock Yards Co. of Omaha v. Chicago, Burlington, & Quincy Railroad, 196 U.S. 217 (1905).

Facts. Union Stock Yards (P) was responsible for moving the switching cars for the railroad (D). One of the cars had a defective nut that could have been discovered by reasonable inspection by P or D. Both P and D were negligent in failing to perform the inspection and P's employee was injured as a result. P sued to recover damages it paid to its employee. Judgment was entered for D.

Issue. Whether one of several wrongdoers can recover against another wrongdoer when it has paid all of the damages for the wrong done.

Held. No. Judgment affirmed.

♦　　There are exceptions to the general rule of noncontribution among wrongdoers where: (i) there is one party primarily responsible for the wrong; (ii) one does not join in the wrong but is held responsible for it; or (iii) the principle cause, resulting in the injury sustained, was the act of the first wrongdoer and the second failed to discover or correct the defect.

♦　　Here, however, the parties' negligence was of the same character and does not fall into the class of exceptions.

Comment. In cases where a tortfeasor has been released, the traditional common law view was that the release of one party destroyed the cause of action against the other parties. The presumption now is that release of one party does not release the cause of action against another absent clear language indicating the intent to do so. Where there is a dispute, the burden is on the party claiming release.

b. **Concurrent causes.** In the case of concurrent causes, strict application of the "but for" rule fails if each cause, by itself, would not have been sufficient to bring about the result or if each cause, by itself, would have been sufficient to bring about the result. Conduct then is considered a cause of the injury if it is a "substantial factor" in bringing about the harm.

c. **Contribution.** At common law, contribution was not allowed between joint tortfeasors—if one had to satisfy a judgment, he could not recover from the others their share. Today under most contribution statutes, each joint tortfeasor is responsible for a share of the judgment. Under standard contribution rules, all defendants are responsible for equal shares regardless of their respective degrees of fault. However, in many comparative negligence states, contribution is not in equal shares, but is based on relative fault.

1) **Proper apportionment of liability--**

American Motorcycle Association v. Superior Court, 578 P.2d 899 (Cal. 1978).

Facts. Glen Gregos (P) sued American (D) and Viking (D) when P was injured in a motorcycle race. American sought to file a cross-complaint against P's parents claiming that they had contributed to P's injury. American alleged that since P's parents were also negligent, Ds' damages should be reduced by the parents' negligence.

Issue. Does the adoption of comparative negligence abolish joint and several liability of concurrent tortfeasors?

Held. No. American may cross-claim against P's parents.

♦ Comparative negligence does not necessarily abolish joint and several liability.

♦ One tortfeasor may remain liable to P for the entire amount.

♦ A tortfeasor who pays a judgment may recover a portion of that loss from other tortfeasors under a theory of equitable indemnity.

♦ The allocation of the judgment among tortfeasors should be based on each person's percentage of fault.

Dissent. This decision may require a marginally negligent defendant to pay a majority of the judgment. Comparative negligence should also require that when a defendant settles a case and his portion of liability is released, his portion of fault should also be released. Any remaining litigation would be based only on the percentage of fault of the defendants still party to the action.

Comment. The question of joint and several liability where marginally responsible defendants are involved has brought about statutory reform in several states. In California, each defendant is now responsible only for the amount of noneconomic damages allocated to that defendant in "direct proportion to that defendant's percentage of fault. . . ."

---

d.   Proportionate responsibility--

McDermott, Inc. v. AmClyde & River Don Castings, Ltd., 511 U.S. 202 (1994).

Facts. The first time McDermott (P) used a crane which had been specially designed to move an oil and gas production platform (the "deck") from a barge to steel bases affixed to the floor of the Gulf of Mexico, a prong of the crane's main hook broke. Both the deck and the crane were seriously damaged. P brought an admiralty action against AmClyde (D1), the crane vendor; River Don (D2), the hook supplier; and three companies that had supplied the supporting steel slings, seeking recovery for both deck and crane damages. Before trial, the three company defendants settled for $1 million. After trial, the jury assessed damages at $2.1 million and allocated 32% to D1 and 38% to D2. The district court denied Ds' motion to reduce the $2.1 million judgment "pro tanto" (*i.e.*, by the $1 million settlement) and entered judgment against D1 for $672,000 and D2 for $798,000. The appeals court reversed the district court's judgment against D1 based on the contract between P and D1, which provided that D1's free replacement of defective parts constituted fulfillment of any and all liabilities and precluded P's recovery against D1 based on tort liability; found the denial of a pro tanto settlement credit improper; reduced the district court's judgment against D2 to $470,000, based on the appeal court's finding that P's full damage award was $1.47 million ($2.1 million jury verdict minus 30% for the responsibility attributed to P and the company defendants); and found that the $1 million settlement should be deducted from P's full damage award.

Issue. Should the liability of the nonsettling defendants be calculated with reference to the jury's allocation of proportionate responsibility?

Held (Stevens, J.). Yes. Judgment reversed and case remanded.

♦   In *United States v. Reliable Transfer Co.*, 421 U. S. 397 (1975), we abandoned the "century-old" divided damages rule regarding damages when both parties to a collision are at fault which required an equal division of property damage whatever the relative degree of fault might have been, and we replaced it with a rule requiring that where it can be reasonably done, damages are to be assessed on the basis of proportionate fault. The old rule was simple, but the new rule is fair and supported by a consensus of the world's maritime nations, respected scholars, and judges.

♦ There is no consensus about the issue before us. There is general agreement that where a plaintiff settles with one of several joint tortfeasors, the nonsettling defendants are entitled to a credit for that settlement. Scholars and judges disagree, however, on how that credit should be determined. The American Law Institute ("ALI") describes the three alternatives as follows: (i) a pro tanto setoff with a right of contribution against the settling defendant; (ii) a pro tanto setoff without contribution; and (iii) the "proportionate share approach," where the settlement amount diminishes the plaintiff's claim against nonsettling defendants by the amount of the equitable share of the obligation of the settling defendant.

♦ The third option is most appropriate for this case. Option 1 discourages settlement. Option 2 is likely to lead to inequitable apportionments of liability, even where there are hearings to determine the good faith of the settlement. Option 3 is more consistent with the proportionate fault approach of *Reliable Transfer, supra*, because a nonsettling defendant ordinarily pays only its proportionate share of the judgment. There is no advantage to Option 2 insofar as promoting settlement because with the proportionate share approach, considerations such as the parties' desire to avoid litigation costs, to reduce uncertainty, and to maintain ongoing commercial relationships should ensure settlements in the vast majority of cases. Option 2 is not more judicially economical unless we adopt it without requiring a good-faith hearing, and no party or amicus advocates that course because of the potential for unfairness to nonsettling defendants who might have to pay more than their fair share of the damages.

♦ We reject Ds' argument that the proportionate share approach violates the "one satisfaction rule" which some courts apply to reduce a plaintiff's recovery against a nonsettling defendant in order to ensure that the plaintiff does not secure more than necessary to compensate him for his loss. There is no rigid rule against overcompensation in the law, and several doctrines, such as the collateral benefits rule, recognize that making tortfeasors pay for the damage they cause can be more important than stopping overcompensation.

B. VICARIOUS LIABILITY

1. **Introduction.** The cases in this section involve situations where the defendant may be held liable for nonfeasance; *i.e.*, failure to control the conduct of third persons over whom the defendant has the power of control. Where the defendant is present at the time of the third person's wrongful conduct, her failure to exercise control is an act of negligence. Where the defendant is not

present, she may be charged with liability for the acts of the third person only in limited situations. These cases involve imputing the third person's acts to the defendant, who is vicariously liable therefor.

2. Vicarious Liability.

a. Master-servant cases. A master-servant relationship is that of employer-employee.

    1) Agency law. It is a fundamental principle of agency law that an employer is vicariously liable for any tortious acts committed by her employee within the scope of the employment. This rule applies whether the acts were committed in the presence of the employer or otherwise; *i.e.*, whether or not the employer had the actual ability to control the employee's conduct.

    2) Crucial requirement—"scope of employment." The doctrine of respondeat superior does not apply where the tort is committed by the employee outside the scope of his employment. Thus, if the defendant's employee leaves the place of employment and, while pursuing some private objective, injures the plaintiff, the defendant cannot be held liable under respondeat superior.

    3) Intentional torts. Batteries and other intentional torts committed by an employee are frequently held to be outside the scope of employment, except where the employee's duties involve the use of physical force on others (*e.g.*, to collect a debt due the employer).

    a) Scope of employment--

Ira S. Bushey & Sons, Inc. v. United States, 398 F.2d 167 (2d Cir. 1968).

Facts. Lane, a seaman assigned to a Coast Guard vessel owned by the United States (D), returned drunk to the vessel. Before boarding the vessel, which was in a dry dock owned by Ira S. Bushey & Sons (P), Lane opened the valves on one side of the dry dock. The flooding caused the vessel to list to one side and to fall against the dry dock, damaging both the dock and the ship. P was awarded a judgment by the district court on the theory of respondeat superior. On appeal, D argued that Lane was not engaged in any activity within the scope of his employment at the time he committed the tort.

Issue. Is an employer liable under respondeat superior for reasonably foreseeable acts of its employees acting within the general scope of their employment, but without any motivation to benefit the employer?

Held. Yes. Judgment affirmed.

- This court does not find D's reliance on the "motive test" of the Restatement helpful. The true basis of respondeat superior is not the purpose for which the employee acted, but rather the deeply rooted sentiment that a business enterprise cannot justly disclaim responsibility for accidents which may fairly be said to be characteristic of its activities.

- Here, Lane's conduct was not so "unforeseeable" as to make it unfair to charge D with responsibility for his tortious activities.

- It was foreseeable that crew members, drunk or not, might do some damage while crossing the dry dock.

- Lane was required to return to the vessel. His presence there was not merely personal. In addition, his activities, although not readily explicable, at least were not due entirely to his personal life.

- Under these circumstances, D should bear the burden of loss.

Comment. The doctrine of respondeat superior is almost universally recognized in the United States. Nevertheless, no one seems to be in agreement as to the rationale for the doctrine, and courts, more probably than not, choose the rationale that will allow them to reach a certain result.

---

b. **Partners and joint venturers.** Persons who engage in a joint enterprise are vicariously liable for the conduct of the other members within the scope of the enterprise. *Rationale:* Those engaged in such an enterprise have an equal right to control its operation; whether all members in fact exercise such control is immaterial.

  1) **Requirements.** A joint enterprise requires: (i) a mutual right to control the management or operation of the enterprise; and (ii) in some jurisdictions, at least, a common business purpose in which all persons involved have a mutual interest.

  2) **Application—automobile trips.** A frequent issue is whether there is a joint enterprise between the owner of an automobile and a rider when they have embarked on a "share the expenses" trip—having reached some sort of agreement that they will take turns driving, will mutually agree on an itinerary, and will split all costs.

     a) Many courts hold this to be a joint enterprise, so that if there is an accident, an injured third person can hold liable either of the persons in the car, regardless of which one was driving at the time of the accident.

    b)   However, some states refuse to find a joint enterprise unless a business purpose is involved. In such jurisdictions, sharing the expenses on vacation or pleasure trips does not amount to a joint enterprise.

c.   Independent contractor cases.

    1)   Liability based on employer's own negligence. An employer may be held directly liable for the torts of her independent contractor if she has failed to exercise due care in selecting a competent contractor. This is liability imposed for the employer's own negligence, and it is immaterial whether there is also a basis for imposing vicarious liability.

    2)   Vicarious liability. As a general rule, one who employs an independent contractor will not be held vicariously liable for the negligent conduct of the latter even while the independent contractor is acting within the scope of the contract. *Rationale:* The employer has no right to control the manner in which an independent contractor performs the contract.

    3)   Exceptions. There are a couple of exceptions where the party that contracts an independent contractor will be held vicariously liable to third parties that are injured by the acts of the independent contractor.

        a)   Nondelegable duties. Certain duties are said to be "nondelegable." Examples include the duty to provide employees with a safe place to work, to refrain from obstructing a highway, etc.

        b)   Dangerous activities. If the activity involved is so intrinsically dangerous that the employer should realize that it involves a peculiar risk of physical harm (*e.g.*, blasting with dynamite), the employer cannot avoid liability by hiring an independent contractor to perform.

            (1)   Contractor's assumption of liability. The fact that the independent contractor "assumes all of the risk" does not change the result. But it does indicate that the employer has a cause of action against the independent contractor if the employer is held liable by a third party.

    4)   Vicarious liability of HMO--

Petrovich v. Share Health Plan of Illinois, Inc., 719 N.E.2d 756 (Ill. 1999).

Facts. Petrovich (P), who died during suit, alleged that her physician and Share HMO (Ds) were responsible for the negligent and untimely diagnosis of her oral cancer. As a member of the HMO, P had to select a physician from the HMO's network of participating physicians in order to qualify for benefits. The HMO does not employ the physicians, but contracts with independent medical groups and physicians that complete the HMO's application procedure and are approved. P received a member handbook from the HMO, which advertises "comprehensive high quality services." Additionally, the handbook refers to participating physicians not as independent contractors but as "our staff" and "Share physicians." P believed that her physicians were employed by the HMO and sues for medical malpractice. The court held for P.

Issue. Can an HMO be held vicariously liable for the negligence of its independent contractor physicians under agency law?

Held. Yes. Judgment affirmed. P is entitled to a trial under the doctrines of apparent and implied authority.

♦ Generally, vicarious liability does not exist for the actions of independent contractors. However, vicarious liability may be imposed for the actions of independent contractors if an agency relationship is established under the doctrines of apparent or implied authority.

♦ Under the doctrine of apparent authority, a principal is bound by the authority it actually gives, or appears to give, to another.

♦ In *Gilbert v. Sycamore Municipal Hospital*, 622 N.E.2d 788 (Ill. 1993), a hospital was found vicariously liable for a physician's negligence. The case set forth the elements necessary to prove apparent authority against a hospital, which is now extended to HMOs for physician malpractice: (i) the HMO must hold itself out to be a provider of health care without informing the patient that the physicians are independent contractors, and (ii) the patient must have jusifiably relied on this holding out by looking to the HMO, and not to a specific physician, to provide health care services.

♦ Here, the record establishes a "holding out" because it contains no evidence that P knew or should have known that the HMO engaged its physicians as independent contractors.

♦ However, the HMO claims that P did not establish justifiable reliance because she did not select the HMO—it was selected by her employer—and thus she could not have relied on it. The court holds that although P had no choice in selecting the HMO, she nevertheless relied on it to provide health care. P had to select a primary care physician from the HMO's network to qualify for benefits and that physician could refer P only to specialists approved by the HMO.

♦ Implied authority exists where the alleged agent retains the right to control the manner of doing the work. Here, the HMO exerted sufficient control over the physicians so as to negate their status as independent contractors.

---

d. ERISA preemption. Congress enacted ERISA, the Employee Retirement and Income Security Act of 1974, to protect the interests of participants in employee benefit plans and their beneficiaries by making uniform federal standards for employee benefit plans, including health insurance. The provisions of ERISA supersede state laws insofar as they relate to employee benefit plans.

1) Mixed eligibility and treatment decisions. In *Pegram v. Herdrich*, 530 U.S. 211 (2000), Herdrich sued her doctor and her HMO for medical malpractice and breach of fiduciary duty under ERISA. Herdrich's doctor, an HMO physician, required her to wait eight days for an ultrasound of her inflamed abdomen, and her appendix ruptured during that time. She claimed that the HMO encouraged and rewarded physicians for limiting medical care and that this involved an inherent or anticipatory breach of an ERISA fiduciary duty. According to the *Pegram* Court, HMO claims should be classified as either pure eligibility, pure treatment, or mixed eligibility and treatment. The Court held that mixed eligibility and treatment decisions by HMO physicians, as in *Pegram*, are not fiduciary decisions for which ERISA provides the exclusive remedy.

2) Pure eligibility decisions. In *Aetna Health Inc. v. Davila*, 542 U.S. 200 (2004), the Court held that a claim under the Texas Health Care Liability Act against an HMO for failing to exercise ordinary care in its determination of whether a physician's treatment recommendation was medically necessary or covered by the plan was completely preempted by ERISA. The Court distinguished *Pegram* because the HMO's coverage decisions in *Davila* were pure eligibility decisions. The Court stated that a benefit determination under ERISA is part of the ordinary fiduciary responsibilities connected to the administration of a plan even though medical judgments infuse the determination.

VI. CAUSATION

A. INTRODUCTION

Causation involves the relationship between the defendant's conduct and the harm to the plaintiff. It encompasses both actual and proximate cause. If the defendant did not cause the injury in fact, he is not liable, but even if the defendant caused the injury in fact, he is not liable if he was not the proximate cause of injury or damage.

Actual causation is always a question of fact for the jury. The court enters into the decision only in deciding if reasonable persons could find such a fact. Proximate cause is a question of law, not concerning facts; it involves conflicting considerations of policy—it comes into consideration only after causation in fact is established. In order to recover, the plaintiff must sustain the burden of proof as to both.

B. CAUSE IN FACT

1. **Sine Qua Non ("But For" Rule).** If the injury to the plaintiff would not have happened "but for" the act or omission of the defendant, such conduct is the cause in fact of the injury.

   a. **Illustrations.**

      1) The omission of one driver to give a turn signal is not a cause of an auto collision when the driver of the other auto was not looking and would not have seen it even if it had been given. In such a case, the defendant is negligent, but his negligence in not signaling his intention to turn was not the actual cause of the damage.

      2) Likewise, the failure to supply firefighting equipment that could not have been used anyway because of no available water is not the actual cause of the plaintiff's loss when his building burns down.

   b. **Cause in fact not found--**

New York Central Railroad v. Grimstad, 264 F. 334 (2d Cir. 1920).

Facts. Grimstad was the captain of a barge owned by New York Central Railroad (D). A tug bumped against Grimstad's barge, knocking him overboard. He did not know how to swim. Before his wife (P) could find a line to throw him, Grimstad drowned. P alleged that D was negligent in not providing life preservers or other necessary and proper safety devices on the barge. The trial court refused D's motion to dismiss the complaint. The jury found for P. D appeals.

Issue. Was D's failure to provide safety devices the cause in fact of Grimstad's death?

Held. No. Judgment reversed.

♦ The most immediate cause of Grimstad's death is his falling overboard and there was no evidence that D was involved in that accident.

♦ Further, there is no evidence that, even if there had been a life buoy on board, P would have been able to get it to Grimstad any more quickly than the line she did throw, or that she would have been able to accurately throw it to him. Even if he had seized it, there is no evidence that he would not have drowned anyway.

♦ In effect, there is no evidence that the lack of safety devices in any way caused or contributed to Grimstad's death. The cause of Grimstad's death was his own inability to swim.

♦ Thus, because D's failure to act was not the proximate cause of Grimstad's death, the trial court should have allowed D's motion to dismiss the complaint.

---

c. **A classic case--**

Zuchowicz v. United States, 140 F.3d 381 (2d Cir. 1998).

Facts. Patricia Zuchowicz (P) had a prescription for Danocrine filled at the local Naval Hospital's (D's) pharmacy. The prescription erroneously directed her to take 1,600 milligrams of the medication, which is twice the maximum recommended dosage. She took the prescribed dosage for one month and subsequently reduced the dosage to 800 milligrams. Side effects that she experienced from the medication include abnormal weight gain, a racing heart, chest pains, and headaches. Several months later she was advised to stop taking the medication, but she continued to have chest tightness and pain. She was diagnosed with primary pulmonary hypertension ("PPH") and was placed on a waiting list for a lung transplant. However, she became ineligible for the transplant when she became pregnant. She died one month after giving birth. Her husband continued this case, which claims that she developed PPH as a result of D's negligence in prescribing an overdose of Danocrine. P was awarded $1,034,236.02 in damages. D appeals.

Issues.

(i) Was Danocrine a "but for" cause of P's illness and death?

(ii)   Was the negligently prescribed overdose of Danocrine a "but for" cause of P's illness and death?

Held. (i) Yes. (ii) Yes. Judgment affirmed.

♦   P's expert testified that he believed to a reasonable medical certainty that P's PPH was caused by the overdose of Danocrine, and that the progression and timing of her PPH in relation to her overdose supports a finding of drug-induced PPH.

♦   This case is a classic example of the tort principle that: if a negligent act was deemed wrongful because that act increased the chances that a particular type of accident would occur, and a mishap of that very sort did happen, it was enough to support a finding by the factfinder that the negligent behavior caused the harm. If such a strong causal link exists, it is up to the negligent party to bring in evidence denying the "but for" cause and suggesting that in the actual case the wrongful conduct had not been a substantial factor.

♦   When a drug has been prescribed in greater than approved dosages, and negative side effects have been shown to be the result, a strong enough causal link has been shown to permit the finder of fact to conclude that the overdosage was a substantial factor in producing the harm.

2.   **Proof of Causation.** Plaintiff has the burden to prove that more likely than not the defendant was a substantial factor in bringing about the result.

a.   **Appellate court standard--**

General Electric Co. v. Joiner, 522 U.S 136 (1997).

Facts. In 1973, Robert Joiner (P) worked as an electrician and his job required him to work around electrical transformers, which used mineral-based dielectric fluid as a coolant. He often had to place his hands and arms in the fluid when making repairs and it would occasionally splash onto other body parts. In 1983, P's employer discovered that the fluid was contaminated with polychlorinated biphenyls ("PCBs"), the production and sale of which had been banned by Congress in 1978 as being hazardous to human health. P was diagnosed with lung cancer in 1991 and sued Monsanto, General Electric, and Westinghouse Electric (Ds) the following year, alleging that the lung cancer was "promoted" by his exposure to PCBs and their derivatives. P was at a heightened risk of developing the cancer because he had been a smoker for eight years and had a history of lung cancer in his family, but claims that absent exposure to PCBs his cancer would not have developed for many years, if at all. Ds removed the case to federal court and moved for summary judgment, which was granted. The trial court held that although there was a genuine issue of material fact that P was exposed to PCBs, there was no genuine issue as to whether P had been exposed to their derivatives. Because P's experts failed to establish a link between his exposure and his cancer, the court deemed the expert testimony inadmissible. The appellate court reversed, holding that the trial court erred in excluding the testimony of P's experts.

Issue. Is abuse of discretion the appropriate standard by which to review a trial court's decision to admit or exclude scientific evidence?

Held. Yes. Judgment reversed and case remanded.

♦ In cases where it is within the trial court's discretion to receive or exclude evidence, an appellate court will not reverse a ruling unless it is manifestly erroneous.

♦ The Federal Rules of Evidence allow district courts to admit a broad range of scientific testimony, but leaves the trial judge in charge of screening that evidence. Abuse of discretion will be applied in reviewing the trial judge's decision—a more stringent review process will not be applied in this case merely because the granting of summary judgment was outcome determinative.

♦ The trial court did not abuse its discretion. The testimony of P's experts relied on studies in infant mice who developed cancer after being injected with massive doses of PCBs. P's exposure to PCBs was far less and no study showed that PCBs caused cancer in any other species. The opinions of P's experts were not sufficiently supported by the animal studies on which they relied and the court did not abuse its discretion by rejecting the experts's reliance on them.

♦ The trial court does not have to admit opinion evidence that is connected to existing data only by the *ipse dixit* of the expert.

Concurrence (Breyer, J.). The trial judge must ensure that scientific evidence is relevant and reliable.

Dissent and concurrence (Stevens, J.). The appellate court decided that the weight of the evidence method was scientifically acceptable, and this methodology is used by other scientific agencies. Ds' experts used the same methodology. It is reasonable that this method could raise an inference that P's cancer was promoted by PCBs.

---

    b.   **Lost chance of survival--**

Herskovits v. Group Health Cooperative, 664 P.2d 474 (Wash. 1983).

Facts. Herskovits went to Group Health Cooperative (D) for a physical examination. D negligently failed to diagnose lung cancer. Herskovits probably had less than a 50% chance of surviving the lung cancer if it had been diagnosed at the first visit. Since the cancer was missed, his possibility of survival was reduced by 14%. When he died, his estate (P) sued D, claiming that the misdiagnosis was the cause of death. D alleged that Herskovits probably would have died anyway, and its negligence was not the cause of death. The trial court granted D's motion for summary judgment and P appeals.

Issue. Can the lost opportunity for survival be considered the cause of death in a tort action?

Held. Yes. Judgment reversed and case remanded.

♦ Although P must prove causation by a "more probable than not" standard, that does not mean that P must prove that the decedent had a probability of survival with a correct diagnosis.

♦ Due to D's negligence, the decedent had a reduced chance of survival, which is actionable. To do otherwise would release the medical profession from all care any time a patient had less than a 50% chance of survival.

♦ The evidence of a 14% reduction in the chance of survival is sufficient to allow the issue of cause to go to the jury.

Concurrence. A patient who lost a chance of survival, although the chance initially may have been less than 50%, should have the opportunity to have the issue of causation considered by the jury. The damages, of course, may reflect the less than 50% chance of survival that the patient had even with proper treatment.

Dissent. A patient who had less than a 50% chance of surviving even with proper treatment will be unable to prove that a "substantial cause" of the death was the negligence.

---

c.   **Apportionment of damages--**

Kingston v. Chicago & Northwestern Railway, 211 N.W. 913 (Wis. 1927).

Facts. One fire, set by sparks emitted from the Chicago & Northwestern Railway (D) locomotive, joined with another fire of unknown origin and together they entered and destroyed Kingston's (P's) property. The fires were of comparatively equal size and the jury found each of them to be the proximate cause of P's damage. The trial court granted P judgment in his action for damages. D appeals.

Issue. If two separate acts constitute the proximate cause of injury, is each tortfeasor liable for the full damage?

Held. Yes. Judgment affirmed.

- Any one of two or more joint tortfeasors whose concurring acts result in injury is individually responsible for the damage.

- Exceptions to the above-stated rule would arise if D's fire joined a much larger fire or one resulting from natural causes.

- Nothing in the record suggested any natural cause of the second fire.

- It is D's burden to show that the fire that joined his fire originated from natural causes.

- While under some circumstances a wrongdoer is not responsible for damages that would have occurred in the absence of his wrongful act, he is responsible where two causes (each attributable to the negligence of a responsible person) concur in producing injury.

- To permit each wrongdoer to plead the wrong of the other as a defense would permit both wrongdoers to escape liability and make it impossible to apportion damages.

---

    d.   Alternative liability. Where there is without doubt fault and alternative liability, the rule of causation is relaxed.

       1)   Disproving causation--

Summers v. Tice, 199 P.2d 1 (Cal. 1948).

Facts. Tice and Simonson (Ds), while hunting quail, shot in Summers's (P's) direction with their shotguns at the same time and a shot hit P in the eye. Obviously, only one of the Ds shot P, but P could not tell which one. Ds therefore argued that P could not show which D was negligent (*i.e.*, that the "but for" test could not be satisfied). Ds appeal judgment for P.

Issue. Has P shown causation?

Held. Yes. Judgment affirmed.

- Ds' acts of shooting in P's direction were negligent and P's injury would not have resulted but for Ds' acts. Ds are joint tortfeasors and each is jointly and severally liable even though only one inflicted the injury. Either D may avoid liability only by proof that he did not cause the injury.

Comment. The effect of the alternative liability rule is to shift the burden to Ds. Each D must disprove causation just as they must disprove breach of duty in *Ybarra v. Spangard, supra.*

———————

2) Examples where rule applies.

    a) Two Ds negligently sell bullets to children and one bullet kills a child. There is joint and several liability.

    b) Two cars driven negligently by A and B collide. Then, a negligent third driver, C, runs into the wreck and a passenger in A's car is hurt. The result is that all three drivers are liable (absent guest statute protection for driver A, etc.), but only because all three were negligent and there is no evidence as to which driver caused the injury.

3) Compare. Distinguish the case where P does not prove a case against one or more Ds from the alternative liability case where P proves he was injured by one of several Ds but does not know which one. The difference is that under the alternative liability rule, both Ds are negligent and only one caused the injury; whereas under the other rule, only one D was negligent. Both Ds must be negligent to apply *Summers v. Tice.*

e. "Market share liability" rejected--

———————

Skipworth v. Lead Industries Association, 690 A.2d 169 (Pa. 1997).

———————

Facts. Dominique Skipworth (P) was born in 1988 and was hospitalized and received outpatient treatment for lead poisoning on five separate occasions during the 22-month period that she lived in the same house, which was built in 1870. Testing of the home revealed the presence of lead-based paint. P filed suit against several manufacturers of lead pigment, along with their successors and a trade association (Ds), alleging that her physical and neuropsychological injuries were caused by lead poisoning from the lead paint in her home. P could not identify the manufacturer of the lead paint in her home and therefore joined substantially all manufacturers of lead pigment used in residential house paint from 1870 until 1977, under various theories of collective liability. Ds were granted summary judgment and the appellate court affirmed. P appeals.

Issues.

(i) Should this court adopt the market share theory of liability in lead paint poisoning cases?

(ii) Did the trial court err in entering summary judgment for Ds on P's alternative liability count?

(iii) Did the trial court correctly enter summary judgment for Ds on P's civil conspiracy claim?

(iv) Did the trial court properly enter summary judgment for Ds on P's concert of action claim?

Held. (i) No. (ii) No. (iii) Yes. (iv) Yes. Judgment affirmed.

♦ The market share liability theory is an exception to the general rule that a plaintiff must establish that the defendant proximately caused the injury.

♦ *Sindell v. Abbott Laboratories*, 607 P.2d 924 (Cal. 1980), was the first case to adopt this theory. In *Sindell*, the plaintiff developed cancer after her mother's ingestion of diethylstilbestrol ("DES"), a drug manufactured by several companies under an identical formula. The *Sindell* court found the theory appropriate when the following elements are present: (i) all named defendants are potential tortfeasors; (ii) the harmful products are identical or share the same defective qualities; (iii) the plaintiff, through no fault of her own, is unable to identify which defendant caused the injuries; and (iv) substantially all of the manufacturers of the defective product during the relevant time are named as defendants. Under the theory, "each manufacturer's liability would approximate its responsibility for the injuries caused by its own products."

♦ The market share theory is a substantial departure from this state's rule that the defendant's negligence must be the proximate cause of the plaintiff's injuries and, if applied to cases such as this, would lead to a distortion of liability resulting in arbitrary and unfair determinations of culpability. Unlike the DES case, which is limited to a nine-month time period during which the patient ingests the drug, the relevant time period here is far more extensive—100 years. Such an extensive time period could result in liability of companies that could not have been responsible for P's injuries (*e.g.*, a company could have entered the market within the 100-year period but after the placement of the lead paint in P's home). Additionally, lead paint pigments had different chemical formulations and levels of toxicity; thus, different brands of the paint could cause different levels of injury.

♦ P's alternative liability theory is inapplicable because Ds did not act simultaneously in producing the paint and P did not join all entities that manufactured lead paint during the 100-year period.

- P's civil conspiracy claim was correctly dismissed because P produced no evidence to establish that Ds acted in concert to commit an unlawful act, or to do a lawful act by unlawful means, and that they acted with malice.

- A concerted action claim "cannot be established if the plaintiff is unable to identify the wrongdoer or the person who acted in concert with the wrongdoer." We adopt these interpretations and find that P failed to establish her concerted action claim, as P is unable to identify any one of the manufacturers as the manufacturer of the lead paint that was ingested by P.

C. PROXIMATE CAUSE

1. **Introduction.** Proximate cause is used to determine the extent of the defendant's liability after actual causation (cause in fact) is established. It is an attempt to deal with the problem of liability for unforeseeable or unusual consequences following the defendant's acts. "Proximate cause" is an unfortunate term since closeness in time and space have nothing to do with the consideration here, which really deals with how far public policy will extend liability to the defendant for the consequences of his act. The Restatement uses the term "legal cause," but this term is not much better.

2. **Direct Results of Defendant's Act.** When there is no intervening force between the defendant's negligent act and the harm to the plaintiff, such harm is said to be the direct result of the defendant's act. For example, if the defendant negligently reaches for his cigarette lighter while driving his car, and the car hits a telephone pole that falls onto the plaintiff's house, the damage to the plaintiff's house is the direct result of the defendant's negligence. Indirect results (discussed *infra*) occur when there is an intervening force (or forces) between the defendant's act and the harm to the plaintiff.

   a. **Foreseeability of harm.** The harm caused the plaintiff as a direct result of the defendant's acts may be either foreseeable (*e.g.*, it is foreseeable that pedestrians and other drivers may be injured if the defendant negligently runs a red traffic light) or unforeseeable (*e.g.*, it is unforeseeable in the preceding example that buildings in the neighborhood will have all their windows blown out by an explosion caused by the defendant running into another vehicle, which turns out to be a gasoline tank truck).

   b. **The opposing views.** There are two opposing views on foreseeability of consequences of the defendant's act: one view is that the defendant's act will be considered the proximate cause of the plaintiff's injury only if such consequences, judged at the time, place, and under the circumstances when the defendant acted, were reasonably foreseeable. Essentially, this view uses the same criteria for foreseeability to determine the extent of liability as is used to determine whether the defendant's act is negligent—is the injury reasonably foreseeable as something likely to happen? The other view, where the injury to the plaintiff is the direct result of the defendant's act, is that foreseeability is important only in determining whether there is negligence; if the injury follows in an unbroken sequence of events, the defendant will be liable for the consequences regardless of the remoteness of the injury.

    c.   Placing limits on remoteness: fire cases.

        1)   One house rule--

Ryan v. New York Central Railroad, 35 N.Y. 210 (1866).

Facts. New York Central Railroad's (D's) engine negligently set fire to D's woodshed. The fire then spread to a number of nearby houses. Ryan (P) sued for the value of his house, which was 130 feet from the shed and was burned down when the fire spread to it. The trial court nonsuited P, and he appeals.

Issue. Does D's liability extend to all damage caused by D's acts?

Held. No. Judgment affirmed.

♦   Destruction of P's home was not the proximate result of D's negligence. It was too remote (*i.e.*, P's house was too far away).

♦   It was not foreseeable that the fire would spread and destroy P's home. D had no control over the spread of the fire.

Comment. This is an arbitrary limit on foreseeability—one home only. If the court did not adopt the foreseeability rule, the defendant would be liable for all the buildings burned. This case represents a policy to spread the burden of the loss.

---

    3.   Violation of a Statute.

        a.   Plaintiff's violation--

Berry v. Sugar Notch Borough, 43 A. 240 (Pa. 1899).

Facts. The borough (D) allowed a chestnut tree to remain standing near a street car line. P was a motorman for the line and was injured when the tree fell on his car. At the time of the accident, P was operating the car at a speed in excess of the allowable rate. D claimed this violation of the statute by P was the cause of his injury. After a judgment for P, D appeals.

Issue. Was P's violation of the statute the proximate cause of his injury?

Held. No. Judgment affirmed.

♦ The fact that his speed brought P to the accident location was mere chance. The proximate cause of the injury was the fall of the tree.

Comment. The violation of a statute by the plaintiff or the defendant will not be conclusive on the outcome of the case. There must still be a determination of which act of negligence was the proximate cause of the injury.

---

b. **Third-party violation--**

Brower v. New York Central & Hudson Railroad, 103 A. 166 (N.J. 1918).

Facts. Brower (P) owned a horse and cart that was struck at a grade crossing due to the negligence of the New York Central & Hudson Railroad (D). The driver of the cart was stunned and was unable to prevent the theft of empty kegs and a barrel of cider. Detectives employed by D to prevent theft on its trains did not act to prevent the theft of P's property. P sued for damages and was given an award that included the value of the stolen items. D appeals, arguing that the theft of the items was due to the unforeseeable intervention of a third party.

Issues.

(i) Is a defendant liable for damage caused by an intervening force?

(ii) Was the intervention of third parties foreseeable?

Held. (i) Yes. (ii) Yes. Judgment affirmed.

♦ A party is liable for the consequence of damages caused by third parties if that damage is foreseeable.

♦ The presence of train detectives on the freight train evidences a knowledge by the railroad that items small enough to be stolen will be taken if unprotected.

♦ It is foreseeable that if a train crashes into a loaded cart, the contents of the cart will be scattered. If the driver of the cart is unable to protect those contents, it is likewise foreseeable that they will be taken unless protected by someone else.

◆   Since D made no effort to protect P's property, it was foreseeable that it would be stolen.

◆   Thus, the theft of P's property as a consequence of D's negligence is not too remote and the trial court judgment that D should pay the value of the stolen property is affirmed.

Dissent. If the defendant's negligence merely provides the opportunity for crime, the continuity between cause and effect necessary to establish proximate cause does not exist. We would not, for example, impose liability for the murder of a passenger where the only negligence of the railroad was in allowing the train to derail, thus giving the murderer access to his victim.

---

4.   **Rescue--**

Wagner v. International Railway, 133 N.E. 437 (N.Y. 1921).

Facts. Wagner's (P's) cousin fell off an overcrowded train as it lurched violently while crossing a trestle. The car stopped at the end of the trestle and P was injured while he attempted to find his cousin. The trial court found that the railroad (D) was not liable unless P was invited by the conductor to go on the trestle. P appeals.

Issue. Were the limitations by the trial court correct?

Held. No. Judgment reversed.

◆   Danger invites rescue. It is a natural human response to seek to rescue others who may be in distress.

Comments.

◆   This doctrine also applies where the defendant negligently endangers himself and the plaintiff attempts to help and is injured in the process. Even rescue of a rescuer is covered.

◆   In *Wagner,* Justice Cardozo (who rendered the opinion) gets by *Palsgraf* (*infra*) by saying that a rescuer is always foreseeable. Is the injury in *Wagner* really foreseeable? How far does this arbitrary rule go?

◆   Contributory negligence may bar a plaintiff rescuer's action, but not always, since under some circumstances even an extreme risk may be justified (*e.g.*, mother sticking her head into a building filled with cyanide gas to see if her baby is inside will not be barred from action against the defendant by a defense of contributory negligence).

- There is no need of real danger to make the plaintiff a "rescuer." An apparent danger that would stimulate a reasonable person to act is sufficient.

- The rescuer can think the act over quite a while. The act need not be a human instinctual response without reflection.

---

5.   **Manner in Which Injury Occurs--**

In re **Polemis & Furness, Withy & Co.,** [1921] 3 K.B. 560.

Facts. Owners of a vessel (Ps) chartered it to Ds. While unloading cargo, Ds' servants dropped a plank into the hold of the vessel. Apparently it caused a spark that, in turn, ignited benzine vapors. The resulting fire destroyed the vessel. Arbitrators found the foregoing and also that the longshoreman who dropped the plank was negligent in doing so. They also found that, although the spark could not have been anticipated, some damage could have been. The court affirmed and Ds appeal, arguing that the particular damage could not have been anticipated.

Issue. Is a defendant liable for unforeseeable consequences of his acts if some damage is foreseeable, but not the damage that actually occurred?

Held. Yes. Judgment affirmed.

- The foreseeability of damages may be important in determining the existence of negligence. But once negligence is established, the negligent party is liable for all damages, regardless of foreseeability.

- Here the arbitrators found that the falling plank was due to the negligence of the defendants' servants. They also found that, although the creation of a spark could not be reasonably anticipated, some damage could be foreseen.

- Ds are liable for the damage actually caused, even though it was not the type foreseen.

Concurrence. Negligence in this case is dependent on whether damages could be anticipated as a result of the falling plank. Once negligence is shown, the negligent party is liable for all damages caused by that act.

Concurrence. If a negligent act is likely to cause damage, the fact that the damage actually caused is different from that anticipated is immaterial as long as the actual damage is a direct result of the negligent act.

---

6. Duty Owed Only to Foreseeable Plaintiffs--

Palsgraf v. Long Island Railroad, 162 N.E. 99 (N.Y. 1928).

Facts. A passenger carrying a package, while hurrying to catch and board a moving train, appeared to the Long Island Railroad's (D's) employee to be falling. The employee attempted to help the passenger and caused a package the passenger was holding to fall on the rails. Subsequently, fireworks in the package exploded. The shock knocked down scales at the other end of the platform, which injured Mrs. Palsgraf (P). P sued D, claiming her injury resulted from negligent acts of the employee. D appeals from a judgment for P.

Issue. May D's negligence toward a third person be the basis of recovery for injuries to P, even though no risk of harm to P was foreseeable?

Held. No. Judgment reversed.

♦   D owed no duty to P, as she was not a foreseeable plaintiff. D may have been negligent toward the passenger holding the package but not to P. D owes a duty of care only to those persons to whom the average reasonable person would have foreseen a risk of harm under the circumstances.

♦   The foreseeability of the plaintiff is an element of the duty owed and is, therefore, a question of law for the court.

Dissent (Andrews, J.). Judgment for P should be affirmed. A wrongdoer should be held liable for all the proximate results of his acts, whether or not the injured person or the manner in which the injury resulted was foreseeable. Any question of foreseeability of injury is a question of fact for the jury.

Comment. The opinion in *Palsgraf* represents the majority view today. Note that *Palsgraf* deals with an unforeseeable plaintiff rather than an unforeseeable risk as the *Polemis* case represented. A third view, based on the holding's dictum, is that even if there is a duty to the plaintiff, liability will not attach unless the average reasonable person would have foreseen a risk of harm to the particular interest of the plaintiff that is actually invaded. Very few cases actually involve direct causation to an unforeseeable plaintiff, although *Palsgraf* is often cited (incorrectly) as a matter of course in cases involving causation issues.

Query. Was the railroad negligent in having the scale there? Since the plaintiff was a passenger, it owed her a duty of the "highest degree of care"—common carrier rule. If the scales were actually knocked down by Mrs. Palsgraf or another passenger scared by the fireworks, what would the decision be? Did the attorney use the correct tactics? Did he stress the right facts? Was it negligent to have scales on the platform that were so easy to knock down? Even under the majority rule as stated in *Palsgraf,* once there is a duty, foreseeability of the type of damage is not necessary if there is foreseeability of some damage present.

---

7. Placing Plaintiff in a Position of Peril--

Marshall v. Nugent, 222 F.2d 604 (1st Cir. 1955).

Facts. Marshall (P) was a passenger in an auto that left the road to avoid a collision with a truck negligently operated by a Socony employee. The employee suggested that P warn other drivers about the danger, while he pulled P's car back on the road. P did so and was struck by an auto driven by Nugent. P sued Nugent and Socony (Ds) for damages and the jury returned a verdict for Nugent but against Socony. Socony appeals.

Issue. May a negligent actor remain liable for the continuing consequences of his act if the jury deems the consequences to be reasonably foreseeable?

Held. Yes. Judgment affirmed.

♦   A negligent tortfeasor may remain liable until the situation has returned to normal. The jury may decide the foreseeability issue as long as reasonable minds can differ on the inferences to be drawn from the facts.

---

8. Actual Results Must Be Foreseeable: A Departure from *Polemis*--

Overseas Tankship (U.K.) Ltd. v. Morts Dock & Engineering Co., Ltd. (Wagon Mound (No. 1)), [1961] A.C. 388 (P.C. Aust.).

Facts. Overseas's (D's) freighter, Wagon Mound, was moored approximately 600 feet away from Morts's (P's) wharf. D's ship negligently discharged oil, which spread across the harbor and under P's wharf. P's workers were welding on the wharf. Molten metal dripped from the welding job, set fire to cotton that was floating on the surface of the water, and this in turn ignited the oil. The ensuing fire damaged the wharf and two ships docked alongside. D appeals a judgment for P.

Issue. Must the actual damage or results be foreseeable?

Held. Yes. Judgment reversed.

♦ The actual type of damage or results must be foreseeable. It is not enough that just any damage or results are foreseeable or follow in an unbroken sequence. Some limitation must be imposed upon the consequence for which a negligent actor is to be held responsible. We, therefore, adopt the view of reasonable foreseeability; *i.e.*, liability limited to what the reasonable person ought to foresee.

Comment. This case represented a repudiation of the direct causation rule of *Polemis*. As a practical matter, the plaintiff was prevented from introducing evidence that it was foreseeable that the mixture of oil, cotton, and sparks would cause a serious fire. If the defendant could have foreseen that result, the plaintiff could also have foreseen it and been barred from recovery by contributory negligence. In an action filed by other ship owners who did not spill oil, yet suffered loss, it was proven that fire was foreseeable. [Overseas Tankship (U.K.) Ltd. v. The Miller Steamship Co., (1967) 1 A.C. 617, (Wagon Mound (No. 2))]

───────────────

9. **Indirect Results of Defendant's Act.** As stated above, indirect results occur when there is an intervening force (or forces) between the defendant's act and the harm caused to the plaintiff. Such forces or causes are of external origin, and do not come into operation until after the defendant's negligent act has occurred. Intervening causes generally do not relieve the defendant of liability unless they are both unforeseeable and bring about unforeseeable results. In such cases, the intervening causes are said to be "superseding." However, the test in every case where there is an intervening force or cause is whether the average, reasonable person faced with like or similar circumstances would have foreseen the likelihood that the force or cause would intervene.

   a.   **Unforeseeable results--**

───────────────

Virden v. Betts and Beer Construction Company, 656 N.W.2d 805 (Iowa 2003).

───────────────

Facts. Virden (P), a maintenance worker in a high school, was reinstalling an angle iron that had fallen from the ceiling of the school's wrestling room. P fell from the top of a 10-foot ladder as he was bolting the angle iron into place. He sustained severe injuries, requiring several surgeries. P sued Betts and Beer Construction and another contractor (Ds) who had installed the ceiling. The district court granted Ds summary judgment, and P appealed. The court of appeals reversed. The Supreme Court of Iowa granted review.

Issue. Was Ds' purported negligence the proximate cause of P's injuries?

Held. No. Judgment vacated.

- ♦ Summary judgment may be rendered in a negligence case where the material facts fail to show a causal link between the negligence and the injury.

- ♦ Before the repairs were attempted, Ds were not contacted. Furthermore, P did not seek help in positioning or securing the ladder even though clear access to the repair site was impeded by wrestling equipment.

- ♦ Ds had a duty to construct a secure ceiling that did not fall on anyone. But P's injury was not caused by the angle iron; he was hurt when the ladder "suddenly kicked out from under" him and he fell.

- ♦ To constitute actionable negligence, Ds' breach of their duty of care must be the proximate cause of P's injury. The two components to the proximate-cause inquiry are: (i) the defendant's conduct must have in fact caused the damages; and (ii) the law must require the defendant to be legally responsible for them.

- ♦ To prove the first component, a plaintiff must prove that the damages would not have occurred but for the defendant's negligence. Here, looking at the facts in the light most favorable to P, but for the fallen angle iron, he would not have been on the ladder. Thus, P survives the motion for summary judgment based on the but-for test of causation.

- ♦ However, P must also prove that Ds' negligent welding of the angle iron was a substantial factor in bringing about the injury. The district court correctly found that Ds' role was remote rather than foreseeable. P's injury resulted from his fall, not from a defective angle iron.

---

b. Extraordinary consequence--

Hebert v. Enos, 806 N.E.2d 452 (Mass. App. Ct. 2004).

Facts. Hebert (P) sued Enos (D) to recover for personal injuries from a severe electric shock he received while on D's property to water D's flowers. P claimed that D's faulty repairs of his second-floor toilet caused the toilet to overflow, and the resulting water reacted with the electrical system. P's expert, a professional engineer, prepared a report for the motion judge. In the expert's opinion, the leaking water caused insulation on wires to break down, allowing leakage current to flow into a grounded surface and through the water piping system. Because P was wet with perspiration from watering his own flowers, a greater amount of electric current flowed through him than would have if he had been dry. According to the expert, this current was a direct result of the water overflow. D's motion for summary judgment was granted. P appeals.

Issue. Is summary judgment appropriate if a plaintiff has no reasonable expectation of proving that his injury was a foreseeable result of the defendant's conduct?

Held. Yes. Judgment affirmed.

♦ P submitted sufficient evidence to show that D's faulty repair of the toilet led to the harm that P suffered. However, the accident that occurred was extraordinary and not foreseeable.

♦ The motion judge held D to the proper standard of care—that which is reasonable under the circumstances.

---

10. **Emotional Injury.** Mental or emotional distress can flow from wrongful acts; claims for this type of injury are common. One defense is to deny the link between the defendant's acts and the distress. Another is that even if the defendant's acts caused the harm, that cause is not the proximate cause.

   a.   **No recovery based on fright--**

Mitchell v. Rochester Railway, 45 N.E. 354 (N.Y. 1896).

Facts. Mitchell (P) was waiting to board one of Rochester Railway's (D's) cars which had stopped where P was standing. Just as P was about to step up, one of D's horse cars came down the street and came so close to P that P stood between the horses' heads when they stopped. P claimed fright and excitement caused her to miscarry, become unconscious, and suffer a consequent illness. Medical testimony supported P's position that her mental shock was sufficient to produce these results. The court found for P. D appeals.

Issue. Can P recover for injuries resulting from fright caused by D's negligence?

Held. No. Judgment reversed and case dismissed.

♦ P cannot recover for injuries occasioned by fright as there is no immediate personal injury. If fright cannot be the basis of an action, no recovery can be had for resulting injuries, no matter how serious the consequences.

♦ A flood of litigation would result if recovery were allowed in this class of cases; the injuries may be easily feigned and damages must rest on speculation. To establish such a doctrine would be against public policy.

♦ P's miscarriage cannot be said to be the proximate result of D's negligence. Proximate damages are such as are the ordinary and natural result of the negligence charged—those that are usual and may be expected. P's injuries were too remote and could not have been reasonably anticipated.

---

11. Dispensing with the "Zone of Danger" Requirement--

Dillon v. Legg, 441 P.2d 912 (Cal. 1968).

Facts. Dillon (P), a mother who watched her child get killed when the child was struck by an auto negligently driven by Legg (D), brought three causes of action: (i) an action for compensation for the loss of the child; (ii) an action for physical and mental suffering by P resulting from the great emotional shock of witnessing the accident; and (iii) an action for similar suffering on the part of P's daughter, Cheryl, who also witnessed the accident. The trial court dismissed the second cause of action, but refused to grant D's motion for summary judgment as to the third count because there was evidence that Cheryl might have been in the zone of danger. P appeals from the dismissal of her cause of action for physical and mental suffering.

Issue. Must a person who suffers trauma upon apprehension of negligent injury to a family member be within the zone of danger in order to maintain a cause of action for damages resulting from the trauma?

Held. No. Judgment reversed.

- ◆ One who suffers physical injury as the result of trauma upon apprehension of harm to another, if the risk of her injury is foreseeable, has a cause of action.

- ◆ Foreseeability will depend on three factors: (i) P's proximity to the scene of the accident, (ii) whether P suffered the direct emotional impact of viewing the accident, and (iii) whether P and the victim were closely related.

- ◆ The court will not deny recovery for a legitimate claim because other fraudulent ones may be urged. This type of claim is no more susceptible to fraud than those well-accepted claims where a person claims that fear of her own injury caused her mental suffering.

- ◆ Of course, P cannot recover if she is shown to have contributed to the accident. The basis of P's claim must be the adjudicated liability and fault of D.

- ◆ This case, which would allow recovery by the daughter but not by P, both of whom suffered the same damage as a result of the same negligent conduct, points out the incongruity of the zone of danger requirement.

Dissent. The majority sets forth artificial and unpredictable distinctions and leaves many questions unanswered.

Comments.

♦ The court here dispensed with the impact rule and the requirement that the bystander actually be in the "zone of danger." This is not yet the majority rule.

♦ In *Molien v. Kaiser Foundation Hospitals,* 616 P.2d 813 (Cal. 1980), Molien's (P's) wife was incorrectly diagnosed by Kaiser (D) as having syphilis. The diagnosis caused emotional distress for P and the dissolution of P's marriage. P suffered no physical harm but sued for the emotional distress. The court held that P was a foreseeable plaintiff and P could recover without proof of physical harm. P was directly injured by D's acts. The court found that where the emotional distress is clear and capable of proof, a requirement of physical harm is unnecessary. D's duty arose because D directed the wife to advise P of the diagnosis; it did not arise because D's misdiagnosis was necessarily involved.

♦ Two types of acts have traditionally resulted in recovery for negligently caused emotional harm in the absence of physical harm: misdelivery of a death notice and mishandling of a corpse.

VII. AFFIRMATIVE DUTIES

A. GENERAL DUTY

1. **Introduction.** This chapter deals with the care a person must show to others, including the duties of owners and occupiers of land.

2. **Act or Omission of Defendant.** As in intentional torts, the act of the defendant must be the external manifestation of his will, *i.e.*, volitional movement, in order to support a cause of action based on negligence. However, liability in negligence can also be based on the failure or omission of the defendant to act if he is under an affirmative duty to act.

3. **Failure to Act.** Generally, there is no legal obligation to come to the aid of others.

B. THE DUTY TO RESCUE

1. **Duty to Warn--**

Buch v. Amory Manufacturing Co., 44 A. 809 (N.H. 1897).

Facts. Buch (P), an eight-year-old boy, trespassed into Amory's (D's) mill, where dangerous weaving machinery was in operation. An overseer ordered P out of the mill, but P, not understanding English, did not comply. No other attempts were made to remove P from the mill. While P's brother, an employee, was teaching him how to operate one of the machines, P's hand became entangled in the machinery and was crushed. P sued for damages. D's motion for a directed verdict was denied. Judgment was awarded for P. D appeals.

Issue. Does a landowner have a legal duty to warn an infant trespasser of patent dangers on his land?

Held. No. Judgment reversed.

♦ Property owners are not required to warn adults of latent dangers. Reason does not suggest they should have to warn infants of dangers they cannot comprehend.

♦ A property owner is under no obligation to come to the rescue of a stranger not on his land. The presence of a trespasser on his land does not impose any duty that is not there when the trespasser is somewhere else. Certainly, by coming onto his land, an infant does not make the property owner his guardian.

♦   If P caused any damage by trespassing, he is liable to D for that damage.

♦   To hold that P is entitled to damages for the results of his own trespass would also require us to hold that a trespasser who harms the landowner's property and is thereby injured can recover for his injuries caused by himself and also that the landowner could recover for the damage to his property.

♦   The attractive nuisance doctrine is not applicable to machinery in a factory. The landowner is not obligated to shut down his mill in order to protect a trespasser.

Comment. If the landowner is aware of the presence of an infant and through the use of minimal force and time could put the child out of the reach of dangerous machinery, is there any reason the law should not impose such a duty on him as a matter of public policy? Isn't this case distinguishable from the attractive nuisance cases that arise from unsupervised nuisances? What if the child here, instead of being eight years old, had been only three years old? Would not the court, in such a circumstance, probably impose liability on the mill?

---

2.   **Misfeasance vs. Nonfeasance and the Good Samaritan Doctrine.** One must distinguish between nonfeasance and misfeasance—between failing to act and acting negligently. Although a person may be under no duty to take affirmative action in the first instance, if he undertakes assistance and is thereafter negligent in what he does or does not do, he is liable.

     a.   **No obligation to practice--**

Hurley v. Eddingfield, 59 N.E. 1058 (Ind. 1901).

Facts. Eddingfield (D) was a duly licensed practicing physician for years before the decedent's death. He held himself out to the public as a general practitioner and had been the decedent's family physician. The decedent became seriously ill and sent a messenger to let D know of the decedent's condition, to give him fees for his service, to tell him no other doctor was procurable in time, and that the decedent relied on him. D refused to render aid without any reason; no other patients required his immediate attention, and D could have gone to the decedent if he chose to. The decedent's death resulted from D's wrongful act. Hurley (P), the decedent's administrator, sued for $10,000 damages for wrongfully causing the death of his intestate. The court sustained D's demurrer to the complaint. P appeals.

Issue. Is a licensed physician liable in damages for the death of a person caused by his refusal to render medical assistance?

Held. No. Judgment affirmed.

- D refused to enter into a contract of employment. The law regulating the practice of medicine provides for a board of examiners, qualification standards, examinations, license requirements, and penalties for practicing without a license. It is a preventive, not a compulsive, measure. Becoming licensed to practice medicine does not require that the licensee practice at all, or that he will practice on other terms than he may choose to accept.

3. Misfeasance--

Montgomery v. National Convoy & Trucking Co., 195 S.E. 247 (S.C. 1937).

Facts. Trucks owned and operated by National Convoy (D) stalled on an icy highway so as to block the entire roadway. The trucks were stalled at the bottom of a hill on a well-traveled road. Vehicles coming down the hill could not see the trucks until their vehicles crested the hill. D was not negligent in causing the trucks to stall. However, D's employees failed to place any warning signals except in the immediate area of the trucks. Montgomery (P) came over a hill and started down toward the trucks. Because of the condition of the road, P was not able to stop before crashing into the trucks. He suffered injuries and sued for damages. The trial court judgment was for P. D appeals.

Issue. Were D's employees negligent in failing to provide warnings that were reasonably calculated to prevent harm to P—*i.e.*, some warning to cars before they came over the hill 50 feet away?

Held. Yes. Judgment affirmed.

- D's employees had a duty to take such precautions as were reasonably calculated to prevent injury resulting from their stalled trucks.

- Placing flares and leaving truck lights on was not reasonably calculated to prevent such injury, since those warning signals would not be observable until an oncoming car was too close to stop.

- Other evidence in the record shows that a signal at the crest of the hill would have prevented P's injuries.

- Because D's employees failed to take those precautions reasonably calculated to avoid P's injuries, D is liable for those injuries.

Comment. The key to what the court is saying is that it is not enough for a person to make just any warning of impending danger caused by a situation he has created. Rather, the warning must be such that those who might be injured are adequately warned.

C. DUTIES OF OWNERS AND OCCUPIERS

1. **Arbitrary Categorization.** In this area, duties are divided into fairly rigid and arbitrary categories depending on the type of plaintiff involved. These duties are generally the result of historical precedent and often would be considered inconsistent with what reasonable persons under the same or similar circumstances would do.

2. **Persons Outside of the Premises.** The person in possession of land is required to exercise reasonable care with regard to her activities on the land for the protection of those outside the premises.

    a. **Natural conditions.** A landowner/occupier is not liable for damages resulting from conditions on the premises arising in a state of nature.

    b. **Public highways or walkways.** The public right of passage on a highway carries with it an obligation on the part of the abutting landowners to use reasonable care for the protection of those on the highway.

    c. **Artificial conditions.** Where the landowner/occupier creates artificial conditions on the land, she is obligated to inspect them and protect against danger to others.

3. **Trespassing Adults.**

    a. **No duty owed.** Trespassing adults enter the land of another with no right or privilege; they must take the premises as found and are presumed to assume the risk of looking out for themselves. Thus, the general rule is that a landowner/occupier is not liable for injuries to adult trespassers caused by the landowner/occupier's failure to exercise due care, to put the land in a safe condition for them, or to carry on activities in such a manner as not to endanger them.

    b. **Discovered trespassers.** In most jurisdictions, the foreseeability of a trespass is deemed to create no duty on the part of the landowner/occupier. However, where the trespassers are known generally (even though the identity or presence of the particular trespasser is not known) and the trespass occurs on a particular part of the property (walking path, etc.) and has been tolerated, there is a tendency on the part of the courts to treat the trespasser as a licensee, requiring the landowner/occupier to warn the trespasser of, or make safe, known natural or artificial conditions or activities involving any risk of harm that the trespasser is unlikely to discover. Other courts in these cases limit the obligation of the landowner/occupier to a duty to discover and warn the trespasser of, or make safe, known artificial conditions and activities that could cause death or serious bodily injury to the trespasser (under this position, there is no duty with respect to natural conditions or artificial conditions presenting a risk less than death or serious bodily injury).

4. Traditional View on Trespassers--

Robert Addie & Sons (Collieries), Ltd. v. Dumbreck, [1929] A.C. 358.

Facts. Robert Addie & Sons (D) operated a haulage system to remove coal ash from mining operations. The field on which the system was located was surrounded by a hedge with numerous gaps. The field was often trespassed onto by both adults and children. D had placed warning signs at the gates to the field and often warned children and adults not to play or walk on the field. The verbal warnings were largely unheeded. At the end of the haulage system and away from the powering motor (and not visible to one operating the motor) was a large wheel around which an endless wire cable passed. The wheel was unprotected except for some boards on top of it. There was at least an eight-inch gap between the bottom of the wheel and the ground. Dumbreck's (P's) four-year-old son, who had been warned by D's employees not to play on the field, was killed when he became trapped in the wheel and cable assembly. P sued in wrongful death. The trial court returned judgment for P. D appeals, arguing that it had no duty of care to a trespasser.

Issue. Does a property owner owe a duty of care to a trespasser on his land?

Held. No. Judgment reversed.

♦ P's son, upon entering D's property, was either an invitee, a licensee, or a trespasser. The evidence indicates he was a mere trespasser.

♦ A property owner owes no duty of care to protect a trespasser, even from concealed danger. He is liable only if he deliberately injures the trespasser.

♦ D's failure to fence off his property does not change the result.

♦ Because P's son was a mere trespasser, D owed him no duty of care and is therefore not liable for P's son's death.

♦ The lines between the classifications of licensee, trespasser, and invitee dictate the liabilities that follow from the classification. A proprietor has no duty to fence off his property. A fence would, however, act as a warning to others that trespassing is not allowed. Here, D did everything he could do in order to discourage P's son and others from using his field. By doing so, D did not allow trespassers to rise to the level of either an invitee or a licensee.

Comment. This is the traditional view. Most modern courts retaining these distinctions would apply the "attractive nuisance" doctrine (below) because the trespasser was a child, or would find that the trespasser had been discovered and thus was owed a duty of care.

---

5. **Trespassing Children.** Except with respect to extrahazardous activities, such as maintaining a turntable, children were treated the same as adults until about the 1920s, when trespassing children began to be recognized as a special class. The rationale for the special classification is that: (i) children are often incapable of protecting themselves because of their inability to perceive the risk, (ii) out of necessity the parent cannot be expected to follow the child around all day, (iii) maintaining an "attractive nuisance" is deemed undesirable, and (iv) the cost to alleviate the risk of harm is usually slight in comparison with the damages that might be suffered.

   a. **Restatement rule on attractive nuisance.** Restatement (Second) of Torts, section 339, sets out the duty of a property owner with respect to artificial conditions when infant trespassers are involved. (Query: What about natural conditions?) A property owner will be liable for injuries to infant trespassers from dangerous artificial conditions on his land under the following circumstances:

      1) If he knows or should know that they are likely to trespass upon the places where the dangerous condition is maintained;

      2) If he knows or should know that the condition involves an unreasonable risk of injury to them;

      3) If the children, because of their immaturity, do not realize the danger involved;

      4) If the utility of maintaining the condition is slight in relation to the risk of injury to the children; and

      5) If he fails to exercise reasonable care to eliminate the danger or otherwise protect the children.

6. **Easement Holder.** Only the actual possessor of land has immunity with respect to injuries suffered by a trespasser.

7. **Independent Contractors.** There is a great division among the cases relating to independent contractors upon the land. The Restatement suggests granting independent contractors immunity only when they come on the land on behalf of the landowner.

8. **Licensees.** A licensee is one who goes on the land of another with the consent of the owner/occupier, through authority of law, or by necessity, and is deemed to take the land as the occupier uses it. However, the owner/occupier must warn the licensee of, or make safe, known natural or artificial conditions or activities involving any risk of harm that the licensee is unlikely to discover, whether existing at the time of entry or arising thereafter. The licensee has the occupier's consent and nothing more.

   a. **Social guest.** "Invitee" (discussed below) is a word of art; it does not include all persons invited onto the premises. A social guest, although invited, is only a licensee. The fact that a guest renders some incidental service or was invited out of economic motives does not remove the guest from the status of licensee.

   b. **Known danger.** The owner of premises is under a duty to warn a known licensee of known dangerous conditions that the owner cannot reasonably assume that the licensee knows or can detect through a reasonable use of her facilities, or to make such conditions safe.

   c. **Duty to inspect.** The duty of a landowner/occupier extends only to known dangerous conditions; there is no duty to inspect in order to discover dangerous conditions.

9. **Invitees.** An invitee is one who goes upon the land of another with the consent of the owner/occupier for some purpose connected with the use of the premises, *e.g.*, a business, or as a public invitee. The duty owed is coextensive with the invitation. The basis of liability is an implied promise that the premises are, or will be, safe or reasonably so. This means that the invitor is under a duty to make a reasonable inspection of the premises and discover any dangers that may exist. Thereafter, the duty owed the invitee is one of ordinary care. The limitations of responsibility of the invitor of the business invitee are generally determined by specific time, length of stay, part of premises visited, etc. Generally, those entering under public authority during nonbusiness hours (*e.g.*, firefighters) are deemed licensees; others, such as postal workers, are viewed as invitees under the modern view.

   a. **Business invitee.** One of the older theories was that to be a business invitee, one must be invited on the premises for potential pecuniary benefit to the owner. Potential gain was not difficult to find and one who loitered in a store was held to be an invitee because she might buy something.

b. **Limitations on invitation.** A person remains an invitee only while in those areas or parts of the premises held open to her for the purposes for which she came. If an invitee goes outside the area of invitation, but under consent of the owner, she becomes a licensee; and if no permission is involved, she may be a trespasser.

c. **Reasonable care required.** The legal obligation of a defendant in all these situations is only to exercise reasonable care. The duty arises only when danger is to be anticipated (*i.e.*, is reasonably foreseeable), and the owner/occupier is not required to do anything unreasonable to risk his life.

d. **Protection against third persons.** The owner/occupier must exercise his power of control over the conduct of third persons to prevent injury to an invitee who may be injured by such conduct.

10. **Overruling Traditional Visitor Classifications--**

Rowland v. Christian, 433 P.2d 561 (Cal. 1968).

Facts. Rowland (P), a social guest in Christian's (D's) apartment, was injured when a cracked water faucet handle in D's bathroom broke in P's hand, causing severe injuries. D knew the handle was cracked and had asked the landlord to repair it, but she did not warn P of the condition of the handle. P sued to recover for the injury and appeals the trial judge's granting of D's motion for summary judgment.

Issue. If the occupier of land is aware of a concealed condition that presents an unreasonable risk of harm to others, is the land occupier's failure to warn or to repair the condition negligence?

Held. Yes. Judgment reversed.

♦ In the past, the common law divided a landowner's visitors into three categories: (i) invitees-business guests, (ii) licensees-social guests, and (iii) trespassers.

♦ While the landowner owed a duty of ordinary care to invitees, licensees and trespassers were obligated to take the premises as they found them. This exception to the rule of liability for negligence grew out of the high place that land has held in English and American law and is no longer justifiable.

♦ Applying negligence liability equally regardless of the visitor's status will eliminate complexity and confusion in the law.

♦ A person's life or limb is not less worthy of protection because he has come upon the land of another without a business purpose or without permission.

♦ The basic policy set forth by the legislature is that everyone is responsible for an injury caused to another by his want of ordinary care. We adhere to it.

Dissent. The judgment should be sustained. The majority opinion allows for decisions on a case-by-case basis bereft of the guiding principles and precedent of tort law. This sweeping modification falls within the domain of the legislature. Social guests ought to take the premises as they find them.

Comment. *Rowland* met with complete acceptance in some states, partial acceptance in others, and rejection in most states. Under *Rowland,* the same basic duty is owed to trespassers as to invitees. This aspect of the case is its most troublesome. In recent years, several states, including Delaware, New Jersey, and California, have enacted statutes to protect landowners from nonpaying guests and trespassers where the landowner has not acted either intentionally or with willful or wanton disregard of others' rights. California limits the landowner's duty to the "nonpaying, uninvited recreational user" to that "owed a trespasser under the common law as it existed prior to *Rowland v. Christian.*"

D. GRATUITOUS UNDERTAKINGS

1. **Introduction.** Certain relationships, due to their nature, impose liability on a defendant to act (or not act).

2. **Volunteers--**

Coggs v. Bernard, 92 Eng. Rep. 107 (K.B. 1703).

Facts. D agreed to move casks of brandy belonging to P. No consideration was given for the contract. While moving them, the casks were damaged. P sued for damages and was awarded a judgment. D moved to arrest the judgment and argued that the failure of consideration should absolve him of liability.

Issue. If a party to an unenforceable contract negligently performs the contract, is he liable for damages caused by his negligence?

Held. Yes. Judgment affirmed.

♦ Any person who undertakes to do something for another, whether he is a common carrier or not, is liable for damages caused by his negligence.

♦ P entrusted D with certain goods. D accepted that entrustment by undertaking what was agreed between the parties. If D had not undertaken to move the casks, the damage would not have occurred.

Concurrence. Consideration existed in P's trusting D with the goods. If D had not undertaken to move the casks, he would not be liable for the damage caused to them.

---

3. Reliance on a Volunteer--

Erie Railroad v. Stewart, 40 F.2d 855 (6th Cir. 1930).

Facts. Stewart (P) was riding in a truck hit at a grade crossing by Erie's (D's) train. D was not required by statute or ordinance to have an attendant at the crossing to warn of approaching trains. However, D voluntarily had stationed an attendant at this crossing and P knew of this practice. The attendant was not present on this occasion and so failed to warn P in this instance. P sued for negligence. D appeals a jury verdict for P.

Issue. Did D's failure to have an attendant at the crossing constitute negligence as a matter of law because P relied on one being present when a train came by?

Held. Yes. Judgment affirmed.

♦ If the company has established for itself a custom of due care and the traveler has relied on this custom, the company will be held liable for injury if it negligently performs or withdraws the service without proper notice.

♦ D's custom of having an attendant at a grade crossing when a train was coming and P's relying on that custom allowed negligence to be inferred as a matter of law.

Concurrence. All members of the public were entitled to rely on D's actions, not just those people who had specific knowledge of the acts.

---

4. Misfeasance--

Marsalis v. LaSalle, 94 So. 2d 120 (La. Ct. App. 1957).

Facts. Marsalis (P) relied upon LaSalle's (D's) promise to keep his cat locked up after it had bitten P. D allowed the cat to escape, and P had to endure the Pasteur treatment for fear of contracting rabies. P sued.

Issue. Is D liable for his misfeasance?

Held. Yes.

♦   D was liable for the personal injury caused to P on the basis of misfeasance.

Comment. The old rule was that a mere gratuitous promise to render service, even though P relied on it, created no duty. Although this rule has been backed by a large body of case law, it actually serves as a point of departure. Many cases, such as *Marsalis,* find that D, through some insignificant act, has actually undertaken to live up to his promise and, therefore, is liable because of his misfeasance in failing to follow through. A few recent cases have decisions that are realistically basing liability on the mere breach of promise.

---

5.   **Duty to Third Party--**

Moch Co. v. Rensselaer Water Co., 159 N.E. 896 (N.Y. 1928).

Facts. The Rensselaer Water Co. (D) contracted with the city of Rensselaer to provide water for, among other purposes, service at fire hydrants. It specifically agreed to provide certain quantities of water and at a certain pressure to the fire hydrants. A fire broke out near Moch Company's (P's) warehouse. Although D was notified of the fire in a timely manner, it failed to provide either the quantity or pressure of water that it contracted to provide. The fire spread and destroyed P's warehouse. P sued for damages, arguing alternative theories of breach of contract, common law tort under *MacPherson v. Buick Motor Co., infra,* or breach of a statutory duty. The trial court denied a demurrer. The appellate division reversed. P appeals.

Issue. Is a third party beneficiary able to recover for damages caused by a promisor's failure to perform his contractual obligations?

Held. No. Judgment of appellate court affirmed.

♦   Contractual liability does not exist because the parties did not originally intend that D should be liable to individual members of the public. Also, D is not an insurer and did not anticipate becoming one.

♦   If D's conduct was such that inaction would normally result in working an injury, it might have owed a duty to P. But D's conduct was not such, and if it were deemed to be so, it would subject such supply companies to an infinite circle of tort claimants.

♦   Finally, there is no statutory basis for imposing liability.

♦   Thus, D is not liable to P for failing to maintain adequate water quantity or pressure.

Comment. Possibly the real reason Judge Cardozo decided this case as he did was out of a belief that fire insurance companies were the proper social institution for bearing the loss in such circumstances.

Query. Compare the decisions in *Palsgraf, MacPherson, infra,* and *Moch.* Cardozo wrote all three opinions. In *MacPherson,* the defendant owed a duty to a remote plaintiff. In *Palsgraf* and *Moch,* the defendant did not owe a duty to a remote plaintiff. Can the decisions be explained in a manner that makes the results consistent?

E. SPECIAL RELATIONSHIPS

1. **Restatement Rule on Special Relationships.** Restatement (Second) of Torts (1965), section 315, sets out the general rule that there is no duty to control the conduct of a third person so as to prevent him from causing physical harm to another unless:

   a. A special relationship exists between the actor and the third person which imposes a duty upon the actor to control the third person's conduct, or

   b. A special relationship exists between the actor and the other which gives the other a right to protection.

2. **Landlord-Tenant--**

Kline v. 1500 Massachusetts Avenue Apartment Corp., 439 F.2d 477 (D.C. Cir. 1970).

Facts. Kline (P), a lessee of 1500 Massachusetts Avenue Apartment Corporation (D), sustained serious injuries when she was criminally assaulted and robbed while in the common hallway of a large, unguarded office-apartment owned by D. P brought an action against D for personal injuries and the court dismissed her complaint. P appeals.

Issue. Should a duty be placed on a landlord to take steps to protect tenants from foreseeable criminal acts committed by third parties?

Held. Yes. Judgment reversed and case remanded.

♦   The general rule that exonerates a third party from protecting another from criminal attack has no applicability to the landlord-tenant relationship in multiple dwelling houses. Since the landlord is the only one in the position to take the necessary acts of protection required, while not an insurer, he is obligated to minimize the risks to his tenants. Here, the risk of criminal assault and robbery of any tenant was clearly predictable. It was a risk of which D had specific notice, that became a reality with increasing frequency, and that materialized on the very premises under D's control.

Dissent. There was insufficient evidence of prior crimes to put D on notice of possible attacks of this type. In addition, D was not negligent.

---

3.   **Psychotherapists--**

Tarasoff v. Regents of University of California, 551 P.2d 334 (Cal. 1976).

Facts. Poddar, a patient of psychiatrists at the University's (D's) hospital, told his psychotherapist at the hospital, Dr. Moore (D), that he was going to kill Tatiana. The doctor had Poddar detained by the police, but Poddar was eventually released because he seemed rational. The psychotherapist's superior at the hospital informed him that he should initiate no further action to detain Poddar. No one informed Tatiana about the threat. In October 1969, Poddar killed Tatiana. Tatiana's parents (Ps) sued the university regents, the psychotherapists, and the campus police on four different negligence theories, all centering around failure to detain Poddar and failure to warn Tatiana. D demurred and the trial court sustained the demurrer. Ps appeal.

Issues.

(i)   Do Ps state a cause of action against the psychotherapists for failing to warn Tatiana of the threat on her life?

(ii)   Did D have a duty to confine Poddar?

Held. (i) Yes. (ii) No. Lower court judgment for D on first issue is reversed and the case remanded.

♦   The general duty rule is that a defendant owes a duty to all persons foreseeably endangered by his conduct, with respect to the risks that make his conduct dangerous.

♦   The general rule is that a third party is not liable for the actions of a tortfeasor, unless the third party has a special relationship with the tortfeasor or the victim. The psychotherapists had such a special relationship with Poddar.

♦   A psychotherapist's judgment must only conform to that degree of skill, care, and knowledge exercised by psychotherapists under similar circumstances.

♦   A psychotherapist has a duty to warn a potential victim of threatened violence.

- That the psychotherapists were working for the state does not relieve them of liability, because governmental immunity covers only basic policy questions. Telling Tatiana of the threat was not a basic policy question that demanded great discretion.

- Government Code section 856 creates immunity from tort liability for all officials relative to the commitment of a person for mental illness, thus protecting the psychotherapists.

- As for the police officers, Welfare and Institutions Code section 5154 relieves the police from liability for confinements of less than 72 hours of an individual ordered confined by a professional person in charge of an institution.

Concurrence and dissent. This action is based on D's knowledge and not whether D "should have" known of the danger.

Dissent. A decision to require disclosure of private facts should be left to the legislature.

Comment. The court also said that punitive damages could not be paid in a wrongful death action. The court said that the patient's confidence should only be revealed when it is necessary to avert danger to others, and then it should be done in such a manner that would preserve the patient's privacy.

———————

VIII. STRICT LIABILITY

A. ANIMALS

1. **Trespassing.** The general rule is that the owner of animals that are likely to stray and do stray onto the land of another is strictly liable for any damage caused by such animals. An exception to this rule was made for domestic pets.

2. **Wild Animals.** The possessor of wild animals is strictly liable for harm done by the animal if such harm results from its normally dangerous propensities. However, if animals are kept under a public duty (as in a zoo), strict liability does not apply—negligence must be shown, although a high degree of care will be required.

3. **Known Dangerous Domestic Animals.** If the defendant has knowledge of the dangerous propensities of his animal (*i.e.,* that the animal threatens serious bodily harm or property damage to others), he will be strictly liable for all injuries resulting from that dangerous propensity.

4. **"Dog Bite" Statutes.** "Dog bite" statutes have been enacted in several jurisdictions. Basically, these statutes reverse the common law rule that every dog is entitled to one bite before it becomes known to be an animal with dangerous propensities, and makes its keeper liable for all damages or harm caused by the animal, unless the plaintiff was a trespasser or was committing a tort.

5. **Dangerous Propensities Unknown--**

Gehrts v. Batteen, 620 N.W.2d 775 (S.D. 2001).

Facts. Nielsen (D) visited the home of Jessica Gehrts (P) to pick up a wreath made by P's mother. D had come directly from dog obedience school with her eight-month-old St. Bernard, Wilbur, who was tied to the back of D's pickup by a harness attached to a restraining device that had been installed in the pickup box. Wilbur could move freely between the sides of the pickup box, but was limited in his front and back movement. P asked D if she could pet Wilbur, and D permitted her to do so. When P reached to pet Wilbur, he bit her in the face, injuring her nose and forehead. P received extensive medical treatment as a result. P sued, alleging negligent failure to restrain or control the dog. D's motion for summary judgment was granted. P appeals.

Issue. Was the trial court's ruling in error?

Held. No. Judgment affirmed.

♦ While owners of wild animals kept as pets are liable for injuries caused by the pet whether or not the owner had prior knowledge of the animal's propensity to cause harm and exercised utmost care to prevent harm, owners of domesticated animals may be found negligent if they knew or had reason to know the pet had abnormally dangerous propensities, regardless of the care exercised. The breach of the duty of care owed to those who may come in contact with the animal may be tempered by the defenses of contributory negligence and assumption of the risk.

♦ A plaintiff must establish knowledge of the animal's dangerous propensities; one attack by the animal generally results in this knowledge being imputed to the owner. The victim need not be injured.

♦ Where the owner does not know of the animal's propensities, the ordinary negligence standard of foreseeability will be applied. P must establish a duty between owner and victim, a breach, that the injurious event should have been foreseen and steps taken to prevent it. Liability depends on the kind and character of the particular animal concerned, the circumstances in which it is placed, and the purposes for which it is employed or kept.

♦ Here, there is no evidence D knew Wilbur was dangerous; neither P nor D knew of any incidents that would have alerted D. P asserts that the scent of her own dog on her made Wilbur act aggressively and D should have known this, but there is no evidence D knew P owned a dog or that its scent would cause Wilbur to attack. When D petted Wibur, he was appropriately restrained. D has not provided sufficient evidence to permit a finding in her favor. Her cause of action for negligence cannot survive.

♦ We decline to adopt a strict liability standard for injuries caused by dogs. The legislature is the proper place to decide such public policy issues.

Dissent. This court has stated a number of times that summary judgment is not appropriate in negligence actions. Whether D properly restrained the dog, was correct in permitting a 14-year-old to pet the dog, or knew the child's mother owned a dog are questions for the jury.

B. ULTRAHAZARDOUS OR ABNORMALLY DANGEROUS ACTIVITIES

1. **Introduction.** *See* II.D.2., *supra.*

2. **Theory of Liability.** In cases involving dangerous or "ultrahazardous" activities, the question is not whether it is lawful or proper to engage in the dangerous or ultrahazardous activity, but who should bear the cost of any

resulting damage—the person engaged in the dangerous activity or the innocent neighbor injured thereby. Public policy has placed the risk of damage
on the person engaging in such activity. The *Spano* case (*infra*) is an example of the circumstances in which strict liability is applied.

3.   Dangerous or Ultrahazardous Activity--

Spano v. Perini Corp., 250 N.E.2d 31 (N.Y. 1969).

Facts. Spano's (P's) garage and a car inside were damaged when Perini (D) set off 194
sticks of dynamite while blasting at a construction site 125 feet away. No negligence
on the part of D could be shown. The trial court held for P; the appellate term reversed
and the appellate division affirmed the ruling of the appellate term. P appeals.

Issue. Is D liable for damages that result from its dangerous activities notwithstanding
the absence of negligence?

Held. Yes. Judgment reversed.

♦   One who engages in blasting must assume responsibility, and be liable without
     fault, for any injury he causes to neighboring property.

---

4.   Ultrahazardous Activities and Indirect Damages. In *Madsen v. East Jor-*
dan Irrigation Co., 125 P.2d 794 (Utah 1942), East Jordan Irrigation Co. (D)
engaged in blasting activity when repairing its irrigation ditch 100 yards
from Madsen's (P's) mink farm. The blasting caused the mink to become
very excited and 108 of the mother mink killed 230 of their offspring. The
court held that although blasting usually entails strict liability, the damages
were too remote and that one who fires explosives cannot be liable for every
occurrence following the explosion. The result in *Madsen* was endorsed in
the Restatement (Second) of Torts, section 519, illus. 1.

5.   Shipment of Hazardous Chemicals--

Indiana Harbor Belt Railroad v. American Cyanamid Co., 916 F.2d
1174 (7th Cir. 1990).

Facts. American Cyanamid Co. (D) manufactured and loaded a hazardous chemical,
acrylonitrile (highly toxic and flammable at and above 30 degrees Fahrenheit), into a
leased 20,000 gallon railroad tanker car at its plant in Louisiana. The car was then
turned over to the Missouri Pacific Railroad for transport to one of D's plants in New
Jersey, which is served by Conrail. Indiana Harbor Belt Railroad (P) is a small switch-

ing line in metropolitan Chicago and had a contract with Conrail to switch cars from other lines to Conrail. Several hours after the car arrived at P's yard, P's employees noticed fluid gushing from the bottom outlet of the car and, after two hours, finally succeeded in stopping the leak. Approximately 5,000 gallons had leaked from the car and decontamination measures that P was required to take cost P over $981,000. P sued to recover these damages from D, alleging that D negligently maintained the leased tank car and that the transportation of acrylonitrile in bulk through the Chicago metropolitan area is an abnormally dangerous activity for which the shipper (here D) should be held strictly liable. The trial court held for P on the strict liability count. D appeals.

Issue. Is the shipper of a hazardous chemical by rail strictly liable for the consequences of a spill or other accident to the shipment?

Held. No. Judgment reversed and case remanded.

♦ This is not a case for strict liability. No reason has been given to suggest that an action for negligence is not perfectly adequate to remedy and deter, at reasonable cost, the accidental spillage of acrylonitrile from the rail car. The leak in this case was not caused by the inherent properties of acrylonitrile but by carelessness. Accidents that are due to a lack of care can be prevented by taking care, and when a lack of care can be shown, such accidents are adequately deterred by threat of liability for negligence.

♦ We note the six factors considered relevant to strict liability as set forth in Restatement (Second) of Torts, section 520, and the policy rationale behind them. There is a distinction between the storer and the shipper of a hazardous chemical because there is more control on the part of a storer than a shipper, thus justifying strict liability in the case of a storer. The difference between a shipper and a carrier points to a deep flaw in P's case, *i.e.,* here it is not the actors or transporters of the hazardous chemicals but the shipper whom P seeks to hold strictly liable. In emphasizing the flammability and toxicity of acrylonitrile rather than the hazards of transporting it, P overlooks the fact that ultrahazardous or abnormal dangerousness is viewed by the law as not a property of substances, but of activities, *e.g.,* the transportation by rail through populated areas.

---

6. ***Rylands v. Fletcher* Regime Defended.** In *Siegler v. Kuhlman*, 502 P.2d 1181 (Wash. 1972), the court found the transportation of gasoline as cargo sufficiently dangerous to justify the imposition of strict liability on those who engage in it. The court noted the extraordinary danger created by the explosive quality of gasoline coupled with the sheer bulk of a truckload. This danger is amplified, stated the court, when it is transported at high speed

and spilled across the highway. Furthermore, an explosion is likely to destroy all evidence of its cause. Gasoline transportation involves a high degree of risk of great harm and creates dangers that cannot be eliminated by the exercise of reasonable care. It therefore meets the Restatement (Second) test of an abnormally dangerous activity to which strict liability applies.

7. **Abnormally Dangerous.** The Restatement (Second) of Torts uses the term "abnormally dangerous" rather than "ultrahazardous," and takes into account the value of the activity and its appropriateness to the location.

C. NUISANCE

1. **Introduction.** Nuisance refers to a defendant's interference with a plaintiff's right or with a plaintiff's use and enjoyment of property. Nuisances are types of damage or harm. It is best considered as a field of liability rather than as a particular tort. Utility versus harm is the key in nuisance. Each possessor of land is privileged to use his own property or to conduct his own affairs at the expense of some harm to his neighbors; if unreasonable, then it will constitute a nuisance.

2. **Private Nuisance.** Private nuisance refers to an unreasonable and substantial interference with the use or enjoyment of an individual's property interest in land. It is distinguished from trespass in that it does not require a physical entry upon the plaintiff's premises. It follows from the principle that everyone should use his property so as not to injure the property of another.

3. **Damages.** The same conduct may constitute both a public nuisance (discussed *infra*) and a private nuisance. However, for a private person to collect damages for public nuisance, he must show some special damages different in kind, not merely in degree, from those of the public in general.

   a. **Types of harm.** Whether or not a nuisance is actionable by the individual is a matter of the nature of the damages suffered. Damages generally can be recovered for the following and similar interferences:

      1) Deprivation of use or enjoyment.

      2) Temporary diminution in value.

      3) Permanent diminution in value.

      4) Personal discomfort.

      5) Injury to health.

      6) Reasonable expenses.

4. **Bases of Liability.** Liability can rest on any of three bases: (i) intentional conduct, (ii) negligence, or (iii) strict liability based on abnormally dangerous activity.

    a. **Abnormally dangerous activities.** Section 520 of the Restatement (Second) of Torts lists six factors to be considered when determining whether an activity is abnormally dangerous:

        1) The existence of a high degree of risk or harm to person, land, or chattel;

        2) The likelihood that resulting harm will be great;

        3) The inability to eliminate risk through reasonable care;

        4) The extent to which activity is a matter of common usage;

        5) The inappropriateness of an activity to the place where it is carried on; and

        6) The extent to which the activity's value to the community is outweighed by its dangerous attributes.

5. **Definition of Private Nuisance Broad and Flexible--**

Vogel v. Grant-Lafayette Electric Cooperative, 548 N.W.2d 829 (Wis. 1996).

Facts. The Vogels (Ps) were members of Grant-Lafayette Electric Cooperative (D), a cooperative association that provided electricity to its members. Ps built a new milking facility on their farm in 1970, and shortly thereafter noticed that many of their cows behaved violently or erratically while in the facility. Additionally, the herd suffered from excessive and chronic mastitis. This caused a decline in milk production and some cows were removed from the herd. Ps attempted to solve the problems in various manners to no avail. In 1986, D installed an isolator on P's farm after P complained that the cows were suffering from excessive stray voltage. The behavior of the cows began to improve immediately after the installation of the isolator. Ps sued D in 1992, alleging nuisance and negligence in the maintenance of its system. D alleged that Ps were contributorily negligent in the design, maintenance, and operation of their electrical equipment. The jury found for Ps on the negligence and nuisance claims and for D on the claim that Ps were contributorily negligent. The appellate court struck the nuisance claim. Ps appeal.

Issue. Did the appellate court err in holding as a matter of law that stray voltage may not be considered a private nuisance?

Held. Yes. Judgment of appellate court reversed.

- The Restatement (Second) of Torts (1979), section 821D, defines nuisance as "a nontrespassory invasion of another's interest in the private use and enjoyment of land."

- Ps' request for electric service does not negate the invasion element of nuisance. Ps did not request excessive voltage and although they benefited from the service, they were harmed as well.

- Detrimental change to the physical condition of the land is not the only type of nuisance. Nuisance encompasses also the pleasure, comfort, and joy derived from the use of land.

- D's invasion was not intentional. Although the systems interconnected, it is the unreasonable levels of stray voltage that gave rise to liability, not the use of the delivery system. D was not aware of the unreasonable levels until 1986, and D immediately responded to alleviate the problem upon notice.

- The trial court did not err by construing the nuisance action as an unintentional invasion and otherwise actionable under negligence, and by not submitting the question of intentional invasion to the jury.

Comment. There is a view that negligence principles have been imported into nuisance law because the interference must be "unreasonable." The Restatement (Second), section 826, provides: "[a]n intentional invasion of another's interest in the use and enjoyment of land is unreasonable if (a) the gravity of the harm outweighs the utility of the actor's conduct, or (b) the harm caused by the conduct is serious and the financial burden of compensating for this and similar harm to others would not make the continuation of the conduct not feasible."

---

6. Encroaching Tree Roots--

Michalson v. Nutting, 175 N.E. 490 (Mass. 1931).

Facts. Property owners (Ps) brought a bill in equity, claiming that roots from a tree on Ds' land had grown into Ps' land, filled up sewer and drain pipes, grown under the cement cellar of Ps' house, and caused damages throughout. Ps sought a mandatory injunction ordering the removal of the roots, a permanent injunction restraining Ds from permitting the roots to encroach on Ps' land, and damages. The trial judge found Ps' allegations to be true; in fact, Ps had had to dig up and remove the roots from the pipes several times and the last time had incurred an expense in the amount of $42.28. However, the judge dismissed Ps' bill with costs. Ps appeal.

Issue. Are Ds liable for the damage to Ps' property caused by the invading roots of a tree on Ds' land?

Held. No. Judgment affirmed.

♦ In *Bliss v. Ball*, 99 Mass. 597 (1868), we held that a landowner has a right to grow trees on his land, and there is no remedy in the courts for injury to adjoining property caused by the shade of the trees. We see no difference in principle between damage resulting from shade and damage caused by overhanging branches or encroaching roots.

♦ An owner may use his land to grow trees, which naturally will lead to intruding branches and roots. A neighbor does not have the right of appeal to the courts, but he may cut the invading branches and roots. To hold otherwise would subject the public to numerous, and often vexatious, lawsuits.

---

7.   Light and Air--

Fontainebleau Hotel Corp. v. Forty-Five Twenty-Five, Inc., 114 So. 2d 357 (Fla. Dist. Ct. App. 1959).

Facts. Fontainebleau Hotel Corp. (D) began building a 14-story addition to its hotel. When completed, the addition would have cast a shadow on the area used for sunbathing by guests of the Eden Roc Hotel, owned by Forty-Five Twenty-Five, Inc. (P). P sought an injunction to prohibit further construction of the addition on various grounds, including the infringement of P's rights to an uninterfered-with flow of light and air onto its property. The trial court granted a temporary injunction based "solely on the proposition that no one has a right to use his property to the injury of another." D appeals.

Issue. May a landowner, absent a contractual or statutory provision, be precluded from using his property in such a way that it interferes with the air and light of another?

Held. No. Judgment reversed.

♦ It is well settled that a property owner does not have the right to use his property in such a way that it will interfere with the legal rights of another.

♦ But no American jurisdiction has ever held that a landowner has any legal right, in the absence of a contractual or statutory provision, to the free flow of light and air across the adjoining property of his neighbor.

- Thus, even if a structure is built partly out of spite, there is no action against an adjoining landowner for the interference with light and air across another's property if the structure serves a useful purpose.

---

8. Standard for Measuring Offensiveness--

Rogers v. Elliott, 15 N.E. 768 (Mass. 1888).

Facts. The manager of a church (D) regularly rang the church bell. Rogers (P) was confined to his house, near the church, due to a sunstroke. D rang the bell on Saturday. P suffered severe convulsions attributed, according to his physician, to the bells. The physician told D of this and asked him not to ring the bell while P was ill. D told the physician that he had no love for P and would ring the bell even if D's own mother were ill. Sunday, D rang the bell and P suffered damage for which he brought this action.

Issue. For something to be a nuisance, must it be offensive to a reasonable person of ordinary sensitivities?

Held. Yes. Judgment for D.

- D's ringing of the bell is reasonable if the people in the densely populated area in which the bell is heard consider it reasonable.

- It is not reasonable that a person's lawful use of his property be affected by people of undue sensitivity.

- Here, P's claims are based on his sensitivities and not on any nuisance that the bell caused to the community.

- D did not act with wantonness or express malice.

---

9. Coming to the Nuisance--

Ensign v. Walls, 34 N.W.2d 549 (Mich. 1948).

Facts. Walls (D) had bred St. Bernard dogs in the city of Detroit since 1926. Ensign and others (Ps) owning property near that belonging to D sued in nuisance. The trial court issued an injunction in spite of D's contentions that her business was not a nuisance and that most Ps had moved to the area long after she began her business. The trial court found for Ps. D appeals.

Issue. May a nuisance be abated if Ps "came to the nuisance" after the nuisance already existed?

Held. Yes. Judgment affirmed.

♦ The record shows that most Ps moved into D's neighborhood after D began operating her business.

♦ One cannot create a nuisance on his land and thereby attempt to control the uses to which surrounding land may be put in future years.

♦ Consideration is given to the fact that Ps came to D's nuisance, but such fact is not controlling. The trial court exercised its discretion in determining that D's nuisance should be abated.

♦ It is probable that the community surrounding D's business will become more populated and thus her nuisance will become even greater. Case law exists supporting the abatement of a nuisance under these circumstances.

♦ D has offered no suggestions on how her business could be conducted in its present location without creating a nuisance to surrounding landowners. Absent such a showing, this court will believe it cannot be done.

Comment. This decision is in accord with the vast majority of decisions involving this fact pattern. The minority view usually is based on some theory that the plaintiffs assumed the risk of a nuisance by voluntarily moving into the neighborhood. Other courts would have allowed the defendant to continue her business if the land on which her business was located and the plaintiffs lived was zoned for industrial, or perhaps commercial, uses.

---

10. Judicial Zoning--

Boomer v. Atlantic Cement Co., 257 N.E.2d 870 (N.Y. 1970).

Facts. Boomer's and others' (Ps') residences suffered damages from dirt, smoke, and vibrations emanating from Atlantic Cement Co.'s (D's) large cement plant. Although the trial court found that D maintained a nuisance that substantially damaged Ps' properties, the court failed to issue the injunction for which Ps brought the action because of the relatively small damage suffered in comparison with the value of D's operation. The trial court did award damages for injuries up to the time of trial and also found the amount of permanent damages for the guidance of the parties in a settlement. The appellate court affirmed.

Issue. If a business is so operated as to be a nuisance that substantially injures nearby residents, and if the value of the business operation is far more than the relatively small damages suffered, may permanent damages be awarded in lieu of an injunction?

Held. Yes. Lower court ordered to grant an injunction, which will be vacated upon payment of permanent damages.

♦ Permanent damages may be awarded in lieu of an injunction if the value of the activities sought to be enjoined is disproportionate to the relatively small damage caused thereby.

♦ Permanent damages are fair because they fully recompense the damaged property owner and at the same time provide an incentive to the business to abate the nuisance and avoid suits by others.

♦ The granting of a short-time grace period in which to solve the problem prior to issuance of the injunction is impractical and will lead to requests for extensions. Furthermore, it puts the burden for correction of an industry-wide problem on one private enterprise.

Dissent. An injunction should be granted to take effect within 18 months unless the nuisance is abated. In permitting the injunction to become inoperative upon the payment of permanent damages, the majority is licensing a continuing wrong. The incentive to eliminate the wrong is alleviated by the majority's holding. The holding of the majority imposes a servitude upon Ps' lands without their consent and is unconstitutional.

Comments.

♦ When a statutory ordinance is in effect, it governs; in its absence, courts such as this one must resort to what is sometimes referred to as "judicial zoning." This case exemplifies judicial zoning.

♦ The "unreasonable" issue in a nuisance action can be handled at the remedy level as well. That is, if the plaintiff asks for an injunction but the value of the defendant's activity is great, the court may deny the injunction and permit the defendant to pay past damages plus future damages (for permanent injury to the plaintiff's interest).

---

11. **Defenses to Nuisance Actions.** The defenses available to the defendant are dependent upon whether her conduct has been intentional or negligent, or whether she is deemed strictly liable for the interference.

a.   **Contributory negligence.** This defense is available only in situations where the nuisance is based on the negligent acts of the defendant.

b.   **Assumption of risk.** This defense is available in situations where the nuisance is based on the negligent conduct of the defendant and where the nuisance is based on strict liability.

12. **Remedies.** An injured plaintiff may bring an action to recover damages or an action to enjoin further interferences by the defendant with the plaintiff's protected interest, or both. Also available to the injured plaintiff is the privilege of self-help to abate the nuisance. The plaintiff must use only reasonable force to abate the nuisance, which, under the prevailing rule, does not include the infliction of bodily harm on anyone.

13. **Public Nuisance.** Public nuisance refers to an act or omission that obstructs or causes inconvenience or damage to the public in the exercise of rights common to all citizens.

a.   **Public rights--**

Anonymous, Y.B. Mich. 27 Hen. 8, f. 27, pl. 10 (1535).

Facts. D had blocked the King's highway in such a manner that P could not get by. P sued for his own injuries.

Issue. May a private person bring an action for a public nuisance?

Held. Yes.

♦   Ordinarily a public representative should bring the action for a public nuisance. If, however, a private person suffers an injury different in kind, then the private person may bring an action for those special losses.

---

b.   **Injury to a greater or lesser degree--**

---

532 Madison Avenue Gourmet Foods, Inc. v. Finlandia Center, Inc., 750 N.E.2d 1097 (N.Y. 2001).

Facts. A portion of a 39-story office building partially collapsed, causing brick, mortar, and other materials to fall onto Madison Avenue at 55th Street. City officials closed 14 heavily-trafficked blocks and adjacent side streets for two weeks, and some businesses closest to the collapse remained closed longer. 532 Madison (P1) is a delicatessen; in a companion case, two other retailers (P2 and P3) sued on their own behalf and on behalf of "all other business entities" affected. Ps complained that shoppers could not gain entrance to their stores. Ds are the building owner and the management company. In another incident, a 48-story construction elevator tower in Times Square collapsed. Again, the city closed nearby streets to traffic and evacuated nearby buildings for various time periods. Three cases—one by a law firm, one by a public relations firm and a third by a clothing manufacturer (P4)—were consolidated. P4 alleged gross negligence, strict liability, and public and private nuisance. The complaints were dismissed at trial. The appeals court reinstated P1's public nuisance and negligence claims, and reinstated P2 and P3's negligence and nuisance claims. It affirmed the dismissal of P4's complaint.

Issue. Was the appeals court order, which reversed the order of the trial court, properly made?

Held. For P1—No (Judgment reversed). For P2 and P3—No (Judgment reversed). For P4—Yes (Judgment affirmed).

♦ Ps suffered only economic loss because streets in the area of their businesses were closed following construction disasters on Ds' property. This is beyond the scope of the duty Ds owed to Ps. Ds have no duty to protect an entire neighborhood against economic loss. The scope of a landowner's duty in disasters such as this is to those who suffer personal injury or property damage.

♦ A public nuisance exists for conduct that amounts to a substantial interference with the exercise of a common right of the public, thereby offending public morals, interfering with the use by the public of a public place or endangering or injuring the property, health, safety or comfort of a considerable number of persons. Only a private person who can show she suffered special injury beyond that suffered by the community at large may seek redress for a public nuisance.

♦ Here, both the buildings' collapse and the city's actions in closing the areas invaded Ps' interest in the land. While an unlawful obstruction of a public street is a public nuisance, and a person who sustains a special loss as a result may maintain an action for public nuisance, here, Ps suffered harm along with the whole community. Ps may have suffered more harm than a local window washer or per diem employee, but in kind the harm was the same. Every business owner, resident or professional in the affected areas suffered a similar economic loss to a greater or lesser degree. Ps did not suffer a different kind of harm and cannot recover for invasion of the public right.

---

c. **Degree of control required--**

Camden County Board of Chosen Freeholders v. Beretta, U.S.A. Corp., 273 F.3d 536 (3d Cir. 2001).

Facts. The Camden County Board (P) alleges that (i) Ds release into the market substantially more handguns than they expect to sell to licensed purchasers; (ii) Ds knowingly (through information available in ATF gun trace reports) distribute through channels that yield criminal end-users; (iii) Ds do not limit the purchase of guns or supervise gun sales; (iv) Ds do not penalize distributors who "facilitate criminal access to handguns;" (v) Ds design and advertise guns in ways that encourage sales to and use by criminals; (vi) Ds make significant profit from the criminal market, thus generating more sales to lawful purchasers who seek to protect themselves; and (vii) Ds fail to take reasonable measures to mitigate the harm to Camden County. P does not allege any criminal act by Ds or any direct link between Ds and any specific criminal act. Ds recharacterize P's allegations as follows: (i) the manufacturers produce firearms at their places of business; (ii) they sell the firearms to federally licensed distributors; (iii) those distributors sell them to federally licensed dealers; (iv) some of the firearms are later diverted by unnamed third parties into an illegal gun market, which spills into Camden County; (v) the diverted firearms are obtained by unnamed third parties who are not entitled to own or possess them; (vi) these firearms are then used in criminal acts that kill and wound county residents; and (vii) this harm causes the county to expend resources to prevent or respond to those crimes. Ds claim they are six steps removed from the criminal end-users and that intervening third parties divert some guns to the criminal market.

P filed suit, claiming that under a public nuisance theory Ds are liable for the governmental costs connected with criminal use of guns in Camden County. The district court dismissed. P filed an amended complaint and alleged that Ds' marketing and distribution of guns contributed to the widespread criminal use of handguns in the county. The district court dismissed, finding no proximate cause in connection with P's negligence claims and a defect in P's public nuisance claim because of P's failure to allege the required element that the defendants exercised control over the nuisance to be abated. P appeals only the public nuisance claim on appeal. P alleges that Ds' conduct endangered public safety and imposed great financial burdens on the county and that Ds knowingly facilitated, participated in, and maintained a handgun distribution system that provides criminals and youth easy access to handguns.

Issue. Did P state a valid public nuisance claim under state law?

Held. No. Judgment affirmed.

♦   A public nuisance claim may be filed against a defendant who exerts a degree of control over the source of the nuisance. Public nuisance claims have generally involved real property or infringement of public rights. Our state courts have never allowed a claim against manufacturers for lawful products lawfully placed in the stream of commerce. In fact, the courts have kept apart public nuisance law and product liability law. To now allow a public nuisance claim involving a product that is not defective would be stretching the law to absurd extremes and would be unprecedented nationwide.

♦ Further, P has not alleged that Ds have sufficient control over the source of interference with the public right. Ds may not be held responsible without a more tangible showing that they were a direct link in the causal chain that resulted in P's injuries, and that the Ds were realistically in a position to prevent the wrongs.

♦ A defendant has no duty to control the actions of a third party.

———————

IX. PRODUCTS LIABILITY

A. INTRODUCTION

1. **Early Common Law.** At early English common law, liability for defective products was grounded in either contract or tort.

2. **Tort Actions.** Originally, the action in tort was in the nature of deceit—an action on the case by the purchaser for breach of an assumed duty.

3. **Contract Actions.** By the beginning of the 19th century, the plaintiff's action gained substantial recognition in contract, but only those injured plaintiffs in "privity of contract" with the manufacturer or supplier of the defective product were permitted a cause of action against them. This cause of action sounding in contract was in assumpsit, either express, implied-in-fact, or implied-in-law, and the recoverable damages were determined by application of the *Hadley v. Baxendale* rules. In 1842, Lord Abinger, in *Winterbottom v. Wright* (below), rejected the claim against a coach repairman by a passenger injured when the coach collapsed (the repairman had agreed with the owner to keep it in repair), stating that the most absurd and outrageous consequences would result if those not in privity of contract were allowed to sue in contract. Thus, early cases sounding in contract developed the "privity of contract" theory as a shield to the manufacturer and supplier of a defective product not in privity with the injured plaintiff.

B. EXPOSITION

1. **Privity Requirement.** In the past, courts required privity of contract between the plaintiff and the defendant as a precondition to a finding of liability. Unless the injured plaintiff was the buyer, no recovery could be had, either in tort or in contract, no matter how negligent the seller's conduct. However, this notion and the concept of privity have been stretched by the courts and in some instances entirely discarded or modified by statute.

2. **Old Rule--**

Winterbottom v. Wright, 152 Eng. Rep. 402 (Ex. 1842).

Facts. D contracted to supply and maintain coaches for use by the Postmaster General in mail delivery. Atkinson, with knowledge of D's contract, contracted with the Postmaster General to supply horses and drivers for the coaches, and P was one of the drivers. P was injured when the coach that he was driving broke down.

Issue. Is a contracting party who has not undertaken a public duty liable to third persons for injuries that result from his negligent performance of the contract?

Held. No. Judgment for D.

♦ If a contracting party has not undertaken a public duty, he is only liable for negligent performance to other parties to the contract, but not to third persons.

♦ A contrary holding would invite an infinity of actions.

♦ It does not matter that P, who may not bring an action against the Postmaster General, is left remediless. He was not a privy to the contract and may not maintain an action upon it.

---

3.   **New Rule--**

MacPherson v. Buick Motor Co., 111 N.E. 1050 (N.Y. 1916).

Facts. MacPherson (P) purchased a Buick from a dealer, who had purchased the car from the manufacturer, Buick Motor Co. (D). While P was driving the car, a wheel with defective wooden spokes collapsed and P was thrown out and injured. The wheel was not made by D, but was purchased from a subcontractor. Evidence indicated that D could have discovered the defect by reasonable inspection, which had not been performed. On a judgment for P, D appeals.

Issue. Did D owe a duty of care to P so that P could recover against D even in the absence of privity?

Held. Yes. Judgment affirmed.

♦ If the nature of a product is such that it is reasonably certain to place life and limb in peril when negligently made, then it is a thing of danger and, if the manufacturer knows or can reasonably foresee that it will be used by persons other than the immediate purchaser (supplier) without new tests, then, irrespective of contract, the manufacturer is under a duty to make it carefully. This position arises from prior cases involving poisons, explosives, and deadly weapons, which had placed a duty on the manufacturer thereof based on the fact that such products were "implements of destruction" in their normal operation.

♦ Negligence of the wheel manufacturer, such as to constitute an actionable wrong with respect to users of the furnished product incorporating the wheel, was a question of proximate cause and remoteness. However, in order for the wheel manufacturer's original negligence to become a cause of the danger, it was necessary for an independent cause to intervene; *i.e.,* the omission of the car manufacturer to fulfill his duty of inspection.

Dissent. D relied on the seller of the wheels to inspect them. The wheel that failed here was the only bad one in over 80,000 supplied to D. Also, there should be liability only where there is privity of contract between the parties. The manufacturer should not be liable for the negligence of one of his subvendees.

Comment. The rule as originally propounded by the court in *MacPherson* was as follows: If a reasonable person would have foreseen that the product would create a risk of harm to human life or limb if not carefully made or supplied, then the manufacturer and supplier are under a duty to all foreseeable users to exercise reasonable care in the manufacture and supply of the product.

---

4. **Extensions of the *MacPherson* Rule.** The *MacPherson* rule has been further developed in subsequent cases to cover the following situations:

   a. Damage to the product sold resulting from its own defects.

   b. Damage to reasonably foreseeable nonusers in the vicinity of the expected use of the product.

   c. Damage caused by defects in design as opposed to defects in manufacture.

   d. Damage to property in the vicinity of expected use, where the product itself is dangerous to life and limb because it is negligently made.

   e. Liability for products negligently manufactured but posing a foreseeable risk to property only.

   f. Liability of a processor of a product at an intermediate stage.

   g. Liability of one who sells another's product as his own (including dealers, distributors, and any other party in the chain of sale).

5. **Causation—Intermediary's Negligence.**

   a. Restatement (Second) of Torts, section 401, places a duty on dealers and distributors to make a reasonable inspection of their products that are inherently dangerous in normal use and to remedy, or warn buyers against, such defects or dangers. The failure of the dealer to inspect, however, does not relieve the manufacturer of his obligations since the dealer's omissions are considered foreseeable.

b.   However, section 402 of the Restatement does not place such a duty on the dealer where the products are manufactured by others and are not inherently dangerous in normal use. In such cases, the manufacturer is still liable under the *MacPherson* rule, and the dealer may be liable under the theory of warranty or the theory of strict liability. But if the dealer ***discovers*** the defect, the common law rule will make him liable to any injured plaintiff who was not warned of the defect prior to the sale. This failure to warn of known defects also will operate as an unforeseeable intervening force with respect to the manufacturer's negligence and will relieve him of liability under a negligence theory.

6.   **Defenses.** The defenses available to a defendant under a typical negligence action (*e.g.,* contributory negligence, assumption of risk, etc.) may be raised by the defendant in a products liability action, such as *MacPherson*, grounded in negligence.

7.   **The Foreseeable Plaintiff.** Gradually, the courts began to make cracks in the privity wall, moving from contracts to torts, and accepting a theory that manufacturers and suppliers of products owe a duty of due care with respect to the condition of the product. Breach of this duty (*i.e.,* supplying the plaintiff with a defective product) was held to be negligence. As the crack opened wider, the courts began to extend this duty to nonpurchasers. At first, special relationships were required between the purchaser and the injured nonpurchaser (*e.g.,* husband-wife, family members, employer-employee, etc.). Later, the rule was relaxed so that in some instances unrelated bystanders could be recognized as the plaintiffs and the concept of the foreseeable plaintiff came into play. The next step in the development of products liability law, which to some extent paralleled the development of negligence theory, was a move away from negligence and into strict liability. The strict liability theory, which at first was applied in cases involving inherently dangerous products (such as firearms, poisons, and explosives) was extended to the area of products foreseeably dangerous by reason of the defendant's failure to exercise due care. Today, both the strict liability and negligence theories have become alternative theories upon which injured plaintiffs often rely in stating their cause of action in tort. While this dual theory approach is common, there is also an increased emphasis being placed on the contract theory of warranty (*see* Warranty discussion, *infra*), both express and implied, especially with respect to commercial loss. Part of this trend toward use of warranty as a basis for recovery lies in the fact that the Uniform Commercial Code ("U.C.C.") has now been adopted in the District of Columbia and 49 of the 50 states and specifically places substantial burdens in the warranty area on manufacturers and suppliers of goods. [*See* U.C.C. §§2-312, 2-314, 2-315]

a.   **Toward strict liability in tort--**

Escola v. Coca Cola Bottling Co. of Fresno, 150 P.2d 436 (Cal. 1944).

Facts. Escola (P), a waitress, was injured when a Coca Cola bottle exploded in her hand. P sued Coca Cola (D). At trial, she relied on res ipsa loquitur to establish D's liability for her injuries and was awarded a jury verdict. An expert testified at trial that pressure tests performed on new Coca Cola bottles were nearly infallible. D did not test reused bottles except for visible defects. D appeals application of the res ipsa loquitur doctrine to P's case.

Issues.

(i)   Will the fact that D had given up control of the instrumentality prior to the injury prohibit the application of res ipsa loquitur?

(ii)   May res ipsa loquitur apply if the accident might ordinarily occur without negligence?

Held. (i) No. (ii) No. Judgment affirmed.

♦   The doctrine may be applied upon the theory that D had control at the time of the negligent act (even though not at the time of the accident) if P first proves that the condition of the bottle had not changed since it left D's presence and that P exercised care in handling it.

♦   It must appear that the accident would not have occurred without negligence.

♦   Here, the injury resulted either from an overcharge of pressurized gas, which could only be the result of D's negligence, or a defect in the bottle. In light of the evidence that the new bottles were not defective, a defective bottle would almost certainly be the result of D's negligence in failing to discover a defective reused bottle. Thus, the accident would not have occurred without D's negligence.

Concurrence. A manufacturer should be absolutely liable when an article that he places on the market knowing that it has not been inspected is defective and causes injury.

_____

8.   **Warranty.**

   a.   **Warranty defined.** As stated previously, a products liability action can be based in contract upon breach of warranty. The "warranty" upon which the plaintiff will rely will generally be a statement or representation, either express or implied, made by the seller (or attributed to him) with respect to the character, quality, function, performance, reliability, or other matter of the item sold.

   b.   **Cause of action.** When a plaintiff brings his cause of action on a warranty theory, he must show the following:

1) Existence of the warranty;

2) Breach of that warranty (sale of the product in a condition that does not comply with the warranty); and

3) Injury proximately caused by reason of the warranty defect in the product. With respect to this last element, if, for example, a warranty states that a widget has five coats of waterproof paint and in fact it has only one coat, the fact that this warranty is breached will forgive the plaintiff a cause of action for physical injuries suffered as a result of some mechanism unrelated to the warranty (though the plaintiff would have a breach of contract action for contract damages based on the failure of the widget to comply with the express warranty).

c. **Privity.** As noted previously, courts in the past considered an action for breach of warranty as a contracts action and required privity of contract between the plaintiff and the defendant as a precondition to a finding of liability.

d. **Express warranties.** An express warranty is an affirmation of fact or a promise made by the seller about the product sold that acts as an inducement to the purchaser to buy the product. U.C.C. section 2-313 states that an express warranty can be created by such an affirmation of fact or promise, by any description of the product that is made part of the basis of the sale transaction, or by furnishing a sample or model where the product is represented to conform to such sample or model. (This U.C.C. section further states that the words "guarantee" or "warranty" need not appear anywhere in the transaction for such a warranty to arise.) The affirmation of fact or promise may be expressly included in the contract by written representations or oral statements made by the supplier, or by a salesperson, or through advertising, or otherwise. The courts, however, have made an exception for statements of opinion or "puffing language"; on the other hand, the risk that such a statement may be construed by the courts as an express warranty is on the seller, and the tendency has been to find that such statements were warranties where such a construction was reasonable.

e. **Implied warranties.** Implied warranties are creatures of the law and become part of a sale of goods by operation of law rather than by the acts or agreements of the parties.

1) **Privity not required.** *Henningsen v. Bloomfield Motors, Inc.,* 161 A.2d 69 (N.J. 1960), disposed of the requirement of privity on the basis that social policy requires that a manufacturer be held liable for defects in its products and that warranty disclaimers and limitations on liability in consumer situations are "unconscionable" because of the relative inequality of bargaining positions.

a) Thus, even an express disclaimer of liability in a contract will not necessarily bar a products liability action. This decision extended the concept of manufacturer's liability beyond consumer products intended for bodily use.

b) Difficulties remained, however, because actions based on "warranty" were still subject to limiting commercial rules that were unsuited to the protection of consumers.

2) **Statutes.** Until adoption of the U.C.C., which was accomplished principally during the 1960s, the principal statute giving buyers implied warranties was the Uniform Sales Act, originally drafted in 1905. The Uniform Sales Act provisions, however, were designed to apply only between the seller and his immediate buyer. The U.C.C., while specifically applicable only to the sale of "goods," followed, in general, the Uniform Sales Act's "privity" rules in sections 2-314 and 2-315. However, one alternative version of section 2-318 attempted to create rights in remote purchasers and any "natural person who may reasonably be expected to use, consume or be affected by the goods and who is injured in person by breach of the warranty." That version of section 2-318 has not been widely adopted, although some states have adopted similar, even more encompassing consumer legislation. [*See e.g.,* Cal. Civil Code §§1790 *et seq.*] Also, the federal government adopted the Consumer Product Safety Act in 1972.

a) **Merchantability—U.C.C. section 2-314.** If goods are supplied by a merchant who deals in goods of that description, the law implies a warranty in the sales transaction that the goods are of fair average quality and reasonably fit for the general purposes for which they were sold.

b) **Fitness for particular purpose—U.C.C. section 2-315.** If goods are supplied by a seller who knows or has reason to know that the buyer is purchasing the goods for a particular purpose and is relying on the seller's skill or judgment in the selection of the goods, the law implies a warranty in the sales transaction that the goods are suitable or fit for the special purpose of the buyer. Fitness of the goods for general purposes will not satisfy this warranty.

9. **Intentional Acts.** If a manufacturer or supplier of a chattel sells it with knowledge, or with reason to know, that it is dangerous or defective, and fails to warn of the danger or defect, he may be held liable for battery to any person injured through use or consumption of the product. The requisite intent is established by showing that the injuries suffered were substantially certain

to result from use of the chattel in the condition as sold by the manufacturer or supplier.

C. THE RESTATEMENTS

1. **Restatement (Second) of Torts.** The Restatement has provided the framework for the development of strict tort liability in products cases. It allows recovery for injuries from sellers of products for use or consumption that prove to be defective and unreasonably dangerous.

2. **Modern Trend.** The Restatement (Third) of the Law of Products Liability addresses a dissatisfaction with some of the current rules. While "casual sellers" are still excluded, the new rules impose an absolute duty to sell products that conform to the manufacturer's design. There is a more limited obligation to make designs, warnings, and instructions "reasonably safe."

3. **No Recovery in Tort for Purely Economic Losses--**

Casa Clara Condominium Association, Inc. v. Charley Toppino & Sons, Inc., 620 So. 2d 1244 (Fla. 1993).

Facts. Toppino (D) supplied defective concrete to be used in the construction of homes. The defect caused the concrete to crack and break off. Numerous homeowners (Ps) sued D, claiming breach of common law implied warranty, products liability, negligence, and building code violations. The circuit court dismissed all counts against D. On appeal, the district court applied the economic loss rule and held that (i) because there was no personal injury or other property damage, Ps had no cause of action; and (ii) D had no duty to comply with the building code. Ps appeal.

Issue. May homeowners recover for purely economic losses from a concrete supplier under a negligence theory?

Held. No. Judgment affirmed.

♦   The basic distinction between tort and contract law is that contract law protects expectations, and tort law is determined by the duty owed to avoid causing physical harm to others. A purchaser's desire to enjoy the benefit of his bargain is not an interest protected by tort law.

♦   In the instant case, there are no physical injuries, and no property other than the structures built with D's concrete has sustained damage.

♦   To determine the character of a loss "which determines the appropriate remedy" one must look not at the product sold by D but at the product purchased by Ps. Here, Ps purchased dwellings, not individual components.

♦   In this case, contract principles provide adequate protections to Ps.

Concurrence and dissent. Without privity with D, Ps' claim for breach of warranty has been denied. The majority has denied Ps access to the courts to remedy the wrongs. The economic loss rule supposes that parties in a business context are able to allocate economic risks and remedies as part of their contract negotiations. That premise does not exist here. Further, I disagree with the majority's view that the defective concrete has not damaged other property.

Concurrence and dissent. I agree with the economic loss theory, but I do not agree that it was intended to defeat a tort cause of action that would otherwise lie for damages caused to a third party by a defective product.

---

4.   Proper Defendants--

Cafazzo v. Central Medical Health Services, Inc., 668 A.2d 521 (Pa. 1995).

Facts. Cafazzo (P) underwent surgery for implantation of a mandibular prosthesis in 1986. In 1992, after it was discovered that the device was defective, P sued the hospital and the physician who performed the surgery (Ds). (P sued Ds because the manufacturer of the device is in bankruptcy.) P claims that the prosthesis was defectively designed, unsafe, and lacked the necessary warnings. P claims that Ds sell, use, or provide certain prosthetic devices and should be held strictly liable as having provided, sold, or placed such devices in the stream of commerce. P appeals dismissal of the complaint.

Issues.

(i)   Are Ds "sellers" under the definition of the Restatement (Second) of Torts, section 402A?

(ii)   May a hospital and a physician be held subject to strict liability for defects in a product incidental to the provision of medical services?

Held. (i) No. (ii) No. Judgment affirmed.

♦   To ignore the ancillary nature of the association of product with activity is to assume that any medical service requiring the use of a physical object is a marketing device for that object. For example, this assumes that the surgery necessary for the implantation of the prosthesis is related to its sale.

♦   Concepts of purchase and sale cannot be attached to the materials supplied by medical personnel for a price as part of the medical treatment. While the prosthesis was transferred from Ds to P, it was not a sale even though it was supplied for a price as part of the medical treatment.

♦   The provision of medical services is different from the sale of products. While the prosthesis was incidental to the implantation procedure, it was necessary to the treatment administered, and fulfilled a particular role in the provision of medical care—the primary activity in this case.

♦   The test to determine supplier liability involves a four-part analysis: (i) which members of the marketing chain are available for redress, (ii) whether imposition of liability is an incentive to safety, (iii) whether the supplier is in a better position than the consumer to prevent the circulation of defective products, and (iv) whether the supplier can distribute the cost of compensation for injuries by charging for it in his business.

> Ds are subject to liability only if the quality or quantity of the services rendered are called into question. Medical personnel must exercise skill and expertise when selecting a product for use in medical treatment. Here, P does not allege that Ds carelessly or intentionally selected the prosthetic device despite knowledge of its defects.

> The safety testing and licensing of medical devices is governed by the FDA. Imposing liability on the doctors and hospitals who use them based on the assurances of the FDA is unlikely to change the safety of the devices.

> Ds have no control over distribution of defective products.

> Relying on cost factors without a logical basis would confine the focus of section 402A to the search for a deep pocket. Medical services are distinguished by factors that make them different from the retail marketing enterprise at which section 402A is directed.

D.   PRODUCT DEFECTS

1.   Manufacturing Defects--

Speller v. Sears, Roebuck & Co., 790 N.E.2d 252 (N.Y. 2003).

Facts. Speller died, and her son was injured, in a fire that originated in her kitchen. Speller's family (Ps) commenced suit against Sears, Whirlpool, and the landlord (Ds), alleging negligence, strict products liability, and breach of warranty in that the fire was caused by defective wiring in the couple's refrigerator. After a fire marshall's investigation that suggested stove-top grease was the cause of the fire, Ds moved for summary judgment. Ps' experts disagreed with the fire marshall and contended that the fire started in the upper right of the refrigerator, an area that houses extensive wiring. A Whirlpool engineer deposed by Ps did not agree that the fire started in the refrigerator, but said a fire would not start there unless it was defective. Ds were granted summary judgment. Ps appeal.

Issue. Did Ps raise a triable issue of fact concerning whether a defective refrigerator that caused the fire resulting in Ps' injuries?

Held. Yes. Judgment reversed.

♦   Ps tried to prove their theory circumstantially by proving the refrigerator started the fire and did not perform as intended. This state has long recognized the circumstantial approach in products liability cases. If a plaintiff's proof is insufficient, the jury may not infer the product caused the harm.

♦   Ds offered evidence that the stove was the cause of the fire. To withstand summary judgment Ps had to exclude the stove as the source of the fire. Ps offered expert testimony from an engineer, a fire investigator, and a former deputy fire chief. All agreed that the refrigerator was the source of the fire and the stove was not.

♦   Both parties offered substantiated, detailed, non-conclusory evidence and material issues of fact.

———————

a.   **Practical view**—*Campo v. Scofield,* 95 N.E.2d 802 (N.Y. 1951). If a manufacturer does all that is necessary to make a product non-defective, function properly for its intended purpose, and safe for its intended user, it has satisfied the law. The manufacturer has no duty to guard against deterioration, accidents, or "injury from a patent peril or from a source manifestly dangerous." A buzz saw manufacturer need not guard against someone being cut by the saw. The manufacturer has the right to expect the user to avoid potentially harmful contact because the very nature of the product gives notice of the consequences to be suffered.

2.   **Design Defects--**

Volkswagen of America, Inc. v. Young, 321 A.2d 737 (Md. 1974).

Facts. Young had stopped his Volkswagen Beetle, built by Volkswagen (D), at a red light. His car was hit from the rear by another car. As Young's car moved forward from the impact, the entire seat bracketing and seat adjustment mechanisms broke away from the body of the car. Young was thrown into the rear seat of the Volkswagen where he suffered fatal injuries. Young's representative (P) brought an action in federal district court, alleging that D's car was "defectively designed, manufactured, and marketed with defects which rendered it structurally hazardous, not merchantable, and not fit for the purpose intended." The federal court certified to the Maryland Supreme Court the question of whether the term "intended use" in this case would include accidents and thus whether a manufacturer was liable for so-called "second collisions" (where the car's occupant collides with a part of the car).

Issues.

(i)   Does the "intended use" of an automobile include accidents?

(ii)   Is a car manufacturer liable for injuries sustained as a result of a "second collision"?

Held. (i) Yes. (ii) Yes.

♦   The "intended use" of an automobile is not only to provide transportation but also to provide reasonably safe transportation.

♦   An automobile manufacturer can easily foresee that its products may be involved in collisions.

♦   *Larsen v. General Motors Corp.,* 391 F.2d 495 (8th Cir. 1968), and the cases following it are the better-decided cases. *Larsen* held that an automobile manufacturer is under a duty to use reasonable care in the design of its vehicle to avoid subjecting the user to an unreasonable risk of injury in the event of a collision.

♦   That the design defect is not the direct cause of the injury is not significant. By analogy, if two persons are negligent and cause an injury, both are liable.

♦   An automobile manufacturer is liable for a defect in design that could have been reasonably foreseen as causing or enhancing injuries in a collision, that is not patent or obvious to the user, and that in fact leads to or enhances such injuries. The standard is the traditional one of reasonableness. The trial court may consider such factors as convenience, design, economy, and utility in determining whether a product is reasonably safe.

♦   This holding does not make the automobile manufacturer an insurer or obligate it to make injury-proof cars.

Comment. *Young* represents the definite trend in "second collision" cases. The automobile manufacturer is not under an obligation to make the car "crash-worthy," so that no injury will occur if the car is in a crash. But it must anticipate clearly foreseeable dangers that could exist if the car is involved in a collision. And, of course, the most appealing lawsuits are those where the plaintiff argues that some small part was defective, rather than that the car itself is unsafe.

---

a. Defective design—test to apply--

Barker v. Lull Engineering Co., 573 P.2d 443 (Cal. 1978).

Facts. Barker (P) was operating a high-lift loader on uneven terrain. The loader turned over and injured P. P alleged a design defect by Lull (D). P alleged that the loader needed roll bars and outriggers. After a verdict for D, P appeals.

Issue. Was the proper standard for design defects applied in this case?

Held. No. Judgment reversed.

♦   Strict liability in tort does apply to design defect cases.

♦   The standard in design cases is the same as that in manufacturing defect cases.

♦   In determining whether a design is defective, the jury must consider the gravity of the danger, the likelihood that the danger will occur, feasibility of a safer design, cost to make it safer, and adverse consequences of changing the design.

---

b. Consumer expectation test--

Linegar v. Armour of America, 909 F.2d 1150 (8th Cir. 1990).

Facts. The widow and children of trooper Linegar (Ps) brought a products liability suit against Armour of America (D) after Linegar was killed in the line of duty. Linegar was wearing a bullet-resistant vest manufactured by D. None of the bullets that hit the vest caused any injury. However, there were gaps under the arms of the vest where the vest panels did not meet the sides of Linegar's body. The fatal bullet entered under Linegar's armpit and pierced his heart. The vest was purchased from D as standard issue for state troopers and the design was obvious. In a district court diversity action, the jury found for Ps. D appeals.

Issue. Is the manufacturer of a bullet-resistant vest liable under a theory of strict liability in tort for defective design if a person wearing the vest was killed when a bullet entered the body at an area not covered by the vest?

Held. No. Judgment reversed.

- In order to recover, Ps must show: (i) the product was sold in the course of D's business; (ii) when sold, the product was in a defective condition, unreasonably dangerous when put to its reasonably anticipated use; (iii) the product was used as reasonably anticipated; and (iv) Ps were damaged as a direct result of the defective condition that existed when the product was sold.

- Regarding element (ii), it defies logic to suggest that D reasonably should have anticipated that anyone would wear its vest to protect body areas not covered by the vest.

- The Missouri "consumer expectation" test provides: "The article sold must be dangerous to an extent beyond that which would be contemplated by the ordinary consumer who purchases it, with the ordinary knowledge common to the community as to its characteristics." [Restatement (Second) of Torts, §402A, comment i]

- Here, the vest's purported defect could not have been more open and obvious. The vest performed as expected. To hold D liable would be to place D in the role of insurer for anyone wearing its vest, regardless of whether any bullets penetrated the vest.

---

c. **Modified consumer expectation test.** In *Potter v. Chicago Pneumatic Tool Company*, 694 A.2d 1319 (Conn. 1997), the court reasoned that a modified consumer expectation test should be applied in cases involving complex product designs for which ordinary consumers may not be able to form expectations of safety. Under this test, consumers' expectations may be viewed in light of various factors that balance the utility of a product's design with the magnitude of its risks. The court also rejected the requirement of the Restatement (Third) of Torts that plaintiffs prove a feasible alternative design.

d. **Consumer expectation test retained--**

Halliday v. Sturn, Ruger & Co., 792 A.2d 1145 (Md. 2002).

Facts. Halliday's (P's) three-year-old son shot himself while playing with his father's gun. The semi-automatic, manufactured by Sturn (D), came with an instruction manual and the offer of a free gun safety course which the father declined. The father disregarded all warnings in the manual and left the gun under his mattress; a loaded magazine was left on a bookshelf in the same room. From watching television, the child was able to assemble the gun and shoot it. P sued D, alleging that the gun was defective and unreasonably dangerous because D had failed to install devices that prevent use by young children (*e.g.*, safety grip, heavy trigger pull, built-in lock, trigger lock, etc.). P alleged that it was foreseeable that the gun would be handled and fired by a child or others, and that the industry had developed a childproof grip safety that D failed to install. P filed a wrongful death suit. The trial court granted D's motion for summary judgment. P appeals.

Issue. Should the court apply a "risk-utility" analysis to guns?

Held. No. Judgment affirmed.

♦　　The consumer expectation test makes the seller of a defective product that is unreasonably dangerous to the consumer liable for the physical harm caused to the consumer by that product.

♦　　The "risk-utility test," generally applied to alleged design defects, regards a product as defective and unreasonably dangerous, for strict liability purposes, if the danger presented by the product outweighs its utility. Where this test is applied, there is consideration of whether a safer alternative design was feasible that would alter the balance by reducing the dangerousness of the product.

♦　　In *Kelley v. R. G. Industries, Inc.*, 497 A.2d 1143 (Md. 1985), involving a gun, we held that the risk-utility test did not apply to a product that did not malfunction. We also found that "Saturday Night Specials" were in a separate category; their short barrels, lightness, concealability, and inaccuracy made them attractive to criminals but useless to lawful consumers. We determined that because it was foreseeable that criminals would be the likely users of these guns, manufacturers could be held liable for injuries to innocent persons. Whether a gun falls into this category is a jury question.

♦　　Under the consumer expectation test, no cause of action has been stated here. The gun did not malfunction. The child's father caused the tragedy.

♦　　Ps ask that we modify the common law and impose liability on gun manufacturers who have failed to incorporate child safety devices into their products— apart from other safety devices, warnings regarding storage, and the offer of a lock box in which to store the gun. Some courts have done that, but our legislature has dealt with more specific issues than those presented here on several occasions and has chosen not to impose liability on gun manufacturers. We respect that policy decision.

Comment. In this case two judges dissented from the trial court's opinion and concluded that the consumer expectation test applied in *Kelley* was no longer state law, that the design defect should be considered under a risk-utility analysis, and under that analysis there was a triable issue of fact.

3.   **The Duty to Warn.** A manufacturer of a product may be held liable when there is a failure to warn of dangerous conditions associated with the product. Two critical issues can be raised in failure to warn cases. First, the courts must determine to whom the warning must be given. In addition, the courts must determine whether the failure to warn is a true strict liability claim or merely negligence.

    a.   **Manufacturers of birth control pills--**

MacDonald v. Ortho Pharmaceutical Corp., 475 N.E.2d 65 (Mass. 1985).

Facts. Ortho (D) was the manufacturer of birth control pills. D supplied warnings to physicians who prescribed the pills and warnings in the packages of the pills. The warnings in the packages met FDA guidelines but did not use the word "stroke." A stroke is a risk associated with using birth control pills. MacDonald (P) took birth control pills for three years and had a stroke. P sued D, claiming a failure to adequately warn. The jury returned a verdict for P, but the trial court entered a judgment n.o.v. The basis of the trial court's decision was that a drug manufacturer fulfills its duty to warn about prescription drugs by providing a warning to physicians. P appeals.

Issue. Is there a duty to warn the actual consumer of prescription drugs?

Held. Yes. Judgment reversed and jury verdict ordered reinstated.

♦   Ordinarily, the duty to warn for prescription drugs is met by warning the physician. Birth control pills, however, are different. They create a high risk of injury due to stroke, and the patient might only visit the doctor once a year for consultation. The manufacturer, therefore, must also warn the user.

♦   This warning was inadequate. Although the warning met the FDA guidelines, that is not conclusive. The lack of reference to "stroke" resulted in the warning failing to adequately alert the user of a clear risk of harm from the pill.

Dissent. Manufacturers of prescription drugs fulfill their duty by adequately warning physicians and complying with FDA regulations.

    b.   **"Hindsight analysis" no longer applied to duty to warn--**

Vassallo v. Baxter Healthcare Corp., 696 N.E.2d 909 (Mass. 1998).

Facts. In 1977, Florence Vassallo (P) underwent breast implantation surgery. The silicone implants that were inserted into P were manufactured by Heyer-Schulte ("Heyer").

After experiencing chest pains, P had a mammogram in 1992, which revealed that the implants may have ruptured. The silicone implants were removed and replaced with saline implants in 1993. During the surgery, it was noticed that the left implant had ruptured and the right implant was intact but had several pinholes. Expert testimony indicated that Heyer knew that the silicone gel could leak and possibly cause detrimental effects in the body, but failed to conduct studies to document the safety of the implants. Instead, Heyer relied on animal testing conducted by Dow Corning, the manufacturer of the silicone gel, despite the fact that the studies "left many questions unanswered." Heyer did conduct toxicity testing on the gel, and the gel failed the 90-day toxicity test; however, Heyer continued to use the gel in its implants and did not conduct further toxicity testing. Heyer did provide warnings to physicians regarding the gel implants. The warning that accompanied P's implants stated that it could cut or rupture easily from excessive stresses, but did not mention normal stresses or the consequences of gel migration in the body. P claims that she would not have undergone the implantation procedure if she had been warned of the complications. She sues Baxter Healthcare and its affiliate (Ds) (who assumed responsibility for the implant products manufactured by Heyer) under theories of negligent design, negligent product warnings, and breach of implied warranty of merchantability, and also included a claim under the Massachusetts Consumer Protection Law. The jury found for P on all claims except the consumer protection claim. The judge held that Ds were liable on the consumer protection claim but awarded only costs and attorney's fees because Ds did not act willfully or with knowledge. Ds appeal.

Issue. Should products liability law concerning the implied warranty of merchantability be changed to adopt a "state of the art" standard that conditions a manufacturer's liability on actual or constructive knowledge of the risks?

Held. Yes. Judgment affirmed.

♦   Current products liability law presumes a manufacturer "was fully informed of all risks associated with the product at issue, regardless of the state of the art at the time of the sale, and amounts to strict liability for failure to warn of these risks." This is based on the public policy that a defective product, unreasonably dangerous because of inadequate warnings, is unfit for its intended use regardless of the absence of fault on the defendant's part.

♦   The majority of states follow the Restatement (Second) of Torts, section 402A, which requires that a seller warn against a danger if he has knowledge, or should have knowledge, of the danger. It further states that a product is defective if it has inadequate warnings if the foreseeable risks of harm could have been reduced by providing reasonable warnings. Although unforeseeable risks from foreseeable use cannot be warned against, a manufacturer has a duty to perform testing and is charged with knowledge of what reasonable testing would reveal.

♦   Massachusetts is among a minority of states that applies a "hindsight analysis" to the duty to warn. We now revise our law to state that a defendant will not be liable under an implied warranty of merchantability for failure to warn or provide instructions about risks that were not reasonably foreseeable or could not have been discovered through reasonable testing. A manufacturer will be held to the standard of knowledge of an expert in the appropriate field, and will remain subject to a continuing duty to warn of risks discovered following the sale of the product at issue.

---

      c.   **Instructions and warnings.** Warnings of risks associated with a product's unintended uses and warnings of dangers that cannot be reasonably reduced by a manufacturer (*e.g.*, side effects of pharmaceuticals) sometimes accompany products. The sufficiency of such warnings has been a common issue before the courts.

      1)   **Adequate warnings--**

Hood v. Ryobi American Corporation, 181 F.3d 608 (4th Cir. 1999).

Facts. Hood (P) purchased a fully assembled Ryobi TS-254 miter saw with a 10-inch diameter blade for home repairs. The blade was controlled by a finger trigger on a handle near the top of the blade. Two blade guards shielded almost the entire saw blade. The owner's manual and warnings affixed to the saw warned in several places to keep the guards in place during operation. When P used the saw the day after he purchased it, he removed the guards to saw a piece of wood. He continued to saw with the blade exposed for about 20 minutes. In the middle of a cut, the blade flew off the saw and back toward P. P's left thumb was partially amputated and his right leg was cut. P admits he read the owner's manual and warning labels, but he believed the guards were meant to prevent clothing or fingers from coming into contact with the blade. P claims he was not aware the blade would detach, but Ryobi (D) was. In fact, D had been sued for such an event. P sued D for failure to warn and defective design. The trial court entered summary judgment for D. P appeals.

Issue. Did D provide adequate warnings on its product?

Held. Yes. Judgment affirmed.

♦   P's argument that D's warnings were insufficient because they did not inform the user of the consequences of using the saw without the blade guards fails. A warning need only be reasonable under the circumstances. A manufacturer need not warn of every conceivable danger.

♦   In determining the adequacy of a warning, we ask whether the benefits of a more detailed warning outweigh the costs of requiring the change.

- The cost of changing labels is not the only consideration. More detail on a label threatens to undermine the usefulness of the warning altogether. Voluminous and technical labels are often not effective.

- D's warnings are clear and unequivocal. Two of the seven labels warn of "serious injury." Had the warnings been followed, injury would have been prevented in this case.

- The only other incident similar to P's occurred 15 years before P's. P has not shown D's warnings to be insufficient.

Comment. In most cases, adequacy of warning is a matter for the jury. In clear cases, however, it may be a question of law.

E. PLAINTIFF'S CONDUCT

1. **Disclaimers.** Liability based on warranty is generally subject to disclaimer by the seller. Since it arises out of contract conditions (either express or implied in law), the seller may limit or exclude such warranties by use of an appropriate statement in the contract of sale, but only in strict accordance with and to the extent allowed by law.

2. **Misuse.** If the plaintiff misuses the product or engages in an abnormal use that was not foreseeable, the defendant will not be liable, even under a strict liability theory.

   a. **When is a use abnormal?** The use becomes abnormal when the plaintiff fails to follow the defendant's directions and instructions.

   b. **Foreseeable misuse.** Where an unusual or abnormal use should be anticipated by the defendant (*e.g.,* sailor walking over containers used for trans-oceanic shipping was injured when he fell through a defective container; this is abnormal but foreseeable), strict liability may apply.

3. **Comparative Fault--**

Daly v. General Motors Corp., 575 P.2d 1162 (Cal. 1978).

Facts. Daly's (P's) decedent was killed when thrown from an automobile manufactured by General Motors (D). P alleged that the auto had defective door locks. Evidence showed that the decedent did not have the doors locked, did not have his seat belt on, was intoxicated, and was driving 50 to 70 miles per hour. After a judgment for D, P appeals.

Issue. Is comparative negligence a defense to strict liability?

Held. Yes. Judgment reversed.

♦ Decedent's own conduct may be used to reduce his damages whether the action is based on negligence or strict liability.

♦ Assumption of risk as a separate defense is abolished and merged with comparative negligence.

♦ Thus, comparative fault must be applied to reduce damages, and the complete bar of assumption of risk should not be applied.

Dissent. The court should not mix the negligence principle of comparative negligence with the strict liability doctrine.

Comment. Section 17 of the Restatement (Third) of Torts follows *Daly*. It does not treat alteration, misuse, or modification as independent defenses. To the extent they are traced to the plaintiff's conduct, they are governed by the comparative fault system in effect in the jurisdiction.

F. FEDERAL PREEMPTION

1. **The Supremacy Clause.** The Supremacy Clause of the United States Constitution states that the Constitution and laws made thereunder and all treaties of the United States shall be the supreme law of the land, notwithstanding any state laws. Laws may be expressly or impliedly preempted. Where there is express preemption, it is for the courts only to determine if the challenged state law is one the federal government intended to preempt. Where there is an implied preemption, the courts look at the federal issue at stake to see if the federal scheme of regulation is pervasive, whether federal goals would be frustrated by the state law at issue, or whether the state law is in direct conflict with the federal law.

2. **Common Law Tort Action Preempted--**

Geier v. American Honda Motor Company, Inc., *et al.,* 529 U.S. 861 (2000).

Facts. Geier, driving a 1987 Honda Accord, was seriously injured when she collided with a tree. P had buckled her shoulder and lap belts; the car had no airbags. Geier and her parents (Ps) sued American Honda and its affiliates (Ds), alleging negligent and defective design because there was no driver's side airbag. The district court dismissed. The court of appeals dismissed for different reasons. We granted certiorari.

Issue. Does the National Traffic and Motor Safety Act of 1966, when taken together with the relevant regulatory standard, preempt a common-law tort action claiming that a car manufacturer, compliant with the standard, ought to have equipped the car with airbags?

Held. Yes. Judgment affirmed.

♦ Under the National Traffic and Motor Vehicle Safety Act of 1966 ("Act"), the United States Department of Transportation promulgated Federal Motor Vehicle Safety Standard ("FMVSS") 208, which, among other matters, required auto manufacturers to equip some, but not all, of their 1987 vehicles with passive restraints. FMVSS 208 gave car manufacturers a choice as to whether to install airbags.

♦ The Act's preemption provision reads: "Whenever a federal motor vehicle safety standard established under this subchapter is in effect, no State or political subdivision of a State shall have any authority either to establish, or to continue in effect, with respect to any motor vehicle or item of motor vehicle equipment[,] any safety standard applicable to the same aspect of performance of such vehicle or item of equipment which is not identical to the federal standard."

♦ The Act's "saving" clause says that "compliance with" a federal safety standard "does not exempt any person from any liability under common law." [15 U.S.C. §1397(k) (1988 ed.)] Thus, the saving clause assumes that there are common-law liability cases to save. Where federal law creates only minimum safety standards, for example, state tort law may operate. The saving clause prevents a broad reading of the express preemption provision that, arguably, might preempt common law tort actions. Such a broad reading would preempt all nonidentical state standards established in tort actions covering the same aspect of performance as an applicable federal standard, even if the federal standard merely established a minimum standard. On that broad reading of the preemption clause little, if any, potential "liability at common law" would remain. We have found no evidence Congress intended such a broad reading.

♦ Conflict preemption principles are not barred by the saving clause. There is nothing in the clause that suggests saving state tort actions that conflict with federal regulations. The words "compliance" and "does not exempt" sound as if they simply bar a defense that compliance with a federal standard automatically exempts a defendant from state law, whether the federal government meant that standard to be an absolute, or a minimum, requirement. This interpretation does not conflict with the purpose of the saving provision, for it preserves actions that seek to establish greater safety than the minimum safety achieved by a federal regulation intended to provide a floor. Further, we have repeatedly declined to give broad effect to saving clauses that would upset the careful regulatory scheme established by federal law, a concern applicable here. The preemption provision itself favors preemption of state tort suits, while the saving clause disfavors pre-emption at least some of the time. However, there is nothing in any natural reading of the two provisions that would favor one policy over the other where a jury-imposed safety standard actually conflicts with a federal safety standard.

♦ This lawsuit actually conflicts with FMVSS 208 and the Act itself. FMVSS 208 was a way to give a manufacturer a range of choices "among different passive restraint systems that would be gradually introduced, thereby lowering costs, overcoming technical safety problems, encouraging technological development, and winning widespread consumer acceptance. . . ." FMVSS sought variety to help develop data on comparative effectiveness, to provide time to overcome safety problems and high costs, and to encourage the development of alternative, cheaper, and safer passive restraint systems, thereby building public confidence necessary to avoid an interlock-type fiasco.

♦ Ps' tort action depends on their claim that manufacturers had a duty to install an airbag when they manufactured the 1987 Honda Accord. Such a state law— *i.e.*, a rule of state tort law imposing such a duty—by its terms would have required manufacturers of all similar cars to install airbags rather than other passive restraint systems, such as automatic belts or passive interiors. It thereby would have presented an obstacle to the variety and mix of devices that the federal regulation sought. It would have required all manufacturers to have installed airbags in respect to the entire District of Columbia-related portion of their 1987 new car fleet, even though FMVSS 208 at that time required only that 10% of a manufacturer's nationwide fleet be equipped with any passive restraint device at all. It thereby also would have stood as an obstacle to the gradual passive restraint phase-in that the federal regulation deliberately imposed. In addition, it could have made less likely the adoption of a state mandatory buckle-up law. Because the rule of law for which petitioners contend would have stood "as an obstacle to the accomplishment and execution of" the important means-related federal objectives that we have just discussed, it is preempted.

Dissent (Stevens, J.). The Court has permitted an interim regulation to prevent Ps' proposition that to be safe a car must have an airbag from being addressed. The rule enforced here was not enacted by Congress and was not found in the text of any Executive Order or regulation. It is the product of the Court's interpretation of a commentary accompanying an administrative regulation. We would have preempted tort actions only if they created a "special burden" on the regulatory scheme as envisioned by Congress. There is no such burden here. Ds have not overcome the presumption against preemption in this case.

———————

X. DAMAGES

A. INTRODUCTION

The rule of damages is based on the principle that a plaintiff is to be compensated for the actual loss that was caused by the wrong of another. [*See* Sullivan v. Old Colony Street Railway, 83 N.E. 1091, 1092 (Mass. 1908)] Although the object of compensatory damages is to give the injured party the equivalent in money for his suffering, there are times when no amount of money can make up for the loss. [*See* Zibbell v. Southern Pacific Co., 116 P. 513 (Cal. 1911)]

1. **Definition.** Damages is the sum of money that may be recovered in the courts by a plaintiff who has suffered damage (*i.e.,* loss, detriment, or injury), whether to person, property, or rights, through the conduct of the defendant.

    a. **Nominal damages.** Nominal damages are a small sum of money awarded to the plaintiff for a technical invasion of her rights (*i.e.,* no substantial loss or injury), in order to make the judgment a matter of record so that prescriptive rights can be avoided and to cover at least part of the costs of bringing the action.

    b. **Compensatory damages.** Compensatory damages are the sum of money deemed the equivalent of the full loss or harm suffered by the plaintiff (*i.e.,* to compensate the plaintiff for the wrong suffered).

    c. **Punitive (exemplary) damages.** Punitive damages are the sum of money over and above what will compensate the plaintiff fully for the loss suffered. The purpose of punitive damages is to punish the defendant and to make an example of him to others in instances when his conduct is of an aggravated nature (*e.g.,* intent to injure, willful and wanton, or gross disregard of the consequences).

2. **Purpose of Damages.** "The rule of damages is a practical instrumentality for the administration of justice. The principle on which it is founded is compensation. Its object is to afford the equivalent in money for the actual loss caused by the wrong of another. Recurrence to this fundamental conception tests the soundness of claims for the inclusion of new elements of damages." [Sullivan v. Old Colony Street Railway, 83 N.E. 1091 (Mass. 1908)]

3. **Legal Measure of Damages.** "No rational being would change places with the injured man for an amount of gold that would fill the room of the court, yet no lawyer would contend that such is the legal measure of damages." [Zibbell v. Southern Pacific Co., *supra*]

B. RECOVERABLE ELEMENTS OF DAMAGES

1. **Personal Injuries.** Where the plaintiff suffers personal injuries, she is entitled to recover a sum that will fairly and adequately compensate her for all injuries that are the direct and proximate result of the defendant's conduct. This can include, among other things, the following: (i) physical and mental pain and future suffering; (ii) loss of earnings and future loss of earnings; and (iii) reasonable expenses incurred in treatment of the injury, including doctor, hospital, and nursing care expenses. Of course, the damages that the plaintiff is expected to suffer in the future must be proved with reasonable certainty.

2. **Pain and Suffering--**

McDougald v. Garber, 536 N.E.2d 372 (N.Y. 1989).

Facts. Emma McDougald (P) had a caesarean section and tubal ligation. During the surgery she suffered oxygen deprivation and severe brain damage. She is now in a permanent coma. In an action for personal injuries brought in her name and her husband's name, she claimed damages for pain and suffering and loss of enjoyment of life. There was a dispute in the evidence as to whether she retained any cognitive ability. The jury awarded separate damages for P for pain and suffering and the loss of enjoyment of life. She also recovered damages for future medical treatment and lost wages. In addition, her husband received damages for loss of his wife's services. The trial judge combined the awards for pain and suffering and loss of enjoyment of life and reduced them by half. On appeal, the appellate court affirmed. Ds appeal.

Issues.

(i) Can damages be awarded for pain and suffering when P is not conscious of the suffering?

(ii) Are pain and suffering and loss of enjoyment of life separate elements of loss?

Held. (i) No. (ii) No. Action remanded for new trial with proper jury instructions.

♦ Damages are to compensate an injured party, not to punish the defendant. The money is to be used to place the plaintiff in the position, economically, that she would have been in had she not been injured.

♦ Damages for loss of enjoyment of life require that the plaintiff be aware that the enjoyment was lost. Awarding money to a plaintiff who is not aware will not allow the plaintiff to spend it to try to have pleasure or gain pleasure by giving it away. Such damages would be merely punitive.

- Pain and suffering and loss of enjoyment of life are, in fact, elements of the same loss. Human suffering cannot be calculated with exact mathematical certainty and it is better to include both of these elements in the same category.

Dissent. Loss of enjoyment of life is substantially different from pain and suffering. A person may lose that enjoyment even though they are not aware of the loss. Pain and suffering, however, may require awareness of the loss in order to be compensable. The two elements, therefore, should be separated by the jury.

Comment. It is up to the jury to estimate future pain and suffering, and the amount that will compensate the plaintiff. Often, counsel for the plaintiff will use a "per diem" argument such as "plaintiff's pain and suffering should be compensated at the rate of one penny per second" because such small amounts seem rather trivial to the jury. However, arguing damages on a unit of time basis has been prohibited by a minority of courts because it tends to deceive the unwary. (In the example, one penny per second equals $315,360 per year.)

---

3. Lost Earnings--

O'Shea v. Riverway Towing Co., 677 F.2d 1194 (7th Cir. 1982).

Facts. O'Shea (P) was injured by Riverway's (D's) negligence. P had been a cook but was unable to work after her injury. P's evidence included an economist who testified to P's lost future earnings. The economist's calculations included a 6% - 8% per year increase in P's wages to account for the effects of inflation. The trial court awarded P $86,033. D appeals.

Issue. Was it appropriate to use an inflation rate to help determine lost future wages?

Held. Yes. Judgment affirmed.

- Future wages may be based on numerous factors.

- Current wages may be increased for expected inflation and reduced to present value.

- Future decisions by trial judges should clearly state the basis of the damages.

Comment. In the calculation of the recovery for the plaintiff, the amount of recovery (such as for future earnings) can be reduced to present value by the courts. This reduction to present value is to actually give the plaintiff the amount of the recovery over the life of the impairment of the earning capacity of the plaintiff.

4. Excessive Verdict--

Duncan v. Kansas City Southern Railway, 773 So. 2d 670 (La. 2000).

Facts. Three sisters were riding in a church van when it collided with a Kansas City (D) train. One of the sisters was killed and one was rendered quadriplegic. The sisters' parents (Ps) sued for wrongful death and personal injury. The jury found the van driver and D responsible and apportioned fault. Ps were awarded over $27 million, which included future medical expenses of $17 million, pain and suffering, mental anguish, and loss of enjoyment damages of $8 million to Rachel, who was rendered quadriplegic. The appeal court affirmed. D appeals.

Issue. Was the jury's damages award so excessive as to be set aside?

Held. Yes.

♦ Because of the discretionary nature of general damages—those for pain and suffering, inconvenience, loss of physical enjoyment, etc.—an appellate court rarely disturbs such an award. The appeals court's role is to review the trier of fact's exercise of discretion. Where abuse is found, a court may look to prior appropriate awards only for the purpose of determining a reasonable range within the trier of fact's discretion.

♦ Here, we do not look at whether the $8 million award to Rachel exceeds the awards to plaintiffs with similar injuries; we look at whether the award is beyond that which a reasonable trier of fact could assess for the effects of a specific injury to a specific plaintiff under specific circumstances.

♦ Before the accident, Rachel was an active 11-year-old, who enjoyed the outdoors. She was an excellent student, had many friends and was planning to attend college. Now she is wholly dependent. She is dealing with the death of her older sister and the injuries to her younger sister. She can no longer go to school or go on camping trips she used to enjoy with her family. She is aware of the effect her injury has had on the family. However, the $8 million award is excessive. The highest award in similar cases is $6 million and we reduce the award here to that amount.

♦ Regarding D's contention that the $17 million award is excessive, such an award cannot be made without medical expenses being established and medical testimony that they are indicated. Here, both Ps and D presented treatment programs. Accurate evidence was presented regarding Rachel's life expectancy. She is a C5 tetraplegic, and her age at the time of trial was 14.6 years. Her treating physician predicted a 57-year life expectancy; this is more realistic and more scientifically accurate than the 81-year life expectancy predicted by Ps' expert. Thus, we reduce the $17 million award to $10,528,722.

C. ATTORNEYS' FEES

1. **Each Party Pays.** Absent a contractual provision to the contrary, each party must pay his own attorney.

2. **Contingent Fees.** A common method of payment for the plaintiffs in tort cases is the contingent fee. This fee arrangement allows the plaintiff to seek legal counsel without the necessity of paying the fee unless the action is successful.

D. COLLATERAL BENEFITS

1. **Generally No Offset.** Absent a statute to the contrary, collateral benefits do not offset a plaintiff's award of damages.

2. **Insurance Benefits--**

Harding v. Town of Townshend, 43 Vt. 536 (1871).

Facts. Harding (P) was injured due to the negligence of the town of Townshend (D). At trial, the only question was that of damages. The trial court instructed the jury that they should subtract from their award the amount that P had received from his insurance company as a result of the injuries he suffered in this accident. P, on appeal, argued that the instruction was wrong.

Issue. May a jury take into consideration, in awarding damages, any money the plaintiff may have received from liability insurance?

Held. No. Judgment reversed.

- ♦ There is no privity between the insurance company and D, and they are not joint tortfeasors or joint debtors so as to make the payment or satisfaction by one operate to benefit the other. In fact, the insurance policy is collateral to P's remedy against D. There is, in short, no reason that D should benefit from the existence of the insurance policy.

- ♦ The real key is to determine who should bear the burden of loss. Because D breached a duty of care owed to P and is thus the wrongdoer, we believe that D should bear the loss, not the injured P.

Comment. The doctrine of collateral benefits, although still the object of divided academic interest, is a firmly entrenched part of American law. There are two major areas of interest that you should be acquainted with. The first is the statutory attempt by about a third of the states to reduce the costs of medical malpractice by providing for an offset for collateral benefits received. The second major area is the problem involved in attempts by the United States Government to offset awards under the Tort Claims Act by the collateral government benefits to which the claimant is entitled.

E. WRONGFUL DEATH AND LOSS OF CONSORTIUM

1. **Common Law.** The common law rule was that all personal injuries were personal and died with the deceased. There was no action for the injuries suffered by the decedent prior to death nor for the losses the family suffered because of the death. Most jurisdictions have, however, now passed statutes that allow recovery for one or both of these losses. Statutes that allow recovery for the death itself are called Wrongful Death Statutes. Statutes that allow recovery for injuries suffered by the decedent prior to death are called Survival Statutes.

2. **Wrongful Death Damages.** Wrongful death statutes typically allow one of two types of recovery. They may either allow loss to the estate or loss to the survivors. Loss to the estate usually allows only the pecuniary loss of the power to earn money. Loss to the survivors may include companionship or other items.

3. **Survival Damages.** Survival statutes allow the estate to recover those damages the decedent could have recovered if death had not intervened (*e.g.*, pain and suffering).

4. **Loss of Consortium.** Most jurisdictions allow recovery by either spouse for loss of love, companionship, services, and sexual relations.

F. PUNITIVE DAMAGES

1. **Introduction.** Because punitive damages are intended to punish the defendant and make an example of him, they may be allowed in a suit for battery, where the defendant intended to injure the plaintiff. They may be allowed in certain cases for defamation, malicious prosecution, misrepresentation, and products liability cases. Punitive damages are not allowed for negligent conduct, although some states permit such damages where the defendant has engaged in reckless conduct, such as drunk driving.

2. **Proof of a Defendant's Worth Not Required--**

Kemezy v. Peters, 79 F.3d 33 (7th Cir. 1996).

Facts. Kemezy (P) sued Peters (D) under 42 U.S.C. section 1983, alleging that D beat him with a nightstick. P was awarded $10,000 in compensatory damages and $20,000 in punitive damages. D appeals the award of punitive damages.

Issue. Does P have to provide the jury with evidence of D's net worth so that the jury can award a just measurement of punitive damages?

Held. No. Judgment affirmed.

♦   There are many reasons for awarding punitive damages, with the most frequent being to punish the defendant for his conduct and deter him and others from engaging in similar conduct.

♦   Compensatory damages may not fully compensate the plaintiff. An additional award of punitive damages assures full compensation and ensures that the tortious conduct is not underdeterred, which would result if compensatory damages do not fully compensate the injury.

♦   An award of punitive damages does not depend on the level of the defendant's income or wealth; therefore, a plaintiff will not be required to introduce such evidence. Such a requirement would encourage plaintiffs to seek punitive damages merely because a defendant has a deep pocket and would force intrusive pretrial discovery regarding the defendant's net worth.

Comment. The controversy over punitive damages has led many states to legislate reforms. Various approaches to awarding punitive damages include: (i) forbidding punitive damages unless authorized by statute; (ii) capping punitive damages; (iii) requiring that a percentage of any punitive damages award be paid to the state; and (iv) ordering bifurcated trials of liability and damages, with punitive damages being awarded by the judge.

---

3.   Grossly Excessive Award--

State Farm Mutual Automobile Insurance Co. v. Campbell, 538 U.S. 408 (2003).

Facts. Campbell, who was insured by State Farm (D), was involved in a multicar accident after he tried to pass six vans on a two-lane highway; one of the other drivers was killed. D rejected the other parties' offers to settle their claims for the $50,000 policy limit. Evidence showed that (i) D's employees had altered the records to make Campbell appear less responsible; (ii) D had disregarded the other parties' likelihood of proving liability and securing a judgment in excess of the policy's limits; (iii) D had assured Campbell and his wife that their assets were safe; and (iv) D told Campbell to put a for sale sign on his house postjudgment. Although Campbell insisted he had not been at fault, a jury found him 100% at fault and returned judgment for $185,849. D refused to appeal. Campbell appealed unsuccessfully, and D paid the judgment, including the excess over the policy limit. Campbell and his wife (Ps) nonetheless sued D, alleging bad faith, fraud and intentional infliction of emotional distress. A jury found D's decision not to settle unreasonable. In *BMW of North America, Inc. v. Gore*, 517 U.S. 559, we refused to sustain a $2 million punitive damages award which accompanied a $4,000 compensatory damages award. The trial court denied D's renewed motion to exclude dissimilar out-of-state conduct evidence. Evidence was introduced that pertained to D's business practices in numerous states but was not related to the type of claims underlying Ps' complaint. Ps were awarded $2.6 million in compensatory damages and $145 million in punitive damages, reduced to $1 million and $25 million, respectively. On appeal, the state supreme court affirmed the $1 million award and, applying *Gore*, reinstated the $145 million award, based on D's decision to take the case to trial as a result of "a national scheme to meet corporate fiscal goals by capping payouts on claims company wide." We granted certiorari.

Issue. Is a jury's award of $145 million in punitive damages against an automobile insurer excessive, in violation of the Fourteenth Amendment's Due Process Clause, where full compensatory damages had been found to be only $1 million?

Held. Yes. Judgment reversed and case remanded for a redetermination of punitive damages.

◆   Punitive damage awards serve the same purpose as criminal penalties, but civil defendants are not given the same protections as criminal defendants. There is great danger of arbitrary deprivation of property where the decisionmaker is given evidence that does not bear on the amount being awarded. The Due Process Clause prohibits the imposition of grossly excessive or arbitrary punishments on a tortfeasor.

◆   In *Gore, supra*, we instructed reviewing courts to consider three guideposts with regard to punitive damages: (i) the degree of reprehensibility of the defendant's misconduct, (ii) the disparity between the actual or potential harm suffered by the plaintiff and the punitive damages award, and (iii) the difference between the punitive damages awarded by the jury and the civil penalties authorized or imposed in comparable cases. In *Cooper Industries, Inc. v. Leatherman Tool Group, Inc.*, 532 U.S. 424 (2001), we mandated appeals courts to conduct *de novo* review of a trial court's application of these guideposts to the jury's award.

◆   D's conduct is not praiseworthy, but the harm to P was economic. It did not involve repeated behavior and did not evince a reckless disregard of Ps' health or safety. A more modest punishment for the insurer's reprehensible conduct could have satisfied the state's legitimate objectives. The case at hand was improperly used by both the trial court and the state supreme court as a platform to expose and to punish D's nationwide operation. The courts relied on out-of-state evidence and other evidence to punish and discourage conduct that bore no relation to Ps' harm. Ps showed no conduct by D similar to the conduct that harmed them.

♦ We decline to impose a ratio which a punitive damages award cannot exceed. However, in practice "few awards exceeding a single-digit ratio between punitive and compensatory damages, to a significant degree, will satisfy due process." A four-to-one ratio might be close to the line. There is a presumption against a ratio of 145 to 1. The $1 million award for one year and a half of emotional distress was complete compensation for Ps. The basis of the emotional distress was an economic transaction, not a physical assault or trauma.

♦ The most relevant civil sanction under the state's law for the wrong done to Ps appears to be a $10,000 fine for an act of fraud.

Dissent (Scalia, J.). The Due Process Clause provides no substantive protections against "excessive" or "unreasonable" awards of punitive damages.

Dissent (Thomas, J.). The Constitution does not constrain the size of awards of punitive damages.

Dissent (Ginsburg, J.). The Court ought to adhere to the view that the laws of a state have to suffice to superintend awards of punitive damages until authorized judges or legislators initiate system-wide change.

Comment. The *State Farm* decision was confirmed in *Philip Morris USA v. Williams*, 127 S. Ct. 1057 (2007). The Court vacated the judgment of the Oregon Supreme Court after it affirmed a $79.5 million punitive damages award in a negligence and deceit lawsuit in which the plaintiff was awarded $800,000 in noneconomic damages. Justice Breyer stated that it would be unfair to permit courts to award punitive damages to "strangers to the litigation." Williams's widow had sued Philip Morris following Williams's death from lung cancer, alleging that the company had engaged in a campaign of deceit as to the dangers of smoking. Breyer did note that the risk of harm to the general public may be considered as a component of the reprehensibility of the defendant's actions, but the award cannot be increased as a direct result of harms inflicted on nonparties.

XI. INSURANCE

A. INDEMNITY AND LIABILITY

1. **Indemnity.** Originally insurance only indemnified the policyholder for his losses. If, for example, a policyholder injured a plaintiff but the policyholder was bankrupt, the plaintiff recovered nothing. The policyholder had to pay a judgment before the insurance company had to pay the policyholder. Dissatisfaction with this system led to statutory changes.

2. **Liability.** Current insurance is in the form of liability policies. If the policyholder injures a plaintiff, the insurance is for the plaintiff's ultimate benefit.

B. SCOPE OF INSURANCE COVERAGE

1. **Pollution Exclusion Clause--**

Dimmitt Chevrolet, Inc. v. Southeastern Fidelity Insurance Corp., 636 So. 2d 700 (Fla. 1993).

Facts. Dimmitt (D) sold used crankcase oil from 1974 to 1979 to Peak. In 1983, the EPA determined that Peak had caused pollution by storing its waste sludge in unlined bins. D was designated as a "potentially responsible party" because it had generated and transported hazardous materials to the Peak site. D agreed to undertake remedial measures without conceding liability. Southeastern (P) provided comprehensive general liability ("CGL") insurance to D. D's policy included a clause excluding coverage for pollution, excepting only a "discharge, dispersal, release or escape" which is "sudden and accidental." P filed a declaratory judgment action against D in federal district court, seeking a declaration that P owed no duty to defend or indemnify D under the policy. D counterclaimed, seeking a contrary declaration. After both parties filed motions for summary judgment, the district court granted summary judgment in favor of P and denied D's motion to alter or amend. D appealed. The court of appeals certified the question to the Florida Supreme Court.

Issue. Can pollution that occurs gradually over a period of years be within the coverage of a CGL insurance policy that excludes coverage for pollution except for that which is "sudden and accidental"?

Held. No. Record returned to the court of appeals.

♦   While state courts disagree on the meaning of the language at issue here, we agree with the majority of federal courts of appeal that have adopted the view that the word "sudden" has a temporal context. When "sudden" is combined with "accidental," the phrase means abrupt and unintended. There is no ambiguity in the context of the specific insurance policy at issue.

♦ We construe the policy to mean that (i) basic coverage arises from the occurrence of unintended damages, but (ii) such damages as arise from the discharge of various pollutants are excluded from the basic coverage, except that (iii) damages arising from the discharge of these pollutants will fall within the coverage of the policy where such discharge is sudden and accidental.

♦ We hold that the pollution damage was not within the coverage of P's policy. The pollution took place over a period of many years and most of it occurred gradually. The spills and leaks were commonplace events that occurred in the course of daily business, and cannot be classified as "sudden and accidental."

Concurrence. Language should be given its plain and ordinary meaning.

Dissent. The majority ignores key factors in determining that the language is not ambiguous, fails to consider the intent of the insurance industry, and allows the insurance industry to abuse the rehearing process.

C. LIABILITY INSURANCE

1. **"Third Party" Liability Insurance System.** At present, most car owners carry insurance against whatever liability they may incur to third parties in connection with the operation of their vehicles (hence, known as "third party" insurance). Such insurance is also carried for homeowners liability, products liability, and malpractice, and the same principles apply. (*Compare:* "No-fault" insurance, discussed in Chapter XII, is "first party" insurance, meaning that the injured person makes a claim against the insurance covering his car and family, or a car involved in the accident, regardless of who is at "fault" in causing the accident.)

   a. **General operation of the "third party" insurance system.** When an accident covered by third party insurance occurs, the defendant's insurance carrier investigates the claim of the injured party (the plaintiff) and pays all the costs of defending any lawsuit that is filed.

      1) **Insurance carrier's role in lawsuit.** The suit is defended in the name of the insured defendant (rather than in the name of the insurance company), and the jury generally is not told whether the defendant is insured.

         a) **Direct actions against insurer.** Most liability insurance policies insure a defendant only against liability established by a judgment against him in a legal action. Therefore, until a judgment is returned, most states provide that the injured party has no direct action against the defendant's insurance company. (A very few states are contra by statute.)

    b)   **After judgment.** Once a judgment is returned, however, the plaintiff is treated as a third-party beneficiary of the defendant's insurance company's promise to pay any judgment against the defendant, and hence can sue the defendant's insurer directly if it fails to discharge the judgment against the defendant.

  2)   **Effect of intentional or "wanton and reckless" conduct.** Most liability insurance policies cover only negligent conduct by the defendant. Hence, in cases where a plaintiff alleges that the defendant was acting intentionally or "wantonly and recklessly" (usually in an attempt to claim punitive damages), the defendant's insurance carrier may refuse to defend, or may defend with a "reservation of rights," meaning that it pays the costs of defense but reserves the right to refuse to pay any judgment that is returned against the defendant if the jury finds his conduct intentional or "wanton and reckless."

b.   **Typical insurance policy clauses.**

  1)   **Omnibus and "drive the other car" clauses.** These clauses are typically found in automobile insurance. The omnibus clause covers the insured when other people drive his car. The "drive the other car" clause covers the insured when he drives cars other than his own.

  2)   **Medical payments.** Medical payments are frequently covered in policies and may be paid immediately.

  3)   **Uninsured motorist clause.** This clause in an automobile policy allows an insured to recover under his own policy when an uninsured motorist causes his injury.

c.   **Insured's duty of "cooperation."** An express or implied provision of every liability insurance contract is that the insured party will "cooperate" with the insurer, so that if the defendant acts collusively with the plaintiff, fails to testify when required, etc., the defendant's insurance carrier may be able to deny coverage as to any judgment against the defendant.

d.   **Insurer's duty of "good faith" settlement.** Every liability insurance policy has a maximum limit—*e.g.,* $25,000 for injury to any one person—and should a judgment be returned that exceeds the limit, the defendant is personally liable for the excess. Hence, courts today recognize that an insurance company owes a duty to its insured (the defendant) to attempt to settle any claims against the defendant within the policy limits, so as to avoid the risk of the defendant being held personally responsible for satisfying part of the judgment. The question is often phrased as to whether the insurer would have settled if the policy had no limits.

1) **Effect of insurer's breach of duty.** If the insurance carrier fails to make a reasonable effort to settle within the policy limits, it may be held liable for the full amount of any judgment subsequently returned against the defendant (including the excess over policy limits).

2) **Obligation to act in good faith--**

Crisci v. Security Insurance Co., 426 P.2d 173 (Cal. 1967).

Facts. Mrs. Crisci (P), a 70-year-old widow, was sued when her tenant fell through P's stairway and suffered a resulting severe psychosis. P had a $10,000 general liability insurance policy from Security (D). D was obligated to defend P in the tort action brought by the tenant against P. D's attorney and claims manager felt that a jury would award the injured tenant at least $100,000. D rejected one opportunity to settle with the tenant for $10,000 and another to settle for $9,000 (with P paying $2,500 of that amount). The tenant sued P and was awarded $100,000 (her husband was awarded $1,000). D paid P $10,000. P and the tenant settled for $22,000 cash plus a 40% interest in some property P claimed, and an assignment of P's cause of action against D. As a result of the judgment, P became indigent, hysterical, suicidal, and her physical health declined. P brought this suit against D for failure to settle the claim. The trial court awarded judgment to P of $91,000 plus $25,000 for mental suffering.

Issue. If an insurer unreasonably fails to settle a claim against the insured, is it liable for any resulting judgment against the insured?

Held. Yes. Judgment affirmed.

♦ In all contracts, there is an implied covenant of good faith and fair dealing. That implied covenant, in this context, has led courts to hold that when the insured's and the insurer's interests are in conflict, the insurance company must give at least as much consideration to the insured's interest as it does to its own. The test for this is whether a prudent insurer without policy limits would have accepted the settlement offer.

♦ Thus, rejecting a settlement that is within the policy limits, when there is a substantial possibility of a judgment in excess of those limits, will result in the insurer's absorbing losses that result from the failure to settle. (Liability is not imposed solely for a bad faith breach of contract; thus, absence of fraud, deception, etc., is not fatal to a plaintiff's cause of action.)

♦ Here, D breached its duty to consider P's interests and is therefore liable.

♦ The trial court's awarding P $25,000 for mental suffering is upheld. P lost her property and suffered mental distress and thus may recover for her mental distress, even though failure to pay under a contract is usually not actionable as a tort. In this case, the breach also constituted a tort.

Comment. Many states follow this court's lead in awarding special damages.

---

3) **Insured may assign its claim against the insurer.** It is further recognized that the defendant's cause of action against his insurance company for failing to make a reasonable effort to settle is assignable. Hence, if the plaintiff recovers a judgment in excess of the defendant's insurance limits, the defendant (in order to avoid personal liability for the excess) will usually assign to the plaintiff his cause of action against his insurance company.

4) **Bad faith breach of contract not necessary.** As the *Crisci* case demonstrates, the insurer has a duty to use due care to attempt to settle within policy limits whenever there is a substantial likelihood of a recovery exceeding those limits. Unreasonable failure to settle under these circumstances is at the insurer's risk of liability for the whole amount of any judgment against the defendant regardless of whether "bad faith" is shown. [Comunale v. Traders & General Insurance Co., 328 P.2d 198 (Cal. 1958)]

5) **Strict liability.** Other courts have suggested the adoption of a strict liability standard, making the insurer liable for every judgment above policy limits if it fails to offer settlement within those limits.

XII. THE NO-FAULT SYSTEMS

A. INTRODUCTION

Employer liability for employees injured at work was the field in which liability insurance first developed. Shortly thereafter, legislation was passed (now every state has such a system) to provide employer contributions to a state fund to compensate injured employees, regardless of fault (known as "workers' compensation"). Benefits are limited in amount and duration. In most states, employers can alternatively insure against these risks, or employees may choose to be governed by traditional fault principles.

B. WORKERS' COMPENSATION

1. **Introduction.** Workers' compensation covers accidents "arising out of and in the course of employment." Typically, workers' compensation is the sole remedy an employee has against his employer. Further, accidents occurring in commuting to and from work are not covered (the "coming and going" rule).

2. **"Arising Out of and in the Course of Employment"--**

Clodgo v. Industry Rentavision, Inc., 701 A.2d 1044 (Vt. 1997).

Facts. Clodgo (P) was a manager in one of Rentavision's (D's) stores. On a slow workday, P and another co-worker began firing staples at each other. One of the staples struck P in the eye and P filed a claim for workers' compensation. D argued that P's conduct was noncompensable but P was awarded full benefits. D appeals.

Issue. Does P's conduct bar him from recovering under Vermont's Workers' Compensation Act?

Held. Yes. Judgment reversed.

♦ An injury arises out of employment only if the responsibilities associated with that employment placed P in a position where he was injured. P needs to establish that he would not have been injured *but for* his employment and his position at work. In this case, P was injured during work hours, therefore the injury would not have occurred but for his employment.

♦ P also must show that his injury occurred during the course of employment— *i.e.*, while P was on duty and fulfilling the duties associated with his employment. To determine whether P was acting within the course of his employment, we must inquire into whether he deviated too far from his duties when engaging in the "horseplay." We need to consider: (i) the extent and seriousness of the deviation, (ii) whether the deviation was commingled with the work, (iii) whether the deviation was an accepted part of the employment, and (iv) whether the nature of the employment includes this type of deviation.

♦ P's injury did not occur during the course of his employment. The conduct engaged in by P and the co-worker was dangerous. Although employees frequently shot staples at each other, it was not an accepted part of P's employment nor did the conduct advance D's interests. Also, there was no commingling with work duties because the injury was unrelated to any legitimate use of the stapler.

Dissent. P's conduct was not a serious deviation because there were no customers at the time and business was slow; therefore, there were no duties from which to deviate. The conduct was a common occurrence in the store and P would not have been fired for such conduct. It was a "tacit" part of the employment.

---

3. **"Coming and Going Rule"--**

Wilson v. Workers' Compensation Appeals Board, 545 P.2d 225 (Cal. 1976).

Facts. Wilson (P) was injured in an accident while driving to the elementary school where she taught. She had with her materials used in an art class, materials graded at home, and a few books. The Workers' Compensation Referee found that her injuries were job-related. The Workers' Compensation Appeals Board reversed, finding that (i) P's home was not her job site, (ii) only convenience motivated the automobile trip (she could have taken public transportation), and (iii) the transportation of work-related items was not a major part of the trip. P appeals.

Issue. Is driving to work with some incidental work-related materials an exception to the "coming and going" rule?

Held. No. Judgment affirmed.

♦ Under the "coming and going" rule, workers' compensation does not cover travel to or from work.

♦ The fact that P, for her own convenience, graded papers at home does not make her home a second job site. She could do the work at school. The commute is not a business trip.

♦ Transporting materials used in an art class, while perhaps necessary, does not warrant an exception to the "coming and going" rule. Such a commute was incidental to P's employment, not part of it.

Dissent. This case comes under an exception to the "coming and going" rule because P was required to furnish her own transportation to the job.

Comment. There are numerous exceptions to the "coming and going" rule. Extensive litigation has dealt with the coverage of the rule and the exceptions.

---

4. **Compensation Benefits.**

   a. **Statutory.** All workers' compensation benefits have a statutory basis. The statutes typically set a formula for the determination of the allowable benefit.

   b. **Amounts.** Using the formula to determine the amount of recovery requires reference to the statutes of the jurisdiction involved. Most states, however, consider the seriousness of the injury, expected length of incapacity, and average weekly wage of the worker. This provides lost wages. States also set a maximum amount allowable.

5. **Exclusive Remedy.** The workers' compensation statutes provide prompt, certain recovery for injured workers. The worker does not have to prove fault and does not risk losing benefits due to contributory negligence, assumption of risk, or other defenses. The employer gains the benefit that the compensation benefits are limited in amount and are the exclusive remedy available to the injured employee.

   a. **Intentional wrongs by the employer.**

      1) **Narrow view--**

Rainer v. Union Carbide Corp., 402 F.3d 608 (6th Cir. 2005).

Facts. Union Carbide and two successive operators managed the Paducah Gas Diffusion Plant, an industrial plant with approximately 1,800 workers. The plant's primary purpose was uranium enrichment. The processing of uranium produced unwanted radioactive byproducts. Employees were kept ignorant of the byproducts, and company documents revealed that workers' safety was disregarded. There were no requirements that workers wash their hands, and into the late 1970s, they were not required to use respirators. Four workers and members of their families (Ps) sued the plant operators and General Electric, the supplier of spent uranium fuel to the plant (Ds). Ps did not display any clinical symptoms, but they claimed that they suffered certain subcellular damage to their DNA and chromosomes. Ps' claims were dismissed by the district court because there was no showing of present harm and because the Kentucky Workers' Compensation Act ("KWCA") provided the exclusive remedy. Ps appeal.

Issue. In the absence of evidence that an employer had the specific intention to injure its employees, does the Kentucky Workers' Compensation Act provide the exclusive remedy for claims brought for injuries?

Held. Yes. Judgment affirmed.

♦ Although Ps acknowledge that the KWCA is generally the exclusive remedy, they argue that their claim falls under one of the Act's main exceptions. This exception reserves a cause of action where a worker is injured "through the deliberate intention of his employer to produce such injury or death." Ps contend that the phrase "deliberate intention" includes conduct undertaken with the knowledge that it will produce a certain result, or is substantially certain to do so.

♦ *Fryman v. Electric Steam Radiator Corp.*, 277 S.W.2d 25 (Ky. 1995), was the first Kentucky Supreme Court case to directly address the meaning of "deliberate intention." The court stated that this phrase implies that the employer must have determined to injure the employee. Subsequent Kentucky cases have adopted this narrow reading. In *McCray v. Davis H. Elliott Co.*, 419 S.W.2d 542 (Ky. 1967), the court refused to equate wanton and gross negligence with deliberate intention.

♦ Ps argue that in other jurisdictions, the phrase "deliberate intention" includes instances where an employer acts with the knowledge that harm might follow. However, this is not the Kentucky Supreme Court's interpretation of the KWCA. The definition of "deliberate intention to produce injury" as used in the KWCA is much narrower than "intent" in general tort law.

♦ The "deliberate intention" exception of the KWCA only applies when an employer had a specific intent to injure an employee. Here, Ps presented no proof that Ds possessed the specific intention to injure the employees.

2) **Broader view.** In *Beauchamp v. Dow Chemical Co.*, 398 N.W.2d 882 (Mich. 1986), the plaintiffs sued Dow, claiming that it intentionally misrepresented and fraudulently concealed the potential danger of exposure to Agent Orange. The Michigan Supreme Court adopted the substantial certainty standard of the Restatement (Second) of Torts. Under this test, an intentional tort is not limited to consequences that are desired. If the employer knows that the injury is substantially certain to occur as a consequence of the ac-

tions the employer intended, he is deemed to have intended the injuries as well. The court held that in such cases, an employee may bring a common-law civil action against the employer, notwithstanding the exclusivity provision of the Workers' Disability Compensation Act.

C. NO-FAULT INSURANCE

1. Automobile No-Fault Insurance.

a. Introduction. About half of the states have adopted statutes changing the handling of auto accident claims through so-called no-fault insurance plans.

b. Advantages to adopting no-fault plans. Eliminating fault as the basis for liability in auto accident cases alleviates the following objectionable features of negligence actions:

1) **"All or nothing" recoveries.** The plaintiff gets nothing unless she can convince the jury that the defendant was at fault; likewise the defendant can convince the jury that the plaintiff was contributorily negligent or had assumed the risk (assuming no comparative negligence standard).

2) **Delays and expenses of litigation.** Proving fault requires litigation, with attendant expenses and attorneys' fees for both parties. Until a judgment is returned (or settlement made), an injured plaintiff gets nothing (although it is in the interim that she needs help the most); also, the increasing burden of such litigation has congested court calendars, so that plaintiffs frequently have to wait years for a trial.

3) **Inaccurate compensation.** There has also been concern that the settlement process has led to the overcompensation of small cases and the undercompensation of large cases.

4) **Cost of insurance.** Insurance premiums have soared due to the costs of litigation and high verdicts.

c. Operation of proposed no-fault plans. Although the plans already enacted or under consideration vary considerably, the following are the essential provisions:

1) **Mandatory insurance.** All car owners are required to obtain (and keep in effect) insurance covering claims arising out of the operation of their cars. Failure to do so usually results in forfeiture of

auto registration and/or driver's license. This policy would cover both liability and no-fault claims.

2) **Scope of coverage.** The insurance extends to all claims arising out of operation of any motor vehicle, without regard to fault.

a) Generally, this includes claims allowed under traditional tort concepts, as well as certain claims not presently allowed; *e.g.,* claims by an injured "guest" in an auto and by the driver who hurts herself by her own fault.

b) But the insurance does not apply to claims arising out of defects in the vehicle itself (*i.e.,* product liability claims, *supra*).

3) **Claims handled on "first party" basis.** Any driver or passenger injured in an auto accident would make a claim against his own insurer (*i.e.,* the policy covering the car the injured party was riding in), so that in the typical two-car crash, the occupants of each car would claim against the insurance covering their own car.

a) Under the present "third party" insurance system, the injured party usually makes a claim against the insurer of the other car.

b) The "third party" procedure would be retained only if the accident is not covered by first party insurance; *e.g.,* a pedestrian injured by an automobile would still make a claim against the insurer covering the car that struck her. (Under a few plans, however, if the pedestrian owned a car, she would claim against her own insurer.)

c) Since fault would be immaterial, the claims procedure is relatively simple; any disagreement between the policyholder and her insurance company as to the amount recoverable (below) is subject to arbitration.

4) **Damages recoverable.** None of the major plans provide insurance coverage for pain and suffering or disfigurement. Coverage is limited to economic losses (lost wages, medical bills, etc.). However, the plans vary considerably as to the amount of such coverage.

d. **Impact of no-fault plans.**

1) **Curtailment of tort litigation.** The plans vary concerning the extent to which traditional negligence actions (with traditional fault principles) would still be permitted:

a) **"Pure" no-fault.** A few proposals would abolish tort actions altogether. However, no state has adopted such a plan.

b) **"Partial" no-fault.** All existing plans currently allow at least certain actions.

   (1) Under some plans, tort actions can still be maintained for all but relatively minor cases. For example, under the Connecticut statute, the plaintiff can sue for pain and suffering whenever the medical expenses exceed $5,000.

   (2) Under other plans, however, only severe cases could ever be pursued in court. In one plan, for example, a tort action could be maintained for economic losses not covered by the injured party's own insurance, and for general damages in excess of $5,000, but only if the accident caused death, permanent injury or disfigurement, or inability to work for more than six consecutive months.

e. **Constitutionality of no-fault insurance--**

Pinnick v. Cleary, 271 N.E.2d 592 (Mass. 1971).

Facts. Pinnick (P) was injured in an automobile collision negligently caused by Cleary (D). He sought damages in excess of the amount permitted under Massachusetts's no-fault statute. The statute proscribes any tort action for personal injuries arising out of an automobile accident to the extent that the injured party is eligible to receive no-fault benefits and further proscribes damages for pain and suffering in any action in which the medical costs are less than $500. D interposed the statute as an affirmative defense. P sought declaratory relief and a declaration that the statute unconstitutionally deprived him of his full tort recovery.

Issue. Does the Massachusetts no-fault statute, in limiting certain tort actions arising from automobile accidents, violate constitutional principles of due process or equal protection?

Held. No. Judgment affirmed; the statute is constitutional.

♦ The statute bears a rational relation to the legitimate legislative objective of decreasing court congestion, the cost of auto liability insurance, and the disparity of the treatment of claimants.

♦ The statute does not eliminate the remedy of an accident victim but merely affords him a more certain, less time-consuming substitute remedy—payment by his own insurance company. Under the statute, tort actions are maintainable for damages beyond the available insurance coverage.

- The $500 in medical expenses threshold for a pain and suffering claim bears a necessary and rational relationship to the legislature's objective of keeping small cases out of court. Otherwise, pain and suffering claims could inflate cases of very small actual damage to exceed the insurance coverage and thus permit a tort action in circumvention of the statute. The $500 requirement is a justifiable departure from equal protection.

Comment. The monetary thresholds in different states vary greatly. Other states require various degrees of disfigurement, ranging from permanent disfigurement to cosmetic disfigurement that is permanent, irreparable, and severe.

---

2. Other No-Fault Systems.

    a. Reasons for expansion. With the success of automobile no-fault insurance, suggestions have been made to use the no-fault principles in other areas.

    b. Medical malpractice. If no-fault coverage were enacted for medical malpractice, several benefits would be gained. Patients would not have to prove fault but would give up other tort recovery.

    c. Vaccinations--

Pafford v. Secretary of Health and Human Services, 451 F.3d 1352 (Fed. Cir. 2006) (en banc).

Facts. Richelle Pafford (P) was diagnosed with Juvenile Rheumatoid Arthritis ("JRA") after she had been given a series of routine childhood vaccinations. P alleged that the JRA was the result of the vaccinations. However, there was no evidence of a proximate temporal relationship between the vaccinations and the JRA. A special master denied the claim. P appeals.

Issue. Did P prove that the harm would not have occurred but for the vaccinations?

Held. No. Judgment affirmed.

- A petitioner can obtain compensation under the vaccine injury program in two ways. In a "table" case, the petitioner must prove an injury listed in the Vaccine Injury Table within the specified time period for there to be a presumption of causation. The burden then shifts to the respondent to prove that a cause unrelated to the vaccination caused the injury or condition. In an "off-table" case, there is no presumption of causation, and the petitioner has the burden to prove that the vaccination caused the injury. P does not allege that she experienced a table injury. Thus, she must prove causation-in-fact or that the vaccine was actually the cause of her injuries.

- ◆ P must prove by preponderant evidence that the vaccinations were a substantial factor in causing the injury or condition and that the harm would not have occurred in the absence of the vaccination. We recently articulated an alternative three-part test. To show causation in fact, the petitioner must show: (i) a medical theory causally connecting the vaccination and the injury; (ii) a logical sequence of cause and effect showing that the vaccination was the reason for the injury; and (iii) a proximate temporal relationship between the vaccination and the injury.

- ◆ The special master correctly applied these tests. He stated that a petitioner must: (i) provide a reputable medical theory that establishes that the vaccination can cause the type of injury alleged; and (ii) prove that the vaccination actually caused the symptoms. He determined that P proved only one of the two prongs by a preponderance of the evidence. P showed that it is biologically possible that one or more of the vaccinations could cause JRA but did not prove that they were the "but for" cause of the disease.

- ◆ There was no showing of a defined time period during which one would expect to see the onset of JRA following the triggering event. Without this, other contemporaneous events might have been the cause of the injury. P tested positive for a bacteria, had a sinus infection, an earlier bout of tonsillitis, and an earlier cold and diarrhea. These multiple potential causative agents make it difficult to attribute "but-for" causation to the vaccinations. Any of the other contemporaneous events could have been the sole cause of the injury.

- ◆ In *Shyface v. Secretary of Health & Human Services*, 165 F.3d 1344 (Fed. Cir. 1999), this court held that, to establish a prima facie case, the petitioners had to show that the vaccination was a but-for cause of and a substantial factor in the infant's death. But it did not have to be the sole factor or even the predominant factor.

- ◆ Here, however, P did not establish that the vaccinations were a but-for cause of her illness. There was no evidence indicating an appropriate time frame in which the JRA manifests after a triggering event.

Dissent. The statute contemplates off-table situations where medically accepted time frames are not required to prove causation. The majority is thwarting the purpose of the statute. There was substantial evidence as to causation without the identification of a medically accepted temporal relationship. To hold that a prima facie case cannot be established in the absence of an accepted temporal relationship is inconsistent with the statute.

d. **The 9/11 Compensation Fund.** Eleven days after the terrorist-related attacks of September 11, Congress and the President enacted the September 11th Victim Compensation Fund of 2001 to provide compensation to the victims' families. Pursuant to the legislation, a Special Master, Feinberg, was appointed. Feinberg created a method for determining awards and provided materials to permit prospective claimants to estimate economic loss awards for annual incomes up to the 98th percentile of their average income between 1998 and 2000. The presumed noneconomic loss for decedents was $250,000, plus an additional $100,000 for a spouse and each dependent. Claimants could obtain individualized hearings at which they could present their own personal circumstances if their income exceeded the 98th percentile, or they could accept the presumed award at the 98th percentile. In *Colaio v. Feinberg*, 262 F. Supp. 2d 273 (S.D.N.Y. 2003), legal representatives of high-income victims who died in the World Trade Center tragedy filed an action objecting to the "sharp truncation of potential damage awards at the top of the earnings distribution, defined as those above the 98th percentile, or $231,000." The court found that the policies, regulations, and interpretive methodologies of the Special Master were reasonable and proper.

e. **The New Zealand plan.** The New Zealand Compensation Act provides a complete no-fault scheme. All personal injuries due to accidents are covered by insurance. Most tort claims have, therefore, been abolished.

XIII. DEFAMATION

A. INTRODUCTION

At common law, every element of the prima facie case of defamation was based on strict liability, except that of publication. Publication had to be intentional or negligent. Substantial changes in the proof requirements for many defamation cases have been brought about by modern constitutional decisions. This chapter is organized to present the common law principles first, with the impact of the constitutional decisions at the end.

1. **The Prima Facie Case Under the Common Law.** The prima facie case is as follows:

    a. There must be a publication.

    b. The matter published must be capable of a defamatory meaning.

    c. It must be understood as referring to the plaintiff.

    d. It must be understood in a sense defamatory of the plaintiff.

    e. It must cause damage to the plaintiff's reputation.

B. PUBLICATION

1. **Introduction.** In order to hold the defendant liable, the plaintiff must show that the defamatory matter was intentionally communicated by the defendant to some third person who understood it, or that the communication to the third person was made through the defendant's failure to exercise due care (*i.e.*, negligently).

    a. **Qualified privilege--**

Doe v. Gonzaga University, 24 P.3d 390 (Wash. 2001).

Facts. John Doe (P) and Jane Doe had a sexually intimate relationship while students at Gonzaga University ("Gonzaga"). After overhearing Lynch's (a student's) conversation regarding P and dissatisfaction with the way the school handled complaints about date rape, League, Gonzaga's teacher certification specialist, told Kyle, Gonzaga's director of field experience for student teachers, what she had overheard. They decided to investigate. League was concerned that the allegations she had overheard about P might affect the dean's ability to submit an affidavit supporting P's application for teacher certification. League, Kyle and Lynch (Ds) met, and Lynch said Jane Doe had told her P had sexually assaulted her three times. Lynch also said that she accompanied Jane Doe to the student health center soon after the last assault, and the nurse concluded that Jane Doe had been date-raped. League instituted an extensive investigation of date rape, which was conducted by Nore, an investigator for the Office of Public Instruction, and which included many witnesses, including Jane Doe. P was never informed of the investigation and was never asked for his side of the story. Jane Doe had told others she had been forced to have sex with P, but she equivocated on the question and refused to make a formal statement. After meeting with Ds and others, the dean concluded there was sufficient evidence of a serious behavioral problem to preclude her from signing the moral character affidavit supporting P's application for teacher certification. P first learned about Gonzaga's investigation the same day he made his final payment of fees and tuition to Gonzaga. After being called to the dean's office, P was given a letter from the dean explaining that in light of allegations of sexual assault, P would not be given the moral character affidavit required to support his application for certification to teach. The dean refused to tell P who had made the allegations against him. P and his parents were told there were no appeal rights. Jane Doe was married and unavailable at time of trial. In a videotaped deposition, she denied P had sexually assaulted her; she also denied that she had made many of the statements that Ds attributed to her and said Lynch had "really blown things out of proportion," and that there were falsehoods in the declarations of other Ds. P was awarded $500,000 for defamation and lesser amounts on other claims including invasion of privacy. Ds appealed. The appellate court reversed the award and remanded the case for retrial on the defamation claim. P appeals.

Issue. Was the jury properly instructed, and is there substantial evidence to sustain the jury's verdict on the defamation claim?

Held. Yes. Judgment affirmed in part and reversed in part. Case remanded to reinstate the judgment on all claims except negligence, which is to be dismissed.

♦   A defamation plaintiff must show falsity, an unprivileged communication, fault, and damages. The defamation must be communicated to someone other than the person defamed; *i.e.*, there must be a "publication" of the defamation. Intracorporate communications are not "published" for purposes of defamation. The corporation is communicating with itself. However, when a corporate employee, not acting in the ordinary course of his or her work, publishes a defamatory statement, either to another employee or to a nonemployee, there can be liability in tort for resulting damages.

♦   Here, it could be found that Lynch was not acting in the ordinary course of her work as an office assistant when she told another student that P had injured Jane Doe during a sexual relationship. It could also be found that League was not acting in the ordinary course of her work as a certificate specialist when she eavesdropped and shared her concerns of possible misconduct with Kyle. Furthermore, it could be found that League and Kyle were not acting in the ordinary course of their work when they questioned Lynch and then disclosed P's identity and details about his sexual relations to Nore.

♦ While there is a qualified privilege for communications made between co-employees, that privilege may be lost if the employees are not acting in the ordinary course of their work. The trial court's instructions fully encompassed the principles of publication and qualified privilege in a corporate context. The jury was properly instructed.

2. **The Restatement.** Comment e to section 577 of the Restatement (Second) of Torts, which defines publication as "communication intentionally or by a negligent act to one other than the person defamed," provides that communication to an agent of the defamer is sufficient actionable defamation. This position has been widely followed. [*See, e.g.*, Hellar v. Bianco, 244 P.2d 757 (Cal. Dist. Ct. App. 1952)]

3. **Liability of Original Publishers, Republishers, and Disseminators.**

    a. **Original publishers.** Anyone who has any part in the original publication is liable.

    b. **Republishers.** Every repetition of defamation is another publication. Republishers are held to the same standards as original publishers since every repetition of the matter can cause harm. They are not, however, strictly liable. The plaintiff must show that a republisher published the matter intentionally (with knowledge) or negligently.

    c. **Disseminators.** A disseminator is someone who deals in the physical embodiment of defamatory matter, *e.g.,* a bookstore. Disseminators are liable only if they know or should know of the defamatory content.

4. **Modification of Web Page Not Republication--**

Firth v. State of New York, 775 N.E.2d 463 (N.Y. 2002).

Facts. Firth (P), former Director of the Division of Law Enforcement for the Department of Environmental Conservation, was responsible for weapons acquisition. The State Inspector General issued a report critical of P's managerial style and procurement of weapons. On the same day, the State Education Department made the report available on its Government Information Locator Service Internet site. P filed suit more than a year after the report was released, alleging defamation. The State (D) moved to dismiss on the grounds that the claim was time-barred. The trial court granted summary judgment to D, rejecting P's argument that the ongoing availability of the report via the Internet constituted a continuing wrong or new publication. The appellate court affirmed. P appeals.

Issues.

(i)   For statute of limitations purposes, is the single publication rule applicable to allegedly defamatory statements that are posted on an Internet site?

(ii)   If so, does an unrelated modification to a different portion of the website constitute a republication?

Held. (i) Yes. (ii) No. Judgment affirmed.

♦   The single publication rule states that publication of a defamatory statement in a newspaper or magazine gives rise to one cause of action and the applicable statute of limitations runs from the date of publication.

♦   If the multiple publication rule were applied to the sale of a book, for example, the statute of limitations would never expire while a copy of such book remained in stock and was offered for sale to the public.

♦   The purpose of a limitations statute is to "bar completely and forever all actions which, as to the time of their commencement, overpass the limitation there prescribed upon litigation." This purpose would be thwarted if the multiple publication rule was applied to mass media publications. Further problems with potential harassment and excessive liability would result in a draining of judicial resources.

♦   The policies underlying the original adoption of the single publication rule are relevant here. The posting of the Inspector General's report on the state's website resembles reports contained in traditional mass media, only on a far grander scale. Those policies are even more cogent when considered in connection with the exponential growth of the instantaneous, worldwide ability to communicate through the Internet.

♦   Republication occurs with a separate publication from the original, on a different occasion. It is not merely "a delayed circulation of the original edition." A second publication is intended to reach, and reaches, a new audience. Here, a modification of D's website cannot be equated to a separate edition of a book or newspaper. Many websites change frequently as newsworthy events occur.

♦   Applying the republication rule here would either discourage the placement of information on the Internet or slow the exchange of such information, reducing the Internet's unique advantages. In order not to retrigger the statute of limitations, a publisher would be forced either to avoid posting on a website or use a separate site for each new piece of information.

---

5.   **Internet Postings.** In *Zeran v. America Online, Inc.*, 129 F.3d 327 (4th Cir. 1997), an unknown party posted messages on an America Online ("AOL")

bulletin board advertising t-shirts with offensive slogans related to the federal building bombing in Oklahoma City using Zeran's name and telephone number. The posting led to Zeran receiving hostile messages and death threats at his home, and he subsequently asked AOL to remove the posting. Zeran later sued AOL for unreasonably delaying the removal of the posting, refusing to post retractions, and failing to screen for similar postings. The court held the Communications Decency Act of 1996 barred plaintiff's claims. Section 230(c)(1) of the Decency Act, 47 U.S.C., provides that "[n]o provider or user of an interactive computer service shall be treated as the publisher or speaker of any information provided by another information content provider." This section bars any suit that would make service providers such as AOL liable for information originating with a third-party user.

C. FALSE OR DEFAMATORY STATEMENTS

1. **Definition.** "A publication, without justification or lawful excuse, which is calculated to injure the reputation of another, by exposing him to hatred, contempt, or ridicule, is a libel." [Parmiter v. Coupland, 151 Eng. Rep. 340 (Ex. 1840)]

2. **Matter Published Must Be Capable of a Defamatory Understanding.**

   a. **Film--**

Muzikowski v. Paramount Pictures Corp., 322 F.3d 918 (7th Cir. 2003).

Facts. Muzikowski (P) attracted national attention after years of coaching Little League Baseball teams in poor sections of Chicago; his activities led to a book and the movie *Hardball*. P found the movie defamatory; a character identifiable as P was negatively portrayed and P claimed this amounted to disseminating falsehoods about him and his league. P had dropped out of school, became an alcoholic and drug user, was arrested after a bar fight and then changed his life. He became active in Little League. The O'Neill character in *Hardball* never stops drinking, scalps tickets, gambles, and commits crimes such as battery, theft, and disorderly conduct; he represents himself as a broker, but he has no license. He is shown to have no interest in children; he becomes involved in Little League only to pay off a gambling debt. No character in the movie is named Robert or Muzikowski and there are no references to Little League Baseball. The movie credits state, "While this motion picture is in part inspired by actual events, persons and organizations, this is a fictitious story and no actual persons, events or organizations have been portrayed." Publicity about the movie referred to the book that preceded it, and P began receiving telephone calls; at least one press release mentioned him by name and stated the movie was about "a former addict turned devout Christian, who coaches a Little League baseball team." P filed a libel suit after the preview of the movie was released and sought a preliminary injunction to prevent its release. Later, P dismissed the suit in California and filed this case in Illinois, asserting claims of defamation and false light invasion of privacy under Illinois law. P also moved for a temporary restraining order to prevent release of the film, which the district court denied. The district court, relying on Illinois substantive and pleading rules, granted D's motion to dismiss. An Illinois defamation claimant may state a claim for defamation per se (so harmful that damages are presumed) or defamation per quod (extrinsic facts required to show defamatory meaning). The district court found P had not stated a per se claim because D's statements were "reasonably capable" of "innocent construction" or of referring to someone other than P. It dimissed the per quod claim because P had not met the heightened pleading standard for special damages and pecuniary loss. P appeals.

Issue. Does Illinois's pleading law apply to P's claim?

Held. No. Judgment reversed and case remanded.

♦	In Illinois, P may recover with a per se claim only if D's statements impute that P (i) committed a criminal offense; (ii) was infected with a venereal disease; (iii) was unable to perform or lacked integrity in the discharge of duties of public office; (iv) fornicated or committed adultery; or (v) used words that prejudiced P in his trade, profession, or business, and if the statements cannot reasonably be innocently interpreted or interpreted as referring to someone other than P. If a statement is capable of two constructions, the innocent one will prevail. This determination is a matter of law and is made by a judge.

♦	The fact that the story is labeled "fiction" or that a character has a different name does not mean it may not be defamatory per se. A character may so closely resemble a plaintiff that a reasonable person would understand the character was meant to represent the plaintiff.

♦	In Illinois, there is a heightened pleading standard where a plaintiff is not named. A plaintiff must state on the face of the complaint that third parties (other than plaintiff and defendant) must have reasonably understood that the allegedly defamatory material was about the plaintiff and related to him. This pleading rule does not apply in federal court, however. P is entitled to notice pleading; his claim was sufficient to put D on notice.

♦	Here, P's character lies when he represents that he is a securities broker. State law provides that alleging or implying that a person is not a legitimate member of his profession is defamatory per se. P has also adequately alleged that D has imputed to him the commission of a crime punishable by imprisonment, theft, which has been held to be defamatory per se.

♦	P may be able to show there is no *reasonable* interpretation of the movie that would support an innocent construction, and that no person other than him was meant. He is entitled to prove his case under a defamation per se theory.

♦	P's complaint did not state a claim for defamation per quod. He did not raise that argument in his opening brief and therefore waived the claim. In addition, he did not itemize his losses or plead specific damages for actual financial injury. We affirm the district court's judgment on that claim.

---

b.   Author's opinion--

Wilkow v. Forbes, Inc., 241 F.3d 552 (7th Cir. 2001).

Facts. Forbes Magazine (D) ran an article on pending complex litigation involving a bankruptcy ruling of interest to the business community. The article concerned a case in which the Court of Appeals had approved a new-value exception to the absolute priority rule to allow equity investors to retain ownership of an office building, in exchange for infusion of about $6 million in new capital over a five-year period, even though the principal lender would fall about $38 million short of full repayment after filing a bankruptcy petition. The author complained that "many judges, ever more sympathetic to debtors, are allowing unscrupulous business owners to rob creditors." The article noted a partnership led by Wilkow (P) had pleaded poverty and "stiffed" the bank, paying $55 million on a $93 million loan while retaining ownership of the building. P's libel suit was dismissed by the district court and P appeals.

Issue. Was P defamed by D's assertion that he was in poverty (or, worse, "pleaded poverty" when he was solvent) and had filched the bank's money?

Held. No. Judgment affirmed.

♦   Illinois law governs the claim and New York law governs the defense of privilege. In Illinois, a statement of fact is not shielded from an action for defamation by being prefaced with the words "in my opinion," but if it is plain that the speaker is expressing a subjective view, an interpretation, a theory, conjecture, or surmise, rather than claiming to be in possession of objectively verifiable facts, the statement is not actionable.

♦   Words like "stiffing" and "rob" convey the author's objection to the new-value exception. She criticizes judicial willingness to allow debtors to retain interests in exchange for new value, not debtors who seize opportunities allowed by law. There is nothing in the article that implies P did anything illegal. Readers were informed that P's proposed reorganization plan was court-approved. The material in the article was largely from public documents. The words "pleaded poverty" do not imply that P was destitute and unable to pay his personal creditors, an allegation that would have been defamatory. In context, the words convey the idea that the partnership could not repay the loan out of rents received from the building's tenants. P's partnership *did* file a petition in bankruptcy, which is one way of "pleading poverty." An author's opinion about business ethics is not defamatory under applicable law.

---

3. **The Matter Must Be Taken as Referring to Plaintiff.** Any living person or other legally recognized entity may sue for defamation.

    a. Ordinarily, an unincorporated association cannot sue. However, some recent cases allow such suits. Further, even if the unincorporated association cannot sue, individual members thereof may sue if it is clearly defamatory of them.

    b. The defamation of a deceased person may also be defamatory of a living person and hence actionable.

D. LIBEL AND SLANDER

1. **Introduction.** The scope of damages recoverable for defamation depends on the form of the publication; *i.e.,* whether it is libel or slander. Special rules limit the recovery in slander actions.

    a. **Libel.** Libel is defamation usually appearing in some written or printed form; *i.e.,* reduced to some permanent, physical embodiment such as in newspapers, a letter, etc.

    b. **Slander.** Slander is usually oral defamation—representations to the ear rather than to the eye. The principal character of slander is that it is in a less physical form.

        1) Defamation in the form of slander is not actionable unless there is a showing of special damages or the defamation is of a class that the law deems actionable "per se."

        2) *See* the discussion of slander per se, *infra,* for a description of the four slander per se categories and the difference between general and special damages.

2. **Difficult Cases.** In some cases, it is very difficult to determine whether the publication is slander or libel. For example, the defamations may be contained on a phonograph record or a videotape.

    a. **Factors considered.** In these cases, the courts usually consider the following factors:

        1) The permanency or nonpermanency of form;

        2) The area of dissemination; and

        3) Whether the publication is deliberate or premeditated.

    b. **Restatement.** The Restatement (Second) of Torts, section 568A, provides that "broadcasting of defamatory matter by means of radio or television is libel, whether or not it is read from a script." Most modern cases follow this rule.

3. **Slander Per Se and Libel Per Quod.**

    a. **Slander damage rules—generally.**

        1) **Note constitutional modifications.** Care must be used in reviewing the damage principles applicable to libel and slander. The constitutional decisions now require proof of actual damages in many cases.

        2) **Two types of compensatory damages.**

            a) General compensatory damages are available where the words are actionable per se and the plaintiff prevails (or in other cases where the plaintiff has also proven special damages). At common law they were presumed to be the natural or probable consequences of the defendant's conduct, so the plaintiff did not need to show actual damages.

            b) Special compensatory damages must be pecuniary in nature and must be alleged in the pleading and proven by the evidence.

        3) **Punitive damages.** Punitive damages were given only when claimed in the pleadings and the evidence showed common law malice.

    b. **Four categories.** It is unnecessary to prove special damages in four (and only four) slander situations:

        1) The defendant charges that the plaintiff has committed a serious, morally reprehensible crime, or that the plaintiff has been incarcerated for such a crime.

        2) The defendant imputes to the plaintiff a presently existing, loathsome, communicable disease (venereal disease, leprosy, etc., but not tuberculosis, insanity, etc.).

        3) The defendant imputes to the plaintiff conduct, characteristics, etc., incompatible with the proper performance of the plaintiff's business, trade, office, or profession.

        4) The defendant imputes unchastity to a woman plaintiff.

    c. **Libel damage rules—generally.** At common law, most jurisdictions presumed general damages from the fact that the defamation was published. However, if the plaintiff proved special damages, he could recover those, too.

1) **Minority view.** To mitigate the common law strict liability imposed on publishers, general damages would not be presumed in libel per quod cases in some jurisdictions. Libel per quod means where the matter published is not defamatory on its face, but only when the matter is linked up with certain extrinsic facts. [*See* Ellsworth v. Martindale-Hubbell Law Directory, Inc., *infra*] A few cases apply the damage rules of slander, *supra,* if the statement is libel per quod.

2) **Retraction statutes.** These statutes generally provide that the news media cannot be held liable for general damages resulting from a publication unless they fail to publish a retraction. However, the plaintiff must demand the retraction. Special damages may still be recovered regardless of demand or retraction.

E. BASIS OF LIABILITY

1. **Pre-*New York Times Co. v. Sullivan.*** Prior to the *New York Times* decision, the basis of liability in a defamation case was strict liability. The plaintiff had to prove that the statement was defamatory and that was sufficient. The statement would be actionable even though the defendant believed it was true or even though the defendant may have reasonably believed that it was not defamatory, the statement would be actionable.

2. **It Matters Who Was Defamed--**

E. Hulton & Co. v. Jones, [1910] A.C. 20.

Facts. Hulton (D), a newspaper, ran an article about a Mr. Artemus Jones, a church caretaker, being with "a woman who is not his wife, who must be, you know—the other thing!" Artemus Jones (P), a lawyer who wrote signed articles for D, sued D for libel. D defended, contending that it had picked the name "Artemus Jones" as a fictitious name and did not intend to imply that P was with another woman. P produced witnesses who read the article and thought it referred to him. P recovered £1,750 in damages at trial. The court of appeals and the House of Lords both affirmed. The excerpt in the casebook comes from the discussion of the case in the House of Lords.

Issue. Is it "who was meant," rather than "who was hit," that matters in a libel action?

Held. No. It matters who was hit. D's appeal is dismissed.

♦ Libel is a tortious act and it does not matter whether or not the defendant, in his heart, intended no harm to the plaintiff. It suffices that others knowing the circumstances would reasonably think it to be defamatory of the person complaining of and injured by the defamation. Here, the jury found that P, who had been employed by D and was well-known in the area in which D's newspaper circulated, was so injured.

F. DAMAGES

1. Proving Special Damages—Slander--

Terwilliger v. Wands, 17 N.Y. 54 (1858).

Facts. Terwilliger (P) sued Wands (D) for slander. D told several people that P, a man, committed adultery. P learned of this, took ill because of it, and consequently could not do his farm work. P brought an action for slander per se. The trial court granted a nonsuit for D at the end of P's case. P appealed to the court of general term, which affirmed the trial court ruling. P appeals to the New York Court of Appeals.

Issue. Is it slander per se to impute unchastity to a man?

Held. No. Nonsuit for D affirmed.

- It is not slander per se to impute unchastity to a man; therefore, to recover for slander, P must prove special damages.

- Slander actions are given by law to remedy a damaged reputation. Generally, this reputation injury is shown through proving special damages. Loss of marriage or of customers, or the prevention of receiving some other benefit the plaintiff normally would receive, is sufficient damage.

- Slander actions are not available to heal wounded feelings. The words must be defamatory in their nature. They must disparage a plaintiff's character. Here, the words could have had that effect if believed.

- Harm caused by a third person's repetition of slander is deemed remote and is not actionable (*i.e.,* A slanders B, and C repeats A's comments).

- In this case, apparently no one believed the slander; hence, there was no damage to reputation.

- P tried to show damage through loss of health caused by the apprehension of damage to reputation. Even if P could have shown that his illness was the direct result of the defamation, the nonsuit would have been affirmed because fear of harm is not sufficient.

Comment. This case also shows how to prove damages. The court bases its holding in part on the consideration that any loss of health (such as occurred with P) is not a "natural, ordinary" consequence of P's character being damaged. Also, the imputation of unchastity to a woman is slander per se (so no special damages need be shown), but this rule has not been extended to men in most states as yet.

---

2.   **Special Damages—Libel Per Quod--**

Ellsworth v. Martindale-Hubbell Law Directory, Inc., 280 N.W. 879 (N.D. 1938).

Facts. In 1926, Ellsworth (P) was rated "a v 5 g" (legal ability very high, very good recommendations, financial worth $10,000 to $20,000, promptness in paying bills very good) by Martindale-Hubbell Law Directory (D). In 1928, the rating went down to "b w 5 f" (second class legal work, second class recommendations, net worth $10,000 to $20,000, and promptness in paying bills fair). P wrote to D a strong letter of protest. In 1929, D completely omitted P's rating from the directory, which P argued was defamatory since it implied that P's skills were too low to be rated. P sued D for libel, claiming that the 1928 and 1929 ratings were defamatory. The trial court granted D's demurrer and P appealed. The state supreme court held that the alleged defamation was not libel per se and remanded the case to allow P to allege special damages. In his amended complaint, P pleaded libel per quod and showed that his earnings were lower for the three years succeeding D's allegedly libelous rating. D demurred and was overruled. D appeals.

Issue. Must P prove the loss of specific clients in order to show special damages?

Held. No. Judgment affirmed.

◆   P received a lot of his clients from forwarders (people who referred clients to P based on his reputation). These people are nearly impossible to track down.

◆   While he has not shown the loss of clients by name, he is able to show a $2,500 reduction in income for the years he claims to be affected by D's libel.

◆   To hold that P had to give the names of lost clients would, in effect, deny P a remedy for D's alleged wrongdoing.

◆   Therefore, the diminution in income is sufficient proof of special damages.

Dissent. Unless P can show the names of clients he lost due to the alleged slander, he cannot prove that the complained-of statement was capable of a defamatory understanding (a requirement of libel per quod).

3. General Damages.

a. Excessive damages--

Faulk v. Aware, Inc., 231 N.Y.S.2d 270 (Sup. Ct. 1962).

Facts. Faulk (P), an actor, brought a libel action against Aware (D), a membership corporation whose purpose was to combat communism in the entertainment and communication industries. D widely distributed statements charging P with communist sympathies and affiliations. A jury awarded P $1 million compensatory damages and $1.25 million punitive damages against each defendant (Aware and Hartnett, its founder/president). D moved to set aside the verdict, contending that the award was excessive.

Issue. Was the award of damages excessive?

Held. No. Motion denied.

♦ Compensatory damages are awarded in libel to compensate a plaintiff for injury to his reputation (both personal and professional), mental anguish and distress, and loss of income.

♦ P presented unrebutted testimony of injury to his future earning capacity (which was $150,000 to $500,000 per year). Multiplying $150,000 by six years (the time period involved), the jury would arrive at $900,000 for loss of future income. The jury could easily take into account injury to P's reputation, mental anguish, etc., and arrive at a total of $1 million as compensatory damages.

♦ Punitive damages may be awarded if the jury finds the defendant's conduct to be malicious, or evidencing a reckless and wanton indifference to the plaintiff's rights.

♦ Here, P's attorney asked for an award of $1 million for punitive damages and the jury awarded a greater amount. There was sufficient evidence for a jury to find D's conduct wanton and/or malicious. As to the amount of punitive damages, taking note of the nature of the evidence, the fundamental issues of this case, and the jury's conclusions, the amount of punitive damages is sustained.

b. On appeal--

Faulk v. Aware, Inc., 244 N.Y.S.2d 259 (App. Div. 1963).

Facts. Same as preceding case. This is the appeal by D to the intermediate appellate court.

Issue. Was the award of damages excessive?

Held. Yes. Judgment reversed unless P consents to a reduction in damages.

♦ The compensatory damages are grossly excessive. Prior to the libel, P never earned more than $35,000 per year. Expert testimony by P's witnesses left plenty of room for speculation. An award of $400,000 is enough for compensatory damages.

♦ Since Hartnett, the chief actor in the libel, was more culpable than Aware, they should not be subjected to the same punitive damages. However, the punitive damages were excessive in each case. Punitive damages are reduced to $50,000 for Aware and $100,000 for Hartnett.

G. NONCONSTITUTIONAL DEFENSES

1. **Truth.** At common law, truth was an absolute defense. The defendant could avoid liability by proving that the statements sued on were true. Modern constitutional decisions still recognize that truth defeats liability, but the burden of proof on that issue has changed. In order to recover, the plaintiff must now prove that the statement was false.

2. **Absolute Privileges.** These privileges are a complete defense to any action for publication of a defamation. They are not affected by a showing of malice, excessive publication, or abuse.

   a. **Governmental privileges.**

      1) **Judicial.** Witnesses, attorneys, judges, jurors, and the parties in an action are privileged to utter defamations that have some relevance to the matter at hand.

      2) **Legislative.** All federal and state legislative members are absolutely privileged to utter defamations while on the floor or in committee. The utterances need not be relevant.

      3) **Executive.** Top cabinet grade executives of state or federal government are absolutely privileged. This includes the President, his cabinet, and department heads. However, relevancy is a requirement.

   b. **Domestic.** A spouse may utter defamations of third persons to the other spouse.

1) **Minority view.** Some courts extend this privilege to utterances among members of the immediate family.

3. **Conditional Privileges.**

   a. **Introduction.** A conditional privilege is recognized in situations where the public is concerned in the matter directly (*e.g.,* zoning hearings, statements made to law enforcement officers, etc.) or indirectly (*i.e.,* the public is concerned through its agent, the press). Also, the protection of certain private interests is condoned through the granting of a conditional privilege.

   b. **Reports of judicial, legislative, or executive proceedings.** Other meetings or conventions in which there is a sufficient public interest (political conventions, medical conventions, etc.) are also covered under the rubric "conditional privilege," as are inferior legislative bodies and inferior executive and administrative officers and people reporting to them.

4. **Applications.**

   a. **Truth of statement--**

Auvil v. CBS 60 Minutes, 67 F.3d 816 (9th Cir. 1996).

Facts. In 1989, CBS's (D's) show "60 Minutes" featured a segment on daminozide, a chemical sprayed on apples. The segment was based on a Natural Resources Defense Council ("NRDC") report that addressed health risks associated with pesticides on fruit and D's broadcast focused on daminozide's carcinogenity. The program focused on the increased cancer risk to children which results from ingesting daminozide. The broadcast included several opinions on the issue and concluded with statements from a scientist, who stated that most manufacturers of apple products no longer use apples sprayed with daminozide, but they could not keep it out of their products completely. Consumer demand for apples and apple products reduced drastically after the broadcast was aired and many apple growers lost millions of dollars. Auvil and others (Ds) are apple growers in Washington and brought suit against D alleging product disparagement. Summary judgment was granted in favor of D. Ps appeal.

Issue. Have Ps raised a genuine issue of material fact as to the falsity of the broadcast?

Held. No. Judgment affirmed.

♦ In the absence of cases dealing directly with product disparagement, the Washington court looked to the Restatement of Torts and recognized that Ps here face a higher burden of proof than do defamation plaintiffs.

♦ To prevail on a claim of product disparagement (*i.e.,* trade libel), Ps must show that (i) D published a knowingly false statement that was harmful to the inter-

Torts - 203

ests of another, and (ii) D intended the publication to harm Ps' pecuniary interest. These requirements force Ps to prove the falsity of the disparaging statements. Here, Ps claim only that animal studies cannot be relied on in establishing cancer risk to humans. While the effects of ingestion of daminozide have not been studied in humans, such evidence is not sufficient to show a genuine issue for trial; lab tests on animals are a valid means of determining cancer risks to humans.

♦ Ps also claim that no studies have been conducted on the cancer risks to children from daminozide, but have not provided any evidence that it does not create a risk to children and therefore have not raised a genuine issue of fact as to the falsity of the statements.

♦ Ps argue that they have met their burden by proving that the broadcast sends a false message, but the analysis of falsity begins with the actual statements made, not from an implied message.

---

h. Protection of private interests--

Watt v. Longsdon, [1930] 1 K.B. 130.

Facts. Watt (P) sued Longsdon (D), a director of a company, for libel. D received a letter from a third party charging that P, an employee of the company, had immoral relations with P's housemaid. D, believing the truth of the statement, wrote to the third party requesting corroboration of the letter. Before the reply, D showed the letter to the chairman of the board of directors and to P's wife. At trial, the court ruled that the publications were privileged and that, absent evidence of malice, P had no action. P appeals.

Issue. Are communications made pursuant to a social or moral duty privileged?

Held. Yes. Judgment reversed and new trial granted.

♦ What would normally be a defamation may be privileged if: (i) the speaker has a duty or interest in the communication; and (ii) the communication is without express malice, so that the occasion is legitimately used instead of abused.

♦ The question arises: are any of the communications (to the original informant, to the other director, or to P's wife) privileged? This question must be answered in light of the facts in the case.

♦ Here, D had a moral or social duty to: (i) verify the truth of the accusation (consequently his letter to the informant requesting corroboration was privileged); and (ii) discuss the matter with the chairman of the board since P was an employee of the company and D and the chairman had a common interest in the affairs of the company.

♦ The communication to P's wife, however, stands on a different footing, and is not privileged. The general rule is that it is not desirable for anyone to interfere in the affairs of man and wife. D did interfere.

♦ Therefore, the appeal with regard to the communication to the informant and the chairman of the board is dismissed. A new trial is ordered on the issue of the communication to P's wife.

Concurrence. There was sufficient evidence of malice in the statement to the chairman of the board and informant to create a jury issue. The jury must decide if the privilege was abused.

Comment. The defendant is conditionally privileged to defame another if he has a correct or reasonable belief that some important interest in person or property is affected. Generally, there must be some relationship between the defendant and the person to whom the defamation is published: either some family relationship, business, or genuine interest in business affairs. For example, a brother is privileged to tell his sister, "Don't marry X; he has a venereal disease."

———————————

c. **Legal proceedings--**

Kennedy v. Cannon, 182 A.2d 54 (Md. 1962).

Facts. Cannon (D) was an attorney representing Charles Humphreys, a black man accused of raping a white woman, Mrs. Kennedy (P). D called Mr. Moore, managing editor of the local newspaper, and asked Moore what information the paper was going to print about Humphreys. After Moore related what the paper was going to print about the alleged rape, D told Moore that Humphreys told him that the woman submitted willingly to his advances. After some discussion, Moore told D he did not have room to print an article long enough to have the accounts by both P and Humphreys of the "rape." D reluctantly agreed to a shorter story. Moore printed a story that concluded, "Humphreys emphatically denies the charge. He says the woman submitted to his advances willingly." P sued D for slander. D argued that the allegedly slanderous statement was privileged as part of D's duty to his client. The trial court directed the verdict for D. P appeals.

Issue. Were D's words protected by a privilege?

Held. No. Judgment reversed.

◆ An attorney has an absolute privilege covering words spoken in a judicial proceeding, provided the words are spoken in good faith. Here, D's words were not made to anyone (judge, witness, jury, etc.) actually involved in the case, so they were not absolutely privileged.

◆ An attorney may have a qualified privilege, which would justify an otherwise slanderous communication to certain other persons, in order to protect the rights of society or his client. However, such a privilege only applies to a communication made in a proper manner and to proper parties only; *i.e.,* to parties having a corresponding interest or duty. D's communication was not qualifiedly privileged since his statement was made to a newspaper rather than to a proper party.

---

d. Reports of public proceedings--

Brown & Williamson Tobacco Corp. v. Jacobson, 713 F.2d 262 (7th Cir. 1983).

Facts. Brown & Williamson Tobacco Corp. (P) received a suggested marketing strategy for its Viceroy cigarettes that focused on trying to get young people to start smoking. This report suggested relating cigarettes to wine, "pot," beer, and sex. P rejected the report and fired the agency that sent it. Later, the FCC was studying advertising of cigarettes and noted that P had adopted many of the techniques in the report. Jacobson (D) did a news report for CBS (D) that discussed this FCC proceeding. The news report quoted from the FCC proceeding and indicated that P and its spokespersons were "liars" when they claimed that they were not selling cigarettes to children. P sued Ds but the trial court dismissed the complaint. Ds appeal.

Issue. Was Ds' report a fair comment on the FCC proceeding?

Held. No. Judgment reversed.

◆ The news report was libelous per se since it accuses P of the immoral strategy of getting children to smoke. It could also affect P's trade or business by leading to further restrictions on sales.

◆ D has the right to report on public proceedings and records, but those reports must be fair comments. Although the FCC had stated that P had adopted many of the ideas from the paper, it was an unfair comment to indicate that P had been trying to sell to children.

Comment. On remand, P won a judgment of $3 million in actual damages and $2.05 million in punitive damages. The trial court reduced the actual damages to $1. On appeal, the actual damages were raised to $1 million and the punitive damages were retained.

---

      e.   **Common law privilege of fair comment.** *Carr v. Hood*, 170 Eng. Rep. 981 (K.B. 1808), raised the issue of whether there was a privilege of fair comment in criticizing literary and artistic works. The court held that there was, and anyone who publishes a book commits himself to the judgment of the public. If a commentator on the merits of a book does not introduce fiction for the purpose of condemnation, he exercises a fair and legitimate right in criticizing the book, even if he uses ridicule or sarcasm.

H. CONSTITUTIONAL PRIVILEGES

    1.   **Public Officials and Public Figures.**

        a.   **Leading case--**

New York Times Co. v. Sullivan, 376 U.S. 254 (1964).

Facts. New York Times Co. (D), a newspaper, published an advertisement that criticized the action of officials in Montgomery, Alabama, with regard to their treatment of civil rights workers. The advertisement stated that the treatment violated constitutional rights of blacks through intimidation and violence. It was uncontroverted that many facts asserted in the advertisement were false. Sullivan (P), a Montgomery City Commissioner with responsibility for the police department, brought a libel suit against D and four black clergymen. P was awarded $500,000 in damages. The trial court held that a false publication is libelous per se if it injures an official in his public office or imputes misconduct to his office. The award was sustained by the Alabama Supreme Court. D appeals.

Issues.

(i)   May a public official recover damages for a defamatory falsehood relating to his official conduct if he does not prove that the statement was made with "actual malice"?

(ii)   May an impersonal criticism of a governmental operation be the basis of a libel suit brought by the public official responsible for the operation?

Held. (i) No. (ii) No. Judgment reversed.

♦   The constitutional guarantees of free speech and press require a federal rule that prohibits a public official from recovering damages for defamatory statements made without "actual malice."

♦   The advertisement here was an expression of protest on a major public issue and hence clearly qualifies for First Amendment protection.

♦   Protection of statements made in the exercise of a First Amendment freedom has never depended on the truth of the statement.

♦   Injury to official reputation affords no more excuse for repressing otherwise free speech than does factual error.

♦   The fact that the Alabama law allows the defense of truth does not save the law from unconstitutionality. A rule compelling a critic of official conduct to guarantee the truth of his statements on pain of a libel judgment imposes self-censorship and a dampening of free debate.

♦   The rule created by this case is analogous to that which protects federal officials from libel suits for their nonmalicious statements about private citizens.

♦   "Actual malice" means with knowledge of the statement's falsehood, or with reckless disregard of whether it is false or not. P's case lacks convincing proof of actual malice.

♦   Prosecutions for libel of the government cannot be brought even by an official who insists that they are a reflection on his conduct.

♦   There was no reference to P in the advertisement either by name or position, and there was no basis suggested at trial to justify P's belief that he was personally attacked by references in the advertisement to the police.

Concurrence (Black, Douglas, JJ.). The First and Fourteenth Amendments do not merely "delimit" a state's power to award damages to "a public official" for libel but also completely prohibit a state from exercising such power. D had an unlimited, unqualified constitutional right to publish the advertisement. Furthermore, the First Amendment leaves people and the press free to criticize officials with impunity.

Comment. This case holds, in effect, that media defendants (as well as nonmedia defendants, according to later cases) can defame public persons as long as the publication occurs without knowledge of the defamation's falsity, or in reckless disregard for the truth. A later Supreme Court case, *Herbert v. Lando,* 441 U.S. 153 (1979), allowed the plaintiff to ask a TV correspondent for "60 Minutes" what his mental state was at the time he did the story. In other words, correspondents can now be questioned as to whether they did the story with "actual malice." As a practical matter, it is not hard for a correspondent to come up with a justifiable reason for doing the story.

b. Public figures--

Curtis Publishing Co. v. Butts; Associated Press v. Walker, 388 U.S. 130 (1967).

Facts. Butts (P) was the athletic director and former football coach at the University of Georgia. Curtis (D) alleged that P "fixed" a football game. Walker (P) was a United States general who was alleged by Associated Press (D) to have participated in a leadership role in a campus disturbance at the University of Mississippi over racial integration at that school. In the state court libel actions, judgment was for Butts, but against Walker in part on the issue of "malice."

Issue. Is the constitutionality test that is to be applied to a public figure the same as is applied to a public official?

Held. Yes. *Butts* is affirmed and *Walker* reversed.

Plurality opinion (Harlan, J.).

♦   *New York Times v. Sullivan* does not preclude a damage award based on improper conduct that creates a false publication.

♦   Neither plaintiff here has any position in the government. (*New York Times* involved a public official.) Neither plaintiff is entitled to a special privilege protecting his utterances against account liability in libel.

♦   Thus, we believe that a "public figure" (such as Butts or Walker) who is not a public official may recover for "a defamatory falsehood whose substance makes substantial danger to reputation apparent, on a showing of highly unreasonable conduct constituting an extreme departure from the standards of investigation and reporting ordinarily adhered to by professional publishers."

♦   This standard is satisfied in *Butts*, but not in *Walker*.

Concurrence (Warren, C.J.). The plurality formula for liability is an unusual and uncertain guide to liability. There should be no distinction between "public figure" and "public official." I, therefore, adhere to the *New York Times* standard. Under that standard, *Walker* must be reversed and *Butts* affirmed.

Concurrence and dissent (Black, Douglas, JJ.). *Walker* and *Butts* should both be reversed. *New York Times* should be abandoned. The press should be free from the harassment of libel judgments.

Concurrence and dissent (Brennan, White, JJ.). *Walker* and *Butts* should both be reversed. The evidence in *Butts* supports a jury award for P under the *New York Times* rule. However, the jury was not properly instructed under the *New York Times* rule, thus that case should be remanded for a new trial.

Comment. The effect of this split decision was the extension of the actual malice test of *New York Times* to public figures. The five justices concurring at least in part prevailed over the plurality opinion.

---

2. Private Parties Suing on Matters of Public Concern.

a. Private individuals--

Gertz v. Robert Welch, Inc., 418 U.S. 323 (1974).

Facts. Gertz (P), a reputable attorney, represented the family of a youth in a civil action against a police officer who had shot and killed the youth. Robert Welch, Inc. (D) published an article in its magazine accusing P of participation in a communist conspiracy against the police and of membership in two Marxist organizations. P sued D for libel and the trial court directed a verdict on the liability issue in P's favor because the statements were admittedly false and libel per se. The jury returned a verdict of $50,000, but the trial judge entered judgment n.o.v. for D on the ground that the article was about a matter of public interest and protected by the *New York Times* rule, absent a showing of malice. An appeals court affirmed.

Issues.

(i)   Is there a constitutional privilege to publish defamatory falsehoods about an individual who is neither a public official nor a public figure?

(ii)   May a private individual who sues for defamation be awarded punitive damages when liability is not based on knowledge of falsity or reckless disregard for truth?

Held. (i) No. (ii) No. Judgment reversed and case remanded for a new trial.

♦   An erroneous statement of fact is not worthy of constitutional protection, but it is inevitable in free debate. Some falsehood must be protected in order to protect important speech and avoid media self-censorship that results when the media are required to guarantee the accuracy of their factual assertions.

♦   Nevertheless, there is a legitimate state interest underlying the law of libel, which is the compensation of the victims of defamation.

♦   The balance of freedom of speech and the state's interest in protecting its citizens from libel requires that a different rule be applied to private individuals than that stated in *New York Times*.

♦ A private individual does not have the access to the media that is available to public officials and public figures to contradict the libel and minimize its impact.

♦ Public officials and public figures by their involvement in public affairs accept the risk of close public scrutiny. Private individuals who are defamed are thus more deserving of recovery.

♦ So long as they do not impose liability without fault, the state may define the appropriate standard of liability for defamation of a private individual.

♦ P, although he had been active in civic and professional organizations, was not a public figure. He had not sought public notoriety. Furthermore, he had never discussed the case with the media.

♦ Because of the competing interest of the First Amendment, state remedies for defamation must only compensate for actual injury, unless malice is proven.

♦ States may not presume damages of this type of case. Actual injury must be shown by competent evidence.

♦ The awarding of punitive damages must necessarily be carefully limited; otherwise, juries have the power to punish the expression of unpopular views.

Dissent (White, J.).

♦ The right of the ordinary citizen to recover for damage to his reputation has been almost exclusively the domain of the state courts. The majority opinion federalizes important aspects of these defamation laws. These sweeping changes ignore the past court history of defamation (where the risk of falsehood was on the publisher's shoulders if P was a private person).

♦ The private person should not have to bear the heavy burden of proving that his reputation has actually been injured (damages should be presumed).

♦ The majority is overly concerned with the potential for immoderate damage assessments by juries. Appellate courts can protect against that.

♦ The Court wrongly rejects the punitive damages (express malice) test in favor of the test requiring P to show intentional falsehood or wrongful disregard ("actual malice"). There is nothing constitutionally wrong with requiring a publisher to adhere to those standards of care ordinarily followed in the publishing industry.

♦ The *New York Times* doctrine is appropriate for public figures but it should not be stretched to cover the private person. Accountability is not forbidden by the First Amendment. People have the right to have their reputation protected by the states (Ninth and Tenth Amendments).

Comment. This case created the following rule: Liability without fault cannot be imposed on mass media. Thus, a plaintiff must prove either that the publisher knew the words were false or was at least negligent in ascertaining their falsity. If the press was negligent in defaming a private person, but did not do so deliberately or recklessly, that person can recover actual damages, but not presumed or punitive damages.

---

b.   **Later modification of *Gertz*.**

1)   ***Gertz* held to apply to matters of public concern.** *New York Times* and *Gertz* both dealt with news media defendants. In subsequent cases, however, a majority of the Justices have indicated that the media-nonmedia distinction is not tenable. The *New York Times* standard was applied in a public figure-nonmedia defendant libel action in *McDonald v. Smith,* 472 U.S. 479 (1985), and in *Dun & Bradstreet, Inc. v. Greenmoss Builders,* 472 U.S. 749 (1985), *Gertz* was reinterpreted as restricting presumed and punitive damages for statements on matters of "public concern," regardless of the status of the defendant

2)   **Summary.** The basis of liability after *Gertz* and *New York Times* has several important requirements:

a)   Public officials and public figures must prove the actual malice standard.

b)   States may use any standard for private individuals in cases to which *Gertz* applies as long as it is not strict liability. A state may, therefore, use negligence or the actual malice standard. Most states have adopted a negligence standard.

c.   **Burden of proof on the issue of truth--**

Philadelphia Newspapers v. Hepps, 475 U.S. 767 (1986).

Facts. Philadelphia Newspapers (D) owned several newspapers that wrote articles indicating that Hepps (P) had ties to organized crime. P sued D for libel. The trial court held that P had the burden of proving either negligence or malice, but the issue of truth was for D. D would have a complete defense if D could prove the statement was true. The jury held for D and P appealed. The Pennsylvania Supreme Court held that the issue of truth was for D, but remanded for a new trial. The Supreme Court granted certiorari.

Issue. Under the Constitution, can the burden of proof on the issue of truth in a defamation case be placed on the defendant?

Held. No. Judgment reversed.

♦ In cases by private figures against non-news media defendants, the constitution may not require change in the common law of defamation.

♦ Where the news media is the defendant, the Constitution requires additional burdens to protect free speech.

♦ Burden of proof problems only arise when neither party can prove the issue. Where, for example, a statement could not be proven either true or false, the placing of the burden of proof will determine the outcome of the case. The Constitution requires that the slight advantage be tipped in favor of free speech.

♦ The plaintiff, therefore, will have the burden of proving that a statement is false.

Dissent (Stevens, J.). Placing the burden of proving that the statement is false on the plaintiff is inappropriate. The plaintiff must already prove that the defendant was either negligent or malicious. The only type of case where this issue will arise, therefore, is where the plaintiff has already proven that the defendant is a wrongdoer. The burden of proving truth should remain on the defendant.

XIV. PRIVACY

A. INTRODUCTION

1. **Introduction.** The gist of the tort of invasion of privacy is not injury to reputation, but interference with the "right to be let alone" that results in injury to feelings, without regard to any effect on property, business, or reputation. Most states recognize this tort by case law, and some do by statute. Some states do not recognize it at all.

2. **The Prima Facie Case.**

   a. **Introduction.** The elements of the cause of action are:

      1) **Act by the defendant.** The act may consist of words or any type of affirmative conduct.

      2) **Serious and unreasonable invasion of the plaintiff's privacy.** This is the crux of most invasion of privacy suits.

      3) **Intent, negligence, or strict liability.** Most invasion of privacy suits involve intentional acts, but this is not essential. Liability may be imposed for negligent invasions and, at common law, even for invasions based on strict liability. Constitutional privileges may affect this element of the case.

      4) **Causation.**

      5) **Damages.**

   b. **Types of actions.** There are four types of actionable invasions of privacy:

      1) Appropriation of another's name or likeness;

      2) Unreasonable publicity given to the other's private life;

      3) Publicity that unreasonably places the other in a false light before the public; and

      4) Unreasonable intrusion upon the seclusion of another.

B. INTRUSION

1. **Unreasonable Intrusion--**

Nader v. General Motors Corp., 255 N.E.2d 765 (N.Y. 1970).

Facts. Nader (P), an author and lecturer on automotive safety and a critic of General Motors (D), brought suit alleging that D conducted a campaign of intimidation against him in order to suppress his criticisms and prevent his disclosure of information about its products. Among other things, P alleged that D had tapped his phone, electronically eavesdropped on private conversations, and kept him under surveillance. D moved to dismiss P's complaint. Two courts upheld the legal sufficiency of P's cause of action. The appellate court certified the question to the New York Court of Appeals as to whether the alleged conduct would constitute a tort for invasion of privacy.

Issue. Does the seeking of confidential information through wiretapping, electronic eavesdropping, and surveillance constitute an actionable invasion of privacy?

Held. Yes. Judgment affirmed.

- There is a cause of action for invasion of privacy based on the right to be free from intrusions in private matters.

- To constitute an actionable intrusion, there must be more than a mere gathering of information. The information sought must be of a private nature.

- Conduct that merely harasses or attempts to uncover information that P has already revealed to others is not an actionable invasion.

- "Overzealous" surveillance designed to obtain private information may be actionable, as well as wiretapping and electronic eavesdropping.

Concurrence. It is not appropriate to characterize several of P's allegations as referable only to intentional infliction of mental distress, a more restricted tort than the common law right of privacy.

---

2.   **No Trespass--**

Desnick v. American Broadcasting Co., Inc., 44 F.3d 1345 (7th Cir. 1995).

Facts. American Broadcasting ("ABC") (D) is sued by the Desnick Eye Center and two of its surgeons (Ps) for trespass and defamation, among other torts, arising out of a segment featured on its program *Prime Time Live*. Prior to filming the segment, which was to focus on large cataract practices, D contacted Dr. Desnick and asked permission to interview doctors, technicians, and patients at one of its locations and to film a live cataract operation. Dr. Desnick consented upon reassurance that the segment would involve other cataract practices and there would be no "ambush interviews or undercover surveillance." However, D sent seven people with hidden cameras to two of Ps' other locations, where they posed as patients. When the segment aired, it focused only on Ps' practice and stated that Ps were performing unnecessary cataract operations, with negative interviews from former patients, employees, and an ophthalmic surgeon. Ps appeal dismissal of their suit.

Issues.

(i)   Is the evidence as presented sufficient to reach the jury on defamation?

(ii)   Did D commit a trespass by sending the seven undercover people into Ps' clinics?

Held. (i) No. (ii) Yes. Judgment affirmed in part, reversed in part and case remanded.

♦   Generally, a journalist does not have a privilege to commit a trespass, and consent is not implied when the express consent given was based on a misrepresentation or omission. Ps would not have consented to the segment had they known that undercover people would be sent into their clinics.

♦   However, consent will sometimes be given effect even if it was procured by fraud if there is no invasion of the interests sought to be protected by the tort of trespass. In this case, Ps' offices were open to the public and the surgeons that were videotaped were engaging in professional conversations with patients; there was no eavesdropping on personal conversations. D gained entry by misstating its purpose, but the entry did not rise to the level of trespass—D did not interfere with Ps' possession or ownership of the property.

C. PUBLIC DISCLOSURE OF EMBARRASSING PRIVATE FACTS

1.   Unreasonable Publicity Given to a Public Figure's Life--

Sidis v. F-R Publishing Corp., 113 F.2d 806 (2d Cir. 1940).

Facts. Sidis (P) was a famous child prodigy in mathematics. Eventually, he was repulsed with his life of fame and went to great lengths to avoid public scrutiny. An article in a magazine published by F-R (D) redirected public attention at P, tracing his attempts to conceal his identity. P sued D for invasion of privacy. The trial judge granted D's motion to dismiss the complaint. P appeals.

Issue. Are damages recoverable for the truthful revelation of the details of a public figure's life?

Held. No. Judgment affirmed.

- When focused upon a public character, truthful comments upon dress, speech, habits, and ordinary aspects of life are permissible.

- As a child prodigy, P was famous. His subsequent history revealing whether he had fulfilled his early promise was still newsworthy and a matter of public concern.

- An article might reveal facts so intimate as to outrage public decency. The newsworthiness of such an article might not be a defense.

Comment. If a reasonable person would find the disclosure of the private facts highly objectionable, then the plaintiff has a cause of action.

---

2. **Facts of Public Record--**

Cox Broadcasting Corp. v. Cohn, 420 U.S. 469 (1975).

Facts. Cohn (P) brought an action for damages against Cox Broadcasting (D), claiming that his right of privacy had been invaded by D's television broadcasts that, in the course of covering a criminal trial, gave the name of his deceased daughter, a rape victim. Relying on a state statute that made the publication of a rape victim's name a misdemeanor, the state supreme court upheld a lower court decision for P. D appeals.

Issue. May a state extend a cause of action for damages for invasion of privacy caused by the publication of the name of a deceased rape victim that is revealed in connection with the prosecution of the crime?

Held. No. Judgment reversed.

- Rather than addressing broader questions of privileges extended to truthful publications, this decision is limited to the facts of this case.

- In preserving our form of government, the First and Fourteenth Amendments command that the states may not impose sanctions for the publication of truthful information contained in official court records open to public inspection. Even the prevailing laws of invasion of privacy generally recognize that the interests in privacy fade when the information involved already appears on the public record.

- Such information contains none of the indicia of those types of communications that are of such slight social value that their importance is clearly outweighed by the social interests in order and morality. To embark on the course of forbidding publication of certain public records would invite timidity and self-censorship, and make it difficult for the press to inform their readers. If there are privacy interests to be protected, the states may do so by means that avoid public exposure or documentation.

Concurrence (Powell, J.). In cases such as this one, where public access to public records is involved, truth should be an absolute defense.

---

3.   **Newsworthiness Outweighs Offensiveness--**

Haynes v. Alfred A. Knopf, Inc., 8 F.3d 1222 (7th Cir. 1993).

Facts. Alfred A. Knopf, Inc.'s author wrote a journalistic history, *The Promised Land*, tracking black migration between 1940-1970 from impoverished rural areas to the cities. The study focused on individuals, one of whom was Luther Haynes's ex-wife. The book revealed Luther's heavy drinking, unstable employment, adultery, and irresponsible and neglectful behavior toward his family. When that marriage ended in divorce, Luther married his current wife. He now has a home, a steady job, and a position as deacon in his church. The Hayneses (Ps) sued the author and Knopf (Ds) claiming libel and invasion of privacy. The district court granted Ds' motion for summary judgment. Ps appeal.

Issue. May summary judgment properly be granted to a publisher who is sued for invasion of privacy after it publishes a journalistic history that includes information about the plaintiff in which the public has a legitimate interest?

Held. Yes. Judgment affirmed.

- The defamation portion of Ps' claim was properly dismissed on the ground that any deviations from the truth were too insubstantial to support a libel action.

- Ps' privacy action is concerned with the propriety of stripping away the veil of privacy with which we shield previous misconduct. This branch of the privacy tort recognizes the possibility of an involuntary loss of privacy and requires (i) that the private facts published be such as would deeply offend a reasonable person, and (ii) that they be facts in which the public has no legitimate interest.

- One of the author's major themes is the transposition of the sharecropper morality to the slums of the northern cities. This morality was characterized by a matriarchal family structure and an unstable marriage bond. The details revealed in the book to which Ps object are germane to the author's legitimate story which is of transcendent public interest.

♦ The public needs the information conveyed by the book, including the information about Ps, in order to evaluate the profound social and political questions that the book raises.

♦ Given the ruling in *Cox (supra),* all of the discreditable facts about Ps contained in judicial records are beyond the power of tort law to conceal. The disclosure of those facts would strip away Ps' privacy as effectively as the book has done.

♦ The questions of offensiveness and newsworthiness are ordinarily matters for the jury, not for a judge on a summary judgment motion, but summary judgment is properly granted to a defendant when, on the basis of the pretrial discovery, no reasonable jury could render a verdict for the plaintiff. That is the case here.

D. FALSE LIGHT

1. Constitutional Privilege of Reporting Newsworthy Events--

Time, Inc. v. Hill, 385 U.S. 374 (1967).

Facts. In 1952, Hill (P) and his family were held prisoners for several hours by escaped convicts. Thereafter, they moved and sought to avoid all publicity about their experience. *Life* magazine, owned by Time, Inc. (D), published an article about a play that was loosely based on this and other incidents. The play, although it varied substantially from the family's experience, was represented by *Life* to be a reenactment thereof. P brought suit for invasion of privacy and was awarded judgment. The judgment was based on a New York statute that gave no protection to fictitious publications about "newsworthy" persons. D appeals.

Issue. Does the constitutional protection for speech and press preclude recovery for false reporting of a matter of public interest in the absence of actual malice?

Held. Yes. Judgment reversed.

♦ Innocent or negligent erroneous statements upon public affairs must be protected if the freedoms of expression are to have the "breathing space" they need to survive.

- We would seriously impair the indispensable service of a free press if we saddle the press with the impossible burden of verifying all facts printed about an individual.

- The constitutional guarantees can tolerate sanctions against knowing falsity or the reckless disregard of the truth, *i.e.,* actual malice.

- The constitutional protections for speech and press preclude the application of the New York statute to redress false reports of matters of public interest in the absence of proof that the defendant published the report with actual malice.

Concurrence (Douglas, J.). Fiction should enjoy broad First Amendment protection.

Concurrence and dissent (Harlan, J.). Actual malice should not be the only standard. P should recover if D was negligent.

Dissent (Fortas, J.). The facts showing the story to be fictionalized prove that the actual malice standard was met.

E. COMMERCIAL APPROPRIATION OF PLAINTIFF'S NAME OR LIKENESS, OR THE RIGHT OF PUBLICITY

1. Right of Publicity--

Doe a/k/a Twist v. TCI Cablevision, 110 S.W.3d 363 (Mo. 2003).

Facts. Tony Twist (P), a former professional hockey player, brought misappropriation of name and defamation claims against Todd McFarlane Productions and the publishers and marketers (Ds) of *Spawn*, a dark fantasy comic book whose villainous character had P's name and his "tough guy" persona but no physical resemblance. P was known during his career as an "enforcer," a violent protector of goal scorers. On two occasions, McFarlane admitted in published responses to fan letters that the Tony Twist character was named for and based on P. In a published interview, McFarlane said he used real people's names to create characters' identities. Beneath the interview, there was a drawing of the Tony Twist character, a photo of Tony Twist's hockey trading card, and an affirmation that the character was named for Tony Twist, described as a "Goon" for the St. Louis Blues hockey team. Because of his popularity with fans, P endorsed products, made radio and television appearances, hosted a talk show, and was involved with a number of children's charities. P set out to create a positive image of himself and prepare for a career after hockey as a sports commentator and product endorser.

At trial, McFarlane denied that the character was based on P and also denied that he had benefited by using P's name. P countered by introducing evidence that Ds had targeted his fan base by manufacturing and selling hockey pucks and jerseys. P also introduced evidence that a diminution in the commercial value of his name as an endorser of products had occurred. A witness testified that after he learned that P's name was associated with the comic book character, his sports nutrition company withdrew a $100,000 offer to P.

The circuit court dismissed the defamation count. The jury trial on the misappropriation count resulted in a $24,500,000 verdict for P. The court, however, granted Ds' motion for a judgment notwithstanding the verdict ("JNOV") and alternatively ordered a new trial should the JNOV be overturned on appeal. The court also denied P's request for injunctive relief. P appeals.

Issue. Is Ds' use of P's name in the comic book protected speech under the First Amendment?

Held. No. Judgment reversed and case remanded. Order for injunction denied.

♦ P seeks recovery of the fair market value Ds should have paid to use his name and for damage done to the commercial endorsement value of his name. Thus, this case should be brought as a right of publicity action, rather than a misappropriation of name action.

♦ Although there are different types of damages that may be recovered in a misappropriation tort and a right of publicity tort, the elements of the two are basically the same. For the first, a plaintiff must show that the defendant used his name, without his consent, to obtain some advantage. In the second, the plaintiff must prove the same elements but also that the defendant used his name to obtain a commercial advantage.

♦ The elements of a right of publicity action include: (i) the defendant's use of the plaintiff's name as a symbol of his identity, (ii) without the plaintiff's consent, and (iii) with the intent to obtain a commercial advantage.

♦ To establish the first element, it must be shown that the name used by the defendant is understood by the audience to be referring to the plaintiff. P presented sufficient evidence to prove this.

♦ The court below held that there was no credible evidence that Ds intended to injure P's marketability or capitalize on the market recognition of his name and no evidence that Ds derived monetary benefit from the use of P's name. However, P did not have to prove that Ds intended to injure his marketability or that they derived a pecuniary benefit from the use of his name.

♦ The commercial advantage focus is on the defendant's intent to obtain commercial benefit from the use of the plaintiff's identity. Whether Ds intended to injure P or actually succeeded in gaining a commercial advantage is irrelevant. P had only to prove that Ds used his name intending to obtain a commercial advantage. Ds' statements and actions reveal their intent to create the impression that P was associated with the comic book. And P presented sufficient evidence to establish Ds' intent to gain a commercial advantage by using P's name to attract consumer attention. P also introduced evidence that Ds' products are marketed directly to hockey fans.

- ◆ *Zacchini v. Scripps-Howard Broadcasting Co.*, 433 U.S. 562 (1977), is the only right of publicity case decided by the Supreme Court. Although the Court's holding was limited to the facts of the case and does not control here, the Court discussed the right of publicity and the competing right to free speech. It explained that the rationale for protecting the right of publicity is to prevent unjust enrichment by the theft of goodwill. The Court also distinguished claims for right of publicity from claims for defamation and stated that the 'actual malice' standard does not apply in a right of publicity action.

- ◆ The threshold legal question in right to publicity cases is whether the use of a person's name and identity is "expressive" or "commercial." The first is protected; the second is not. The use of a person's identity in news or creative works to communicate information or express ideas about that person is protected expressive speech. But the use of an identity to advertise goods or services or the use of a person's name on merchandise is commercial speech and is rarely protected.

- ◆ The Restatement (Third) of Unfair Competition distinguishes between commercial and expressive speech by means of a "relatedness" test. Use of a name or identity in a work that is "related" to the person—such as in news reporting, creative works, and unauthorized biographies—is protected. If the name is used only to attract attention to a work not related to the individual, the user may be subject to liability. California courts use a "transformative" test. If the work at issue adds significant creative elements that transform the likeness into more than a celebrity likeness or imitation, it is protected.

- ◆ Both tests fail to consider that many uses of a person's identity have both expressive and commercial elements. These tests preclude a cause of action whenever the use is in any way expressive. They do not really balance the interests involved. But a "predominant use" test addresses speech that is both expressive and commercial, and its advantages can be seen in this case. P showed that the use of his identity was for a commercial advantage, but there is an expressive component. However, there is little literary value compared to the commercial value. Ds used P's name predominantly to sell books and other products, not as an element of artistic expression. Thus, free speech must give way to the right of publicity.

- ◆ Because the trial court's errors allowed the jury to find for P without a finding that Ds intended to obtain a commercial advantage, and because the jury might have determined that Ds gained a commercial advantage even though Ds did not intend it, the verdict is set aside.

♦ The trial court was correct in denying P's request for a permanent injunction because it was overbroad. The requested injunction tried to keep Ds from taking part in a variety of expressive activities that are not related to this lawsuit and are protected by the First Amendment, *e.g.,* a parody of P or a factual report on this action.

Comment. At the second trial, the jury found in Twist's favor and awarded him $15 million in damages.

---

2. **Appropriation After Death--**

Factors Etc., Inc. v. Pro Arts, Inc., 579 F.2d 215 (2d Cir. 1978).

Facts. Factors (P) purchased exclusive rights to exploit the name and likeness of Elvis Presley. Pro Arts (D) published a poster of Elvis after his death. P sued D and sought an injunction. The trial court enjoined D from distributing the poster. D appeals.

Issues.

(i) Did the exclusive license to the right to publicize Elvis Presley continue after his death?

(ii) Was Elvis Presley's death such a newsworthy event that D had a First Amendment right to publish the poster?

Held. (i) Yes. (ii) No. Judgment affirmed.

♦ The right to publicity is a valid property right which may survive death.

♦ The poster did not seek to "celebrate" a newsworthy event but merely to appropriate the publicity value.

Comment. The law on this point is not entirely clear. Other circuits have reached the opposite conclusion and held that the "right of publicity" does not survive death.

XV. MISREPRESENTATION

A. INTRODUCTION

1. **Scope of Tort.** Misrepresentation is a specialized area of the law where the plaintiff is seeking damages for some economic loss suffered because of reliance on a false statement. Although some recovery for a negligently made false statement is allowed, the traditional common law action for fraud or deceit required a knowingly made false statement.

2. **Basic Elements for Fraud.** The basic elements for fraud are:

   a. A false representation of a material fact;

   b. Scienter or knowledge that the statement is false;

   c. Intent to induce reliance;

   d. Justifiable reliance on the statement; and

   e. Damages.

3. **Negligence Elements.** The above elements apply to the action for fraud. Negligence actions change the requirement of scienter to failure to use reasonable care. Negligence also reduces the class of possible plaintiffs. Further details of the action for negligent misrepresentation will be discussed after the section on fraud.

B. FRAUD

1. **Common Law Action in Deceit--**

Pasley v. Freeman, 100 Eng. Rep. 450 (K.B. 1789).

Facts. Pasley (P) sold goods on credit to Falch. This sale was based on an assurance from Freeman (D) to P that Falch was a person "to be trusted and given credit." Falch did not have money and was unable to pay. P sued D, alleging that D had known that Falch would not pay. D appeals a verdict for P.

Issue. Can an action lie for a false statement made by a person who was not a party to the transaction?

Held. Yes. Judgment affirmed.

- ◆ (Buller, J.). When a statement is made while knowing that it is false, an action will lie. The law does not require the defendant to speak, but if the question is "answered at all, it shall be answered honestly."

- ◆ (Ashhurst, J.). The importance of the action is the plaintiff's injury. It does not matter that the defendant sought no personal gain.

- ◆ (Lord Kenyon, C.J.). The plaintiff needed the information for a business purpose. If he had not been injured, there would be no action. He did, however, clearly suffer loss.

Dissent (Grose, J.).

- ◆ There should be no action against the defendant since he was not party to the sale.

- ◆ This type of action gives the plaintiff an additional security where he should have only one.

- ◆ The plaintiff should have asked more than one person about Falch's credit.

---

2.   **Statement Must Be of Facts--**

Vulcan Metals Co. v. Simmons Manufacturing Co., 248 F. 853 (2d Cir. 1918).

Facts. Vulcan (P) bought the machinery and patents necessary to produce Simmons's (D's) vacuum cleaners. Subsequently, P sued D, claiming that D misrepresented the quality and performance of the machine, and lied about the fact that it had never been put on the market. P appeals from a directed verdict for D.

Issue. Can "puffing" ever render D liable for misrepresentation?

Held. Yes. Judgment reversed.

- ◆ There are some statements that no person takes seriously, unless he suffers from credulity. Some statements, like the claims of campaign managers before elections, are rather designed to allay the fear that would attend their absence.

- ◆ It makes much difference whether the parties stand on equality. In the case at bar, since P was allowed full opportunity to examine and test the cleaner, the parties must be considered equal in bargaining power. P has no right to treat statements like these as material in his determination, since D justifiably should have expected P to make an independent and adequate inquiry.

♦ As to the representation that the cleaners had never been put on the market, the question of its materiality is unsettled enough to put to the jury.

---

3. **Misrepresentations of Law.** Misrepresentations as to law or matters of law are not actionable under the general rule, since everyone is presumed to know the law and such misrepresentations are thus treated only as opinions. However, the plaintiff's reliance on the defendant's representations of law is usually justified when the representation is factual in nature.

4. **Failure to Disclose--**

Swinton v. Whitinsville Savings Bank, 42 N.E.2d 808 (Mass. 1942).

Facts. Whitinsville (D) sold a house to Swinton (P) knowing it to be infested with termites, but made no mention of the fact to P. P could not readily ascertain the condition and later incurred considerable expense for termite control. P brought suit against D for fraudulent concealment. P appeals from a judgment for D.

Issue. Does a seller's mere nondisclosure of a known defect in a home constitute fraudulent concealment?

Held. No. Judgment affirmed.

♦ A vendor who fails to disclose a latent defect is not liable therefor. Mere nondisclosure when dealing at arm's length is no basis for an action for misrepresentation.

♦ There was no fiduciary relation between the parties. D did nothing to prevent P from discovering the defect. The law does not require sellers to disclose every known nonapparent defect any more than it requires buyers to disclose every known nonapparent virtue.

Comments.

♦ This rule has been changed in many jurisdictions by statute or case law where a home sale is involved. Typical is the California statute, which requires a termite inspection by a licensed exterminator before the home may be sold.

♦ When the plaintiff seeks equitable relief (*e.g.,* rescission of contract), courts have been much more liberal and often grant relief. When the parties stand in some confidential or fiduciary relationship, the defendant may be liable for nondisclosure. Also, a confidential relationship may be found to have been created by certain types of contracts (*e.g.,* suretyship, joint adventure insurance), such that the defendant will have a duty to make a full and fair disclosure of all the material facts.

---

5.   **Nondisclosure of Virtue by Buyer--**

Laidlaw v. Organ, 15 U.S. 178 (1817).

Facts. Organ (P) was a tobacco merchant. He learned that the war between the United States and England had ended before the general public became aware of that fact. He entered into a contract to purchase tobacco from Laidlaw (D), but did not tell him that the war had ended. When the information became generally available, the price of tobacco rose 30 to 50%. D refused to deliver for the contract price. D appeals from a judgment for P.

Issue. Was the failure of P to relay the important information sufficient grounds to invalidate the contract?

Held. No. Judgment reversed.

♦   P had no duty to relay information that might influence the price of tobacco.

Comment. Although modern cases are beginning to require sellers to notify buyers of latent defects which may reduce values, there is no duty for the buyer to notify a seller of latent virtues.

---

6.   **False Statement of a Material Fact--**

Edgington v. Fitzmaurice, 29 Ch. 459 (1885).

Facts. D sought to raise money by sale of debentures. The prospectus indicated that a £21,500 mortgage was the sole mortgage and would be paid off in installments. In addition, the prospectus indicated that the new money would be used for additions to buildings, horses, and vans. P advanced £1,500. In fact, D had a second mortgage, at least £18,000 of the first mortgage could be called at once, and the new money was to be used to pay existing debts. P sued for deceit and received a judgment. D appeals.

Issue. Were these false statements actionable?

Held. Yes. Judgment affirmed.

- The action requires a knowing or reckless false statement that was intended to induce and did induce reliance by the plaintiff.

- The false statement that the mortgage could be paid in installments was not actionable because there was no fraud.

- The statement that there was only one mortgage was also not dishonestly made.

- The statement that new money would purchase new additions was actionable.

- D did not intend to buy new additions when the statement was made. The statement was, therefore, a knowingly made false statement.

- The use to which the money would be put was material for inducing P to advance the money.

---

7.   Plaintiffs' Claims Should Have Been Subrogated--

Laborers Local 17 Health and Benefit Fund v. Philip Morris, Inc., 191 F.3d 229 (2d Cir. 1999).

Facts. Laborers (Ps) provided health care to their union members, thousands of whom became ill or died from smoking cigarettes produced by Philip Morris (D). Ps sued D, alleging that D's advertising was misleading to the public regarding the dangers associated with cigarette smoking. Ps also claim that D concealed information related to health risks from smoking. Ps claim damages for money spent to provide medical care for their members suffering from tobacco-related diseases, and state they have expended millions of dollars in providing such care. Additionally, Ps claim losses due to the Fund's inability to control costs, promote safer alternatives, and educate members to not use tobacco products, and allege RICO violations and fraud. The district court granted D's motion to dismiss in part. D appeals.

Issue. Is the chain of causation linking D's alleged wrongdoing to Ps' alleged injuries too remote to permit recovery?

Held. Yes. Judgment reversed and case remanded with orders to dismiss Ps' complaint.

- To maintain standing to sue under RICO, a plaintiff must show that the defendant's act was a "but for" cause of the injury *and* the proximate cause of the injury.

- Proximate cause limits liability only to the harms that bear a reasonable connection to the defendant's actions. There must be a direct relation between the injury and the wrongful conduct. For example, a plaintiff cannot seek compensation for injuries suffered by a third person—the harm to the plaintiff is too remote. In this case, the harm to Ps' fund devolves from the harm suffered by its members as a result of using tobacco products. Ps' fund would not have incurred financial losses if its members had not been injured. Ps' cause is indirect because it is contingent on the harm to third persons, thus negating proximate cause. Ps therefore lack standing to bring suit under RICO.

♦ Assessment of Ps' damages would be speculative. Although Ps allege losses from D's affirmative misconduct, it is difficult to determine what damages arose from Ps' failure to act (*e.g.*, the fund may have been inefficiently managed, or the smokers may have suffered from health problems not related to smoking). Damages would be impossible to determine.

♦ The fund may still bring a subrogation action and individual participants may bring independent causes of action.

C. NEGLIGENT MISREPRESENTATION

1. **Basic Elements.** A negligent misrepresentation occurs when there is:

   a. A false representation of a material fact made by the defendant in a business or professional capacity.

   b. Failure on the part of the defendant to use reasonable care to determine the truth of the statement.

   c. Duty to the plaintiff who relied on the misrepresentation.

   d. Justifiable reliance.

   e. Damages.

2. **Leading Case--**

Ultramares Corp. v. Touche, 174 N.E. 441 (N.Y. 1931).

Facts. Touche (D), a firm of public accountants, was hired by Fred Stern & Co. to prepare and certify a balance sheet exhibiting the condition of its business. Stern was involved in the importation of rubber, which required extensive credit. D knew that the balance sheet would be used by banks and creditors who dealt with the company, and so presented Stern with 32 certified copies. Although the sheet showed a net worth of $1,070,715, the business was actually insolvent. Further, D certified that in its opinion, the balance sheet presented a true view of the financial condition of Stern & Co. Ultramares (P) loaned Stern & Co. money in reliance on the audit certified by D and suffered losses when Stern & Co. went into bankruptcy. P brought suit against D for negligence and fraud. A jury awarded P damages, but the trial judge granted D's motion to dismiss without entering the judgment. An appellate court reversed and reinstated the verdict. D appeals. P cross-appeals the dismissal by the trial court of the cause of action for fraud.

Issue. May damages be recovered by a person who is injured by the negligent misstatement of another with whom he has no contractual relationship?

Held. No. Judgment for P reversed.

- Liability for a negligent misstatement extends only to the other parties to the contract pursuant to which the statement was given.

- To allow recovery without privity would expand liability for negligent speech to that of liability for fraud.

- Stern & Co. sought D's services primarily for its own benefit and only collaterally for the benefit of those to whom the balance sheet might be exhibited.

- *Glanzer v. Shepard*, 233 N.Y. 236 (1922), is distinguishable because, in that case, transmission of information to the third party was the sole reason for the transaction and not merely a possibility.

- This holding does not limit liability for misstatements that are reckless or insincere, but means only that liability for honest blunders is bounded by contract.

XVI. ECONOMIC HARMS

A. INDUCEMENT OF BREACH OF CONTRACT

1. **Common Law Origin.** Originally, this action was intended to protect master-servant relationships. A master could seek damages if a servant was induced to leave his position.

   a. **Liability--**

Lumley v. Gye, 118 Eng. Rep. 749 (K.B. 1853).

Facts. P contracted for the exclusive services of a certain opera singer. D, knowing of the contract, induced the singer to break the contract and perform for him. P sued for damages and D demurred.

Issue. Is there an action for interference with contract?

Held. Yes.

♦ An action will lie against a person who maliciously procures a breach of contract, resulting in loss to P. D, by procuring a violation of P's rights, has harmed P.

Dissent (Coleridge, J.). There should be no separate tort remedy. Any action by P should be in contract against the opera singer.

Comment. This was the first case that set out the general principle of liability based upon interference with contract. Subsequent cases have extended this principle to cover interference with advantageous relations of pecuniary value.

2. **Modern Elements.** The modern development of this action recognizes several elements.

   a. There must be an existing contractual relationship.

   b. The defendant must have been aware of that relationship.

   c. The defendant must have acted to cause a breach of that relationship.

B. INTERFERENCE WITH PROSPECTIVE ADVANTAGE

1. **Basic Elements.** The action for interference with the prospective advantage

differs from inducement to breach a contract in one distinct manner. This action does not require a presently enforceable contract. It is sufficient if some prospective or future relationship is disturbed. The elements of this action, therefore, are as follows:

a. A prospective or future advantageous relationship;

b. The intentional interference with that relationship; and

c. Damage caused by that interference.

2. Intentional Interference--

Tarleton v. M'Gawley, 170 Eng. Rep. 153 (K.B. 1793).

Facts. Tarleton was the name of a ship owned by Ps. It was trading with natives off the coast of Africa. The natives were fired upon by M'Gawley (D) for the sole purpose of preventing them from trading with anyone else. D claimed that the natives owed him a debt. D also claimed that Ps had not obtained the proper license from the African coastal nation to carry on the trade. Ps sued and obtained a verdict. D appeals.

Issue. May D prevent the natives from trading with others?

Held. No. Judgment affirmed.

♦ D cannot intentionally interfere with trade. Neither the debt owed nor the absence of the proper license by Ps would justify D's actions.

3. Negligent Interference--

People Express Airlines, Inc. v. Consolidated Rail Corp., 495 A.2d 107 (N.J. 1985).

Facts. Consolidated Rail's (D's) negligence caused a dangerous chemical to escape from one of its tank cars. The surrounding area had to be evacuated to avoid harming the health and safety of those in the area. This caused an interruption in People Express's (P's) commercial airline business and resulted in economic losses. P brought suit against D and lost. P appeals.

Issue. Can a plaintiff recover for a purely economic loss to its business caused by a defendant's negligence?

Held. Yes. Judgment reversed and case remanded.

- The traditional rule, which prohibited recovery for economic losses, was created because of fears of fraudulent claims, mass litigation, and limitless liability. A better rule would be to allow valid claims.

- If the risk of harm is foreseeable and the plaintiff is a member of a clearly identifiable class, recovery for purely economic harm is allowed.

C. UNFAIR COMPETITION

1. **Introduction.** Unfair competition may take several forms, but all forms are designed to gain an advantage in the marketplace that the law considers unfair.

2. **Predatory Pricing--**

Mogul Steamship Co. v. McGregor, Gow, & Co., 23 Q.B.D. 598 (1889), *aff'd*, [1892] A.C. 25.

Facts. McGregor (D) was a group of shippers that joined together to fix low prices for tea shipping. Their goal was to gain control of the shipping to the exclusion of all others. Mogul (P) sued for his loss of business. The trial court found for D. P appeals.

Issue. Is the combination of businesses to gain a competitive advantage over other businesses an unlawful act?

Held. No. Judgment affirmed.

- Lowering prices to obtain business is not an unlawful act. There was no malice or ill will, only an attempt to gain business.

- The fact that several businesses joined together to carry out this scheme does not make it unlawful.

Dissent (Lord Esher, M.R.). The conspiracy was not carried out merely to gain business. Its purpose was to drive others out of business. This purpose was wrongful and should be actionable.

Comment. Attempts to lower prices below costs in order to drive others out of business is called "predatory pricing."

---

3. **Intellectual Property--**

International News Service v. Associated Press, 248 U.S. 215 (1918).

Facts. Associated Press (P) was gathering news and selling the stories to 900 daily newspapers. International News Service (D) was engaged in a similar business and supplied 400 newspapers. In order to obtain P's stories, D engaged in the following activities: (i) employees of newspapers receiving P's stories were bribed to forward them to D, (ii) newspapers receiving P's stories were encouraged to forward those stories to D, and (iii) D copied P's stories from early editions of newspapers. P sued and sought injunctive relief. The trial court enjoined the first two activities and the court of appeals enjoined the third activity. Only the injunction that prevented the use of stories obtained from early editions of newspapers (the third activity) was argued before the United States Supreme Court.

Issue. Can D use, for profit, news stories gathered by P and already published?

Held. No. Judgment affirmed.

♦ The news stories were gathered by P and have a value attached to them. These stories are in the nature of quasi-property.

♦ D has taken P's work and sold it as its own.

Dissent (Brandeis, J.). News is not property that can be owned. Once it is published, it is available for free use by anyone.

---

4. **Real-time Transmissions--**

The National Basketball Association v. Motorola, Inc., 105 F.3d 841 (2d Cir. 1997).

Facts. Motorola, Inc. (D) manufactures Sports Team Analysis and Tracking Systems's ("STATS") (D) paging device, while STATS supplies the game information that is transmitted to the pagers. When the pager is in the "current" mode, it shows NBA (P) games in progress and updates game information every two to three minutes, more often closer to the end of the game. The pager is fed data by STATS reporters who watch the games on television or listen to them on the radio and input statistics and key information into a personal computer. Via modem, the information is relayed to STATS's host computer, which formulates data for retransmission. The information then goes to a common carrier, which then sends it via satellite to various local FM radio networks that emit the signal received by the individual pagers. P brought suit, alleging copyright infringement, commercial misappropriation, and false advertising. P sought and was granted a permanent injunction which prohibits Ds, absent authorization from the NBA, from transmitting scores or other data about NBA games in progress via the pagers, STATS's site on America On-Line's computer dial-up service, or "any equivalent means." Ds appeal.

Issues.

(i)   Does the state law "hot-news" misappropriation claim survive preemption by the federal Copyright Act?

(ii)   Have Ds unlawfully misappropriated P's property by transmitting "real-time" NBA game scores and statistics taken from television and radio broadcasts of games in progress?

Held. (i) Yes. (ii) No. Judgment reversed on the misappropriation claim; injunction vacated.

♦   Technology's advances have increased the speed and quantity of information transmission of all kinds of events. While state law attempted to address the challenges, federal copyright law did not come into play in this area until 1976. Prior to then, it was generally understood that live events such as baseball games were not copyrightable. There was even doubt as to whether a recorded broadcast or videotape of such an event was copyrightable. In 1976, federal legislation expressly afforded copyright protection to simultaneously recorded broadcasts of live performances such as sports events. The protection was not extended to the underlying events.

♦   The law contained provisions preempting state law claims that enforced rights "equivalent" to exclusive copyright protections when the work to which the state claim was being applied fell within the area of copyright protection. A "hot-news" claim survives preemption, *e.g.*, an East Coast news service lifting factual stories from a competitor's bulletins and sending them by wire to its West Coast papers that had yet to publish them because of time differentials. However, much state law involved here goes well beyond "hot-news" claims and is preempted.

♦   The extra elements in addition to elements of copyright infringement that allow a "hot-news" claim to survive preemption are: (i) factual information is time-sensitive; (ii) the defendant is "free-riding" on the plaintiff's efforts; and (iii) the existence of the plaintiff's product or service is threatened. The pager does not meet this test.

♦   New York's misappropriation doctrine is based on amorphous concepts such as "commercial immorality" or society's "ethics." It is too broad, and it is preempted.

♦   Only a narrow "hot-news" misappropriation claim survives preemption for actions concerning material within the realm of copyright.

♦ While P meets some of the elements of a "hot-news" claim, its product or service is not threatened. P is in the business of producing live basketball games and licensing copyrighted broadcasts of those games. Ds are collecting and transmitting factual material about those games, similar to television sports news summaries or newspaper box scores. P has shown no competitive effect or free-riding. If Ds were to collect data from P's pager and retransmit them to its pager, that would be free-riding and might result in P's pagers being unprofitable, but that is not the case here. P and Ds both bear their own costs in collecting factual information on NBA games. The better product will be more successful.

---

5. **Passing Off.** This action is similar to misrepresentation. It involves one business selling its own goods in such a way that they appear to be the goods of someone else. In this way, the first business may take advantage of the good name of the second.

   a. **Manufacture and sale of another's product--**

Ely-Norris Safe Co. v. Mosler Safe Co., 7 F.2d 603 (2d Cir. 1925).

Facts. Ely-Norris (P) made and sold safes with a patented special explosion chamber, which made it dangerous for thieves to attempt to open them. Mosler (D) sold some safes with explosion chambers (infringing on P's patent) and some with metal bands on them that made them appear to have explosion chambers. P sued D, claiming that D was taking P's customers by "passing off" safes that appeared to be like P's. The trial court dismissed P's complaint. P appeals.

Issue. Can D sell safes that appear similar to P's in order to take P's customers?

Held. No. Judgment reversed.

♦ Customers who bought D's safes obviously wanted P's explosion chamber. D's attempt to pass off a safe like P's to take P's customers is actionable. P can recover for lost customers.

---

   b. **On appeal--**

Mosler Safe Co. v. Ely-Norris Safe Co., 273 U.S. 132 (1926).

Facts. Same as preceding case. In addition, other safe manufacturers were making safes with explosion chambers. The Supreme Court granted certiorari.

Issue. Can P complain of D's action when others also had the right to make similar products?

Held. No. Judgment of court of appeals reversed.

♦ P was not the sole business entitled to make safes with explosion chambers. The mere fact that D sold such safes, therefore, does not mean that D was "passing off" its safes as P's.

───────────────────

6. **Patents and Trademarks.** Two types of property that are protected by federal legislation are patents and trademarks. Patents protect inventions. Trademarks protect marks or symbols associated with products.

7. **Trade Secrets.** The trade secret is often used to protect unpatentable materials, or patentable "processes" whose patenting might reveal secrets to the competition.

XVII. TORT IMMUNITIES

A. DOMESTIC OR INTRAFAMILY TORT IMMUNITY

1. **Parent and Child.** Although no such immunity was recognized under the English common law, the early American decisions held that a child could not sue her parents (nor a parent her child) for personal torts. *Rationale:* To preserve family harmony and parental authority.

    a. **Limitation.** The immunity was recognized only as to personal torts. It never applied to bar causes of action by a child against a parent for damage to the child's property.

    b. **Modern trend rejects immunity.** Because of its obvious unfairness in many cases, the clear trend of authority today is to restrict or reject the concept of parent-child immunity. But even when abolished, courts do not permit actions by a child against the parent when the parent's act involves the exercise of reasonable parental authority over the child or reasonable parental discretion with respect to providing support or maintenance for the child.

2. **Husband and Wife.**

    a. **Common law rule.** The common law regarded the husband and wife as a single legal entity and accordingly provided that the husband and wife could not sue each other for torts committed by one against the other, whether before or during marriage.

    b. **Abolition of immunity in most states.** Most jurisdictions today have rejected the doctrine of interspousal tort immunity entirely and have denounced the common law fiction of a single legal identity for husband and wife. Some have abolished the immunity only as to intentional torts, while others have abolished it as to all torts, intentional or negligent.

        1) **Rationale.** Liability insurance is so widespread today that the claim is really against an insurance carrier, rather than against the other spouse, so there is no great danger to the marriage.

    c. **When immunity not applicable.** Even when interspousal immunity has been retained, it does not apply in the following situations:

        1) **Both spouses are deceased.** If H and W are both killed in a traffic accident caused by H's negligence, W's heirs are permitted to maintain suit against H's estate for the wrongful death of W. In such a case, the beneficiaries of W's estate are usually the same persons

who are the beneficiaries of H's estate, and the action is really one in which the children are suing themselves. However, the courts tacitly recognize the existence of insurance in such cases and permit this type of suit.

2) **Premarital torts.** Either spouse may maintain an action against the other for premarital torts on the theory that because the tort did not prevent the parties from marrying, there is no reason to assume that the action will cause family discord.

3. **Other Relationships.** Even where still recognized, the doctrine of intrafamily tort immunity does not extend to relationships other than husband-wife and parent-child. Thus, for example, brothers and sisters can sue each other on any type of claim or cause of action.

B. CHARITABLE IMMUNITY

1. **Common Law Doctrine.** A separate ground for tort immunity was recognized at common law for nongovernmental, charitable organizations and enterprises. This immunity is related in theory to governmental tort immunity; *i.e.,* the notion is that the charity is working for the public good and should therefore be entitled to the same immunity as a public agency.

   a. Thus, it was held for many years that private charities—hospitals, schools, community organizations (*e.g.,* the Y.M.C.A.)—were not liable for torts committed by their agents or employees.

   b. Another rationale sometimes advanced for the doctrine of charitable immunity is that the funds on which a charity operates are donated, and subjecting such funds to the payment of tort claims would divert the funds from the purpose intended by the donor.

2. **Status Today.** The doctrine is clearly on the wane today. It has been repudiated entirely in many states, with courts finding that any interest in protecting a "good Samaritan" is outweighed by the need to provide compensation to the Samaritan's victims. Even when retained, the doctrine is riddled with exceptions.

C. MUNICIPAL CORPORATIONS

A great deal of law has developed regarding the tort liability of municipal corporations, resulting from the dual character of such entities: On the one hand, they are subdivisions of the state and therefore its agents in the exercise of certain functions and responsibilities; but on the other hand, they are also corporate bodies capable of the same acts as private corporations, and having certain local interests not shared by the state at large.

1. **Rule Applied.** The law has attempted to distinguish between this dual character of municipalities, and limits tort immunity to the "governmental" or "public" functions. A municipality's "proprietary" or "private" functions are not immune and may therefore result in tort liability.

2. **Problem.** The difficulty arises, of course, in attempting to determine which city functions are "governmental" (*e.g.,* police and fire protection) and which are "proprietary" (*e.g.,* transportation and utilities).

D. SOVEREIGN IMMUNITY

1. **Historical.** At common law, the doctrine evolved that "the King can do no wrong." Thus, when a plaintiff attempted to sue the state for a wrong done to him, the state was held to be immune from tort liability.

2. **Statement of Doctrine.** Whereas the government is liable or may consent to liability in suits of some other nature, its tort immunity is said to rest upon public policy—*i.e.,* the idea that the people as a whole cannot be guilty of a tort.

    a. **State and federal.** Following this doctrine, it is usually held that not only are state and federal governments immune from tort liability, but so are various state and federal agencies (*e.g.,* hospitals, schools, etc.).

    b. **Not applicable when state sues.** Most modern jurisdictions take the position that sovereign immunity applies only when an individual is suing the state; *i.e.,* it does not apply when the state has sued the individual defendant, who then seeks to assert a counterclaim or offset against the state. In such a case, it would be unfair to allow the state to assert its immunity to bar the individual defendant's counterclaim.

3. **Status of Doctrine Today.** The doctrine of sovereign immunity has been firmly implanted in our law and is retained in the majority of states today. Even so, the doctrine frequently operates harshly and inequitably, depriving injured persons of any right to compensation for torts inflicted upon them by the sheer coincidence that the wrongdoer was a governmental employee. Thus, some states recognize exceptions, while others tend to reject it.

    a. **The Federal Tort Claims Act.** The Federal Tort Claims Act, 28 U.S.C. sections 2671-2680 ("FTCA"), provides that, subject to certain enumerated exceptions, the federal government can be held liable in tort to the same extent as a private individual under like circumstances.

        1) **Private person standard--**

United States v. Olsen, 546 U.S. 43 (2005).

Facts. Two mine workers who were injured in a serious accident at an Arizona mine alleged that the negligence of federal mine inspectors helped bring about the accident. The workers and a spouse (Ps) brought suit against the United States (D) under the Federal Tort Claims Act ("FTCA"). The FTCA allows private tort actions against the United States under circumstances where the United States, if a private person, would be liable to the claimant in accordance with the law of the place where the act or omission occurred. The district court dismissed the lawsuit, in part because Ps' allegations were not sufficient to show that Arizona law would impose liability upon a private person in the same circumstances. The court of appeals reversed. The Supreme Court granted certiorari.

Issue. Does the FTCA waive the federal government's sovereign immunity only where local law would make a private person liable in tort, not where local law would make a state or municipal entity liable?

Held. Yes. Judgment vacated and case remanded.

♦ The court of appeals reasoned that the FTCA waives sovereign immunity where unique governmental functions are at issue if a state or municipal entity would be liable in the place where the incident occurred.

♦ This interpretation is too broad. The FTCA waives sovereign immunity where the United States, if a private person, not a state or municipal entity, would be liable. We have maintained this "private person" standard consistently. In *Indian Towing Co. v. United States*, 350 U.S. 61 (1955), we rejected the government's argument that there was no liability for negligent performance of uniquely governmental functions. We held that, where the government has performed activities that private persons do not perform, the FTCA requires the court to look at the state law liability of private entities, not public entities, when determining the government's liability.

♦ The court of appeals also reasoned that federal mine inspections, being regulatory in nature, are unique governmental functions because there is no private-sector analogue for mine inspections. The court of appeals then held that Arizona law would make state and municipal entities liable in the circumstances alleged and thus the FTCA waives the United States's sovereign immunity.

♦ The second basis for the court of appeals decision rests upon a reading of the FTCA that is too narrow. The FTCA makes the United States liable in the same manner and to the same extent as a private individual under like, not necessarily the same, circumstances. The language requires courts to look at analogous circumstances. Like the federal mine inspectors in this case, there are private persons who conduct safety inspections. The court of appeals should have looked for such an analogy.

- Because there is disagreement between Ps and D about which Arizona tort law doctrine applies, we remand this case.

---

2)   Determing whether act is discretionary--

Berkovitz v. United States, 486 U.S. 531 (1988).

Facts. Berkovitz, age two months, was given a polio vaccine and developed polio. In an action by him and his parents (Ps) against the United States (D), Ps claim that D wrongfully approved the release of the vaccine batch. D's motion to dismiss the action on the basis that the FTCA retains an immunity if the act by the governmental agency is "discretionary" was denied by the trial court. The appellate court reversed. Ps appeal.

Issue. Does the "discretionary act" exemption in the FTCA apply to approval of drugs by the Division of Biologic Standards?

Held. No. Case remanded for decision by the trial court.

- The exemption for discretionary acts is intended to provide immunity when a governmental agency has a choice in its decision where public policy considerations must be taken into account.

- This only applies to actual choices based on public policy and does not cover every regulatory decision.

- In this case, the Division of Biologic Standards had certain clear guidelines that had to be followed in order to reach a decision on whether to release the vaccine. There was no discretion as to whether to require that certain data be supplied.

- If the action is based on a claim that the Division of Biologic Standards reached an incorrect decision based on the information supplied, then no claim exists. That type of decision is within the sound discretion of the agency.

- If the action is based on a claim that the Division of Biologic Standards failed to comply with its own regulatory standards for reaching a decision or released the drug after determining that it was not safe, then the discretionary exemption does not apply.

- The case must be remanded to allow the trial court to hear the facts.

E. OFFICIAL IMMUNITY

1. **High-Ranking Officers.** Judges, legislators, and the President are completely immune from tort liability for acts carried out within the scope of their duties, even if they involve "malice" or "abuse of discretion."

2. **Unofficial Acts--**

Clinton v. Jones, 520 U.S. 681 (1997).

Facts. Jones (P), a state employee, was working at a registration desk at an official conference in a hotel where Clinton (D), then Governor of Arkansas, delivered a speech. P alleges that Ferguson, a police officer, encouraged her to leave her desk and visit D at a suite in the hotel. P claims that D made sexual advances towards her, which she rejected, and that she was punished for doing so by her superiors at work, who subsequently treated her in a rude manner. After D was elected President, P claims that Ferguson defamed her by implying that she had accepted D's advances. P seeks actual damages of $75,000 and punitive damages of $100,000. D moved to dismiss on immunity grounds, but the trial court allowed discovery and stayed the trial until the termination of D's term as President. The appellate court affirmed denial of D's motion but reversed the stay. D appeals.

Issue. Does D have official immunity from a civil suit brought while he is President, but which arose out of events that occurred before he became President?

Held. No. Judgment affirmed.

♦ Immunity protects public servants from suits for pecuniary damages arising out of their official acts; it does not apply to unofficial conduct.

♦ Immunity for official acts serves the public interest by allowing officials to perform their duties without fear of personal liability.

♦ D argues that the separation of powers doctrine limits the authority of the federal judiciary to interfere with the executive branch, and that such interference would occur by not staying the suit against him. However, separation of powers is concerned with allocation of power, and here, there is no suggestion that the judiciary is being asked to perform an executive function. The judiciary may review the President's official actions and direct appropriate process to the President himself; therefore, it follows that it has the power to determine the legality of his unofficial actions.

♦ The district court abused its discretion in allowing such a lengthy stay because it failed to take into account P's interest in bringing the matter to trial. Such a delay would increase the danger of loss of evidence, inability of witnesses to remember facts, or the death of a party.

♦   Furthermore, granting of the stay was premature. D has the burden of establishing that a stay is necessary, but the trial court ordered the stay before discovery was completed; thus, it could not be determined whether one was even necessary. The trial court was concerned that allowing the trial to proceed would give rise to unrelated civil actions that would interfere with D's official duties. However, it should have denied the stay and dealt with those issues if they arose.

TABLE OF CASES
(Page numbers of briefed cases in bold)

NOTES

NOTES

NOTES

NOTES

NOTES

NOTES

NOTES

NOTES

NOTES